T0369509

Woman,
The Actuality

A.K. Pant

iUniverse, Inc.
New York   Bloomington

Woman, The Actuality

iUniverse books may be ordered through booksellers or by contacting:

iUniverse
1663 Liberty Drive
Bloomington, IN 47403
www.iuniverse.com
1-800-Authors (1-800-288-4677)

ISBN: 978-1-4502-7176-9 (pbk)
ISBN: 978-1-4502-7177-6 (ebk)

Printed in the United States of America

iUniverse rev. date: 11/12/10

Entirely based on the personal surveys and extensive work done on the subject:-

Woman, The Actuality

यां चिन्तयामि सततं मयि सा विरक्ता
साप्यन्यमिच्छति जनं स जनोऽन्यसक्तः।
अस्मत्कृते च परिशुष्यति काचिदन्या धिक्
तां च तं च मदनं च इमां च मां च॥

My fiancée, whom I love more than my life, desires the sexual proximity of another man. Whom she adores for attaining sexual pleasure is sexually seduced by other lady. The lady, who is sexually available to that person, offers her sexual services to me by spreading her arms. Hence, shame to the source of lust or women as well as the creator of lust or *Kamdeva*.

I am thankful to my wife Rajani for helping me write this. I should be thankful to Manoj, Jeevan(Poison Guru) and Gunjan for their kind cooperation. Thanks to all of my friends for understanding my honest feelings and thoughts.

Preface

From the ancient period till the present era, the structure as well as the environment of society has changed uncountable times and all of such drastic changes have bestowed some peculiar changes to women temperament. It was a long period of revolution and women adopted numerous changes in their behavior and attitude. It was the crucial period for ladies because as the originator, they have to sustain their virtuous qualities while suppress their awful desires and performances. As the incoming of the new generations has to happen through women hence they are responsible for all probable awakenings and deteriorations of the morals as well as the ethics of the society. Again while changing the social circumstances, women also adopted the changes but unfortunately they could not maintain their chastity and other qualities and got involved in immoral sexual debauchment. It is an unspoken but proved truth that only women were having the capacity to ameliorate the society from the moral degradation and ethical deteriorations but unfortunately women were proved incapable in realizing and sustaining their true power of giving birth to virtuous offspring as well as the ethics and got involved in performing entire devastation of the morality and chastity. Even at present if anyone has the capacity and strength to re-establish or resuscitate the lost social norms and morals then this is women but again regrettably they have been mere an object to achieve sexual pleasure because of their wide involvement in illicit acts. The graph of moral degradation of women remained increasing and hence they have crossed all the limitations of moral and physical harlotry. At present around eighty percent ladies have become morally and physically adulterated and hence less that twenty percent ladies could maintain their chastity and dignity. Women take birth to spend their life span and die like a mortal creature and this eternal truth is sustained but in context of them the more preferential truth is that what kind of ethics and morals they teach to their children in the role of the mothers of the new generation, up to what extent they follow the codes of purity and ethics and what sacrifice they do for their families.

Women are willing to live in the snares of lies made by them. They are afraid of accepting the truth because it discloses their own physical and moral nudity. The basic problem is that if one dares to write truth of women then they blame him for keeping mean and disgusting mentality. In fact all about women starts from sexual perversion and ends on sexual perversion. Somewhere redundancy of phrases and figures can be seen in the book because almost aspects of women are directly or indirectly affiliated to their sexual disposition hence I apologize for that because it would have been impossible for me to write this without repetition of few instances. I did an attempt to express the thoughts of innocent men, who scare to disclose their feelings regarding women because of living under the shade of women's terror.

Different surveys have been conducted on women and it is found that less than one percent women speak truth when they are interviewed or surveyed. Hence to get the veracity of the life style and attitude of women, surveys are conducted very secretly by scrutinizing the past and present of ladies without bringing it in their knowledge that their statements might be used as their confessions. This book is based on such personal surveys conducted by me and my team in past eight years and it also includes my personal experiences regarding women. I am extremely sorry to the ladies whose thoughts and opinion I mentioned here without taking their prior permission but taking utmost precautions, I have not mentioned any details which may disclose the identity of anyone. All morally corrupt ladies are welcomed to question and put objection on the authenticity of mentioned surveys and other details.

I pay my heartily reverence to the ladies who are morally high and who follow the codes of conduct and chastity thereby maintaining the dignity of their parents and husbands because I believe that the balance on the earth is not maintained because of it's base being supported by the expanded hood of some snake named *Seshnag* as per Hindu methodology or by the logics of gravity and universe given by scientists instead I am quite determined that the balance of earth is because of the morally high and unadulterated ladies, who are around less than twenty percent of the total count of the ladies. As Hindu religion states that one should also pay honor to devils before performing any ritualistic or pious act hence I also pay my honor to the ill character and disgusting natured ladies, who performed a major role in devastating their spouse, families and the society by performing moral or physical adultery and who are responsible for the degradation of social respect of virtuous women.

The book is in continuation of my previous book Woman, The Myth.

Index

Childhood

Women conceive the fetus and at the completion of the pregnancy, they give birth to child. To know the gender of an infant, the relatives impatiently wait for the nurse or maid, who comes and reveals the information. When the child comes out of mother's womb and enters the world, he starts crying which pleases the family members. Relatives express their pleasure only when the gender of the infant is exposed. This is the biggest example of gender discrimination seen almost everywhere. After the gender of the child is known, relatives congratulate each other. A girl child is blessed as being the form of goddess *Lakshmi*, the symbol of wealth hence her parents are wished for the probable affluence and good fortune. Parents of the financially middleclass or lower class families, who are already having daughters, get depressed on consecutive birth of a girl child. It is usually found that people, belonging to any community or religion or financial status, desire a male child. It is considered that a complete family must consist of at least one boy and one girl child. When an infant comes to this world, all the necessary items are brought for him without differentiating between a boy and girl child. Few parents, who give birth to female child, slay their own child with the help of nurses or secretly exchange their new born girl child with the new born male of some other lady by giving sufficient money to nurses. It is also found that many people leave their new born girl child in hospital or drop it in the dust-bins on the way to home. Though such incidents are seldom found but it happens in the society and this is a bare truth. In a survey done among just married ladies and gents, it is found that seventy one percent of men want there first child to be a girl child whereas only six percent of women desire for a girl child. On consecutive birth of girl child in a family, the mother and grandmother of newborn child express grief, anguish and negligence for her whereas men on this subject are found to be neutral.

Parents become soaked by a kind of feeling of responsibility at the time of birth of a daughter while such feelings are not seen in them when they give birth to a male child. The birth of a daughter doesn't confer any kind of guilty conscious to them but still a kind of strain can be seen in their face expressions. A father of a female infant becomes anxious because he has to take care and protect his daughter till her marriage while a mother becomes anxious because she has to nourish a daughter and spend money as well as efforts on her to ultimately give her to another's hand.

The attachment of umbilical cord produces the arousal of sensations which is felt by children when they go near to their mothers. This feeling is carried out by a child from the womb of mother. This is mostly like the feeling of musk sensed by musk dear. It is a kind of pleasure that is felt by deserts when the rainfall occurs. This is the feeling of deserts and is inexpressible. Similar pleasure is achieved by a true devotee when he confronts his God. These are also umbilical cord relations and are inexpressible. This is the first attachment or sensation that a child carries from the womb.

During the initial stage, infant is found insensitive to all other worldly items except for his mother's breast. Gradually in few months, due to the direct contact with other family members, feelings of imminence arise in him. When a baby is lifted-up in the arms by strangers or comes in contact with them, he expresses his fear by crying, though such tendency is mostly seen in male child. Almost all the kids become uneasy when picked by strangers from the arms of a familiar one and this tendency sustains in them up to the span of two years. If parents make a habit to hold their kid in arms to make him walk and to make him asleep then this habit is immediately grasped by the kid and he cries if not taken in arms regularly and does not sleep unless made a walk by guardians. This is the period when the sensation towards excretion of urine and stool is increased in kids. A very little and cute smile can be seen on the face of a sleeping child when he achieves satisfaction. Though as per the opinions of few scholars, such smiling expressions in kids during the sleep are because of remembrance of former bodily existence or pre-existences. It is considered that up to the first seventy-two days of the life span, every kid has reminiscence of his previous birth. This is the period when kids are often found to be staring towards front without moving eye bowls. During the excretion of urine or stool, child feels shivering and hence becomes uncomfortable while when the process is over, he smiles to express his relief. The moment he finds himself to be wet, he starts crying. The sensation for pain or uneasiness and to express it by weeping is seen in kids from the birth and is considered to be the second sensation that they achieve. This also includes the feel of hunger which he expresses by crying. The third sensitivity which a child carries is for the physical soothing touch therefore a child is patted to make sleep. The fourth sensitivity which arises is for excretion of shit and urine. The fifth sensitivity is invoked for mother's breasts. The sixth sensitivity is generated for melodious sound. The seventh sensitivity, which arises, is for moving items. The eighth sensitivity is for colorful items or toys. The ninth sensitivity arises for familiar and strange persons. Colorful moving objects or toys become the center of attraction for the child. He shows more sensitivity and attraction towards colorful toys producing melodious sound. He expresses spasmodic laugher when tickled on the soles of his foot or stomach. He feels pleasure when excretes gas by farting. He feels very adventurous while searching mother's nipples or playing with his mother's breasts during breastfeeding. In this situation, he is always succeeded and gets excited in finding out the nipples of mother's breast. He sucks milk of one breast and plays with the nipple of the other breast. Usually such kind of playing with the breasts of mother is done by male child while in girl child, such playing is seen at the age of approximately two years which remains till her adolescence if not stopped and becomes the primary cause of evoking homosexual tendency in her.

All children, at the age of around eight months, are attracted more towards movable colorful toys than the still one. In this stage they want to move here and there in the arms of relatives and seek pleasure in that. The boundaries of bed appear to be a confinement to them and they become eager to cross that frontier. In fact in this age group, the kids do not have any liking or disliking instead parents guess about their taste or aversion for anything by looking their normal activities and responses. In this stage, they achieve sufficient physical strength for turning over while resting or sleeping hence they try to move on the bed with the help of hands and legs. Gradually they learn to step out of bed and sit by taking help of their hands and legs. The moment they become expert in crawling on the floor, they start walking with the help of others. The expressions of happiness and pain are found on their face while they slumber but this is in fact because of their natural internal feelings and at this stage, it has nothing to do with reminiscence of past incarnations. When the teeth start growing, they feel an itching as well as irritating pain at gums therefore while sucking

3

the milk from mother's breast they try to cut their nipples and from that instant, aggressiveness appears in their behavior. Though as per the opinion of many brilliant scholars, the difference in gender through the activities of kids is seen after the age group of nine years but in actual, the extent of aggressiveness, the liking or disliking for something and the expressions or the behavior shown for these, get influenced by their gender and can be seen even during the age group of eight to ten months. The dissimilarity in the way of loving and behaving to mothers shown by a boy child and a girl child at such a small age can be seen easily and this typical attitude of them is sufficient to differentiate in their gender just by looking at their performances. Hence the natural aggressiveness and the behavior shown in achieving the pleasure are governed by their gender. Again up to the age of breastfeeding, the boy child is found to be more aggressive while after the age span of breastfeeding, the girl child is found to be more aggressive.

When children start walking without any support they attain the stage of boys or girls depending on their gender. This is the time when the difference could be seen in the behavior of family members for the boys and girls. It is generally found that the relatives or guests are attracted more towards the girl child among the boy and girl of same age-group hence the girl child is more loved by them either by the gifts as chocolates and toys or by emotional expressions. Even parents are more attracted to their girl child and she is more lovable to them. At the time of functions and festivals, parents provide colorful attire to their boy child but to girl child, they even decorate her like a doll besides the beautiful wearing. When a small boy is praised for his attire, he is seen almost unaffected whereas when a small girl is applauded for her dress, she feels happy and reveals shyness by her face. A small girl embraces her father to demand for her new desires. In comparison to the demands of a son, parents find it easier to fulfill the desires of their daughter because they seem to be financially comfortable. Again a girl child becomes very happy when her small desires are fulfilled while for satisfying the desires of a boy child, more investment is needed.

The grooming and the kind of make up done by the mother is keenly observed by the girl child and thus due to her feminine character, she too curiously desires for the same kind of grooming and prefer to use bangles, bracelets and spangle ornamenting the forehead etc. To make the coordination of her small desires with the external world, she prefers small baby-utensils of clay as a symbol of original utensils used to prepare food, decorated dolls as a symbol of herself and materials for adornment or grooming. Every time watching her mother as a housewife, cooking food in the kitchen, she also pretends making food in the clay utensils like her with her friends of same age group. A girl alone or with some boy or girl, performs the role of the parents of that baby-doll and another group performs the role of the parents of a male doll. Thus they perform the dolls' wedding and some girls even arrange a small party of few friends with the help of parents. In this dolls' wedding, marriage procession from the house of male doll or bridegroom to the residence of baby doll or bride takes place. Kids enjoy their party of very small scale and it is assumed that the marriage is done. At the moment of the most dramatic and sentimental scene, when bridegroom doll takes away the bride doll from her house, girls of the side of bride doll start weeping. For them, the process and its objectives of marriage are accomplished at that moment. Except this, they don't know anything about wedlock. Boy-children are found to be more attracted in the outdoor games like cricket and they know almost all of the rules of their favorite games. The names of the players are learned by heart to them. Boys belonging to financially low class, are more attracted towards the games like *Kanche* and *Gilli danda* while at the age of thirteen to fourteen years, their interest is developed in kite flying etc. The boys of financially stable families get diverted towards video games and comics-magazines in the age group of around thirteen years. Few senseless parents provide motor-bikes to their sons at this age and cause life loss of their sons and the kids of others in accidents. It is surprising that never any action is taken against those parents while the other innocent drivers are punished if any accident occurs, even by the mistakes of such underage guys. Along with all the aforementioned stuff, children go to school and study there. If in early period of primary education they show interest in schooling then this is because of being the only place where they can meet the children of their age-group and enjoy with them. It is found that up to the age group of ten years, if parents develop the interest in their children for the studies, make them learn to live a disciplined life and build up a tendency to fairly compete in the exams to achieve top rank in the class, then in future they do not have to bother about the further studies, educational guidance and career of them. The career of the girls mostly has been decided up to this age group. If a girl achieves highest marks and is the topper of her class · then often teachers praise her by ludicrously menacing guys that they should be shame on them as a girl is a topper among them. This is more found in female teachers. If a girl is brilliant in studies and is of assiduous nature then also her mother or the other aged ladies of family make believe her that she is a girl and hence studies are not meant for her. The brilliant girls, who are the toppers in their schooling, often listen the comments or advices mentioned by senior experienced ladies as "What will you do by studying".

Girls are seldom found participating in outdoor sports with the boys. The teachers as well as parents keep on demoralizing girls, who are interested in playing such outdoor games with the guys by saying, "What will you gain by involving yourself in games as you are girls." Such criticism discourages their feelings hence they realize themselves as well as are made realize by others that physically they are weaker than boys. In almost schools, the games or sports teachers appointed are male and hence this also makes the situation for the girls participating in the sports little bit uncomfortable. Even after facing continuous discouragement done by the other matured ladies, a girl in this age group gets acquainted with the fact that if she does continuous efforts and practices then she is no less than boys but now at this age she comprehends that it is good for her to be evaluated lesser in comparison to guys. She has to sustain such situations and utilize them all over her life. In future she has to represent herself as an innocent and virtuous lady thereby taking the credits of good deeds while putting the responsibilities of immoral deeds done by her on others especially on men. This is her first step of the education of women psychology where she learns representing herself as *Abla* or the one who is always harassed by men and is unable to perform anything immoral, even after committing transgressions and adultery thereby falsely blaming men hence proving them responsible for all those immoral acts which have nothing to do with men.

When a small girl is bathed by her mother, she takes it as an amusement. This sustains up to the age group of four years. After four years, she remains quiet while bathing. In the absence of mother, if she is bathed by her father then due to nakedness, she feels embarrassing. If that girl is having elder sister then father does not have to participate himself in this. Though if she is regularly made bathed by her father from the beginning then she does not feel shy till the age of around thirteen years. In the same way, a small boy is also helped by his mother while bathing and till the age of around twelve to thirteen, he does not feel shy.

When a small child has to excrete urine, he does it anywhere without thinking of the presence of other persons or the special facilities. This tendency remains in the kids irrespective of their gender up to the age till they are not able to sense and express the pressure of natural calls. As a continuous rhythmic sound resembling to be the sound of a whistle is produced when young ladies pass urine hence ladies pronounce that sound while making a child to pass urine and surprisingly it is adopted by every person while making a kid to excrete urine and this method almost succeeds. Often the kids start indicating before the excretion at the age of around two years. When they learn properly to pass urine or stool, they undergo different feelings. A boy just has to make his penis out for passing urine while a girl has to lift her skirt up and pull her underwear down and sit to excrete urine which is an uncomfortable process in comparison to the boys. This way of passing urine sometimes makes girls embarrassing hence for excretion, if they do not seek a lone place, they feel shy and anxious. Gradually as they grew, they have to find a lone as well as safe place for urine excretion. In future, they have to take such security measures while bathing, changing the wearing and during excretion. As a girl grows up, she is told by mother or other elders to change her cloths in a lonely place. This is the initial stage where she is made realized about the presence of *Yoni* or vagina. At the domestic level, it can be considered as her first experience to realize the physical difference among her and boys. Many girls, even at the age of twelve-thirteen, do not undergo such feelings of getting instructed by the family members hence change their attires in front of family members. Such girls are instructed when the accumulation of the flesh as a symptom of breasts starts appearing. When a small boy finds a small girl excreting urine in a sitting posture, he feels very strange and surprises and hence sometimes lifts her skirt up to see what she is doing. Contrary to this, when a small girl finds a small boy excreting urine while standing, she is lost in thoughts. A penis and the stream of urine coming out of it give her a thought of water tap.

As the penis is attached outside the body therefore it is easy for guys to excrete and it is also very hygienic as the last drops of urine are execrated by them through vibrating the penis by hand. In girls, this kind of facility is not available and hence their vagina remains wet after excreting which even soaks their undergarments. This is the reason that some hygiene conscious ladies wash their vagina with water after excreting urine. Small boys, while excreting on the boundaries of schools or at the sides of road, ridiculously try to cut the stream of the urine of others by their own. The boys of even fifteen-sixteen years are seen betting on the distance up to which they can let their urine stream go. They make different kinds of drawings and write different names with the help of this. While opposite to this, a small girl on urgency excretes inside her clothes feeling embarrassing. If she finds a corner, she sits and excretes there. After that, she wears her cloth and turns to see the urine excretion done by her and then bashfully smiles and runs away from that place.

Small girls while sleeping put their hand inside their mother's bra and keep that on their breast. This tendency of girls does not come to an end with the growing age. This behavior of playing with the mother's breast can be seen in the girls of the age group of fourteen-fifteen and even somewhere above that age group. It gives pleasure to both of the mother and daughter. Gradually this tendency, which may become a prime cause to incline towards homosexual attraction, diminishes in the girls when mothers strictly deny or prohibit for it. Though the habit of sucking the thumb and excreting urine on bed while sleeping are strictly removed in children by the parents still some girls of even the age group of twenty to twenty-one, who live in their imaginary world of roaming in thoughts beyond the practical life, are found to be sucking the thumb and excreting urine under their passion of imaginary world of fairies. In the small boys, the reasons of excreting urine while sleeping are excitement and wonder while in the small girls, the reason behind this is fear. The girls, who submerge themselves in the imaginary, mystical and emotional world of fairy tales, have to do a lot effort to come out of such phobia.

Small boys and girls perform the acting as if they are doing sexual intercourse though they are fully dressed. This is like a game for them in which they feel the same ineffable pleasure that a kid experiences while sucking mother's breast. Small boys can also be seen playing like this among them but this time they become almost naked. There is a very peculiar game played between such small girls and boys in which a boy acts as a doctor and pretends of perking injection on their hips. Acting like a doctor, he removes the lower garment of girls and boys. They feel happy on the sight of sexual organs of each other. The small girls, while removing their clothes in front of boys of same age group, undergo through an intermingled feeling of curiosity, embarrassment and pleasure. Again this kind of bizarre sensation is also felt by an infant when she plays with her mother's breast or when excretes urine or shit. This kind of pleasure is also felt by small kids when they are kissed at stomach or at lips by the parents. Small boys holding their penis and keep on moving it with there hands also feel the same pleasure. In the grownup age, when girls sit by putting their one thigh on the other, seek such kind of pleasure. This is the same pleasure which an adult man and a woman attain just before performing sexual intercourse and is inexpressible.

The compliments given to small boys and girls on their normal performances make them feel happy. Though almost appraisable activities done by them are lost or neglected because of the image of their childhood. They often try to draw the attention of parents and others towards them. Though for them, the measures or standards of right and wrong are limited still if they are ignored by the parents in the usual life or not complimented on the good deeds then they feel depressed and become arrogant. The boys and girls of this age group become introvert if they do not have brothers, sisters or friends of approximately same age group. Somewhere it is found that the only child, when not properly cared by parents or ignored by them, becomes mentally sick. The initial symptoms of such disorder or mental strain can be observed in the children who undergo such situations. Some of such children face the pain of solitude even after the full attentiveness of parents. The major symptoms of this arise at the age of seven to eight years in guys while in girls such abnormalities are seen after the span of fourteen years and remain in them for whole of the life span. Kids possess a normal tendency to draw the attention of the parents. If parents do not appraise the good deeds done by them or ignore them then they start involving in wrong doings. Though by performing negative activities, they face the anguish of parents, still they become successful in drawing the attention of the parents. Again in such circumstances, they find that wrong job done by them pull the attraction of their parents and thus they commit the wrong deeds. It is also found that if parents do not pay attention to first child because of new born second child, the same situation arises. In such matters, the peculiar kind of behavior shown by first child can be seen as a kind of visible aggression in his nature. It is found that when a male child is alone or is neglected by the parents without any cause as in the first case, aggressiveness appears in his temperament in the later years and it ultimately evokes rebelling tendencies in him but in case of girls, this makes them to tend towards illicit sexual relations when they are grown up. While in later case, when the negligence is due to presence of other child, the male child gets introverted but female child adopts the habit of pilferage which sustains in her for the whole span of her life.

The children of irresponsible parents are often seen involved in theft. Small boys and girls steal money from their house to fulfill their needs of buying different kinds of candies and sweets from shops. They steal money to spend it with friends to show-off their richness among them and the money stolen by them is mainly utilized in buying candies and chocolates etc. Though at present, small boys can also be seen watching movies without informing their parents for which they get money by pilfering it from their residences. Generally small girls are not involved in stealing at this age while maximum percentage of boys is involved in this. With the growing age, the tendency of stealing rises in the girls while in the boys, who are not utilizing this habit in the public or as a source of earnings, this ends-up. When boys and girls are caught red handed while stealing, there is a difference in the attitude shown by them. Boys admit their mistake but girls do not accept their mistake and start weeping. The tendency of speaking lies arises in the girls by this age of seven to nine years and in future is considered as their good quality of elegance, practical wisdom and boldness. From this age, a small girl learns to be satisfied by considering and defining the bad deeds or awful habits of herself as virtuous conduct by her own typical feminine interpretation by discarding and neglecting other's ethical opinions. This becomes very helpful to ladies when they have to live under strict moral control of elders because almost in the past or seldom in present, ladies are seen to be living under the restrictions or bindings of the elders of the family but in fact they can never be kept in ethical control because they never consider themselves to be wrong by any means.

Mothers of financially lower-class families teach their small daughters all the household jobs. This is somewhere also found in the parents of middle-class families but now since past decade, the medium-class men have been sufficient wealthy because of their involvement in bribes in their government jobs or by other illegal activities of money-making. Almost such middleclass men, who have been rich and achieved the level of lower upper class, hide their actual financial status from the government for evasion of taxes and pretend to live a simple life. It includes almost all of the middleclass government employees, a sufficiently big lobby of the businessman, who seems to be doing lower-class business and the persons involved in illicit ways of earnings. In such families, small girls are never taught the household jobs. In the families residing in the very interior villages or who are financially hand to mouth, daughters are not educated with a thought that same cast groom are seldom found for the educated girls. Small girls belonging to financially very low class and low class families are found working with their mothers and other ladies of the house. They work in the residences of so called medium-class and high-class families. They earn by washing utensils, sweeping the floor and wiping in the other's residences. Though the money earned by them is either taken by mother for the family use or snatched by fathers for drinking alcohol or gambling. In such low class families, mostly small girls work for earnings while their same age brothers are not engaged in any work and spend their time here and there playing with friends. That does not mean that the guys of such families go for schooling. If somehow such parents arrange their sons to go for schooling then also this is done till they just become primary level educated while girls are only taught till they learn to write their names and be able to count money. If some small boy or girl of such families is given higher education because of his keen interest then this happens very rarely. Poor parents having only boy child, send their small boys to work in low class hotels, motor repairing centers and garages where such small guys achieve the practical experience of the disgusting life. They are regularly abused, physically tortured and sexually molested by the owners. In this age group, working small boys are physically as well as sexually molested numerous times more than working small girls. Usually sexual harassment is also faced by the small boys of rich families who are taught in boarding schools and live in hostels. In such schools, the facilities are available for living in the school premises hence the newcomer guys are bound to suffer sodomy either by the night staff or by the senior students. Gradually they learn such abnormal sexual activities including various ways of masturbation and unnatural sex and feel pleasure to commit sodomy.

Educated parents are found to be aware of the education of their children and do not discriminate between boy child and girl child while providing them education. In a normal family, after completing the initial studies, girls are told by their mothers to carry their further studies after marriage. It is found in a survey that eighty-seven percent of fathers are willing for their daughters to be properly educated while only thirty-one percent of mothers want their daughters to study. Again mothers are often seen telling their daughters, "What will you do by studying." Most of the mothers keep the opinion that spending money in studies of a daughter is mere misusage of it but when they find their husbands strictly being in the favor of educating daughters, they become helpless. If a girl gets excellent marks in her exams or becomes the topper in some other schooling activity related to studies, she in not applauded by her mother. Mother behaves quite impassively at the moment of the success of her but if she fails or gets poor marks, she is publicly menaced by mother and criticized with the comments like, "This was destined to happen." On such kind of situations, almost mothers are found to be of the view of discontinuing the education of their daughters while fathers are found to be standing in the favor of their daughters but to avoid conflicts with their wives, they avoid saying anything clearly on this subject. Mothers try to stop their small daughters, who are unwilling to study, to go to school or college while a small boy is by-force send for schooling. This is extremely unfortunate that the continuous labor done by the girl child for her studies is found to be negligible in a mother's opinion in comparison to the little effort done by her son to just pass in his exams. Parents are always found to be anxious about the future of their sons and eagerly wait for their exam's result but they are seldom worried for their daughter's result. The parents, who do not have male child, expect from their daughters for having good academic record. Wherever the parents become hopeless from the poor level of intellect and the lack of caliber of their sons, they teach their daughters and provide them higher education. While providing the education to the daughters, parents do not expect them to earn in future while such kind of expectation is always seen in the parents for their sons. Boys are almost confused in the primary stage of education for their aims or future plans while such dilemma is not seen in the brilliant girls. Though it is the duty of parents to educate their children irrespective of their gender but parents involved in business finding their sons not interested in studies, allow them to join family business. Again financially very low-class parents educate their sons and daughters just to make them able to write their names and to calculate money but if they seek their kids having deep interest in studies then they permit them to achieve further education as per their financial capacity. In the middleclass and upper class families, if parents find their daughters doing well in studies then in future seeking their hobby in the fields of science, art and music etc, they help them to move in their desired field. Opposite to this, the willingness of small boys for going school is not considered to be noticeable and they are by-force send to schools. Hence if a boy child does not show his interest towards studies then he is pushed to go to school by some kind of bribe or fear. Very rare parents allow their sons to choose the career of their own liking while most of the parents want to mould their sons to accept the field in which they themselves are or the fields which were their own goals but they could not achieve and now desire their sons to go in that. Financially capable parents of the girls allow them to get any kind of higher education but again they want their sons to follow their instructions while choosing the career. In the very initial period of schooling, almost boys and girls are found to be unwilling to go to school and hence to prevent themselves from going to study, they express same kind of behavior. They cry bitterly by hitting the floor by foot or even lie down on the floor and float on it and try to break the utensils or other items and do all possible things so that they can stay at home.

When a small girl unfortunately becomes orphan, she is adopted by the relatives of her late parents. Sometimes she even has to go to orphanage. Mostly it is seen that illegitimate children, children of unmarried ladies and infants who are abandoned by the parents because of being girl child, are send to orphanage. The prostitutes, who are living in groups or in an organized red-light-area or in a brothel, keep their children with them. A child, whose parents have died, is seldom found in orphanage hence percentage of such orphans in the orphanages is found to be least. Such small orphan girls are adopted by some relatives after the demise of their parents or adopted from orphanages by parents who are unable to give birth to child and from then they live under the patronage of new guardians. If the parents, who take the liability of orphan girls by adopting them, give birth to their own kids in future then the life of such adopted girls become painful. The orphan girls adopted by the relatives, who are already having their own kids, also suffer a lot grief. In such circumstances, almost adopted girls have to do all the household work and are kept like servants. These girls are usually physically harassed by such stepmothers and unfortunately very less, out of the numerous, of such instances come in to the notice of administration and judiciary. The survey done in such forty-seven cases, where step parents were having their own daughters in parallel to their step daughters, disclosed the horrible truth that in thirty-nine of such families, the harassment of adopted girls and inhuman conduct with them was done by the stepmothers and the real daughters of the stepmothers while stepfathers were helpless. In one matter, the stepfather was found to be involved in sexually abusing the adopted daughter. In the case of four families, the step daughters of the age group of twelve to fifteen years were compelled by the parents to commit harlotry thereby earning for the step parents. In the rest of three families, the situations were normal and adopted daughters were living happy life because of strict control of their stepfathers over their stepmothers. Though the orphan girls adopted by the childless or barren parents seldom suffer such harassments but again if such stepmothers conceive later and give birth to female children then the aforementioned situations start arising with the adopted daughters. If the parents adopting the girl children already have some boy children or give birth to boy children then in almost cases, the adopted daughters are found to be safe. The worst conditions start appearing if the step-parents have a real daughter along with the step daughter. Hence if the parents are allowed to adopt orphan girls with the restriction that they must not have their own girl child at that moment and even should not have the same in future then the position of step daughters almost remains safe under the patronage of step-parents. Again in some matters, it was found that mothers compel their step daughters to perform prostitution. If fathers were found exploiting their adopted daughters sexually then this was because of sexually perverted temperament of them but such cases were extremely rare.

If either of the mothers or fathers of small girls die then almost of such widowers or widows remarry in future. If father of a small girl dies and her mother does not remarry then she becomes arrogant and in future keeps illicit sexual relations with number of boyfriends to seek the affection of a father in them. In this case, almost boyfriends of her are found to be quite elder to her. If such a girl bears the financial problem then she accepts the help of some rich man of her surrounding by providing him sexual services. Though in all of such matters, the widow young mothers, who do not remarry, are found to be involved in illicit sexual relations and this has nothing to do with their financial status. Again the only guidance of widow mother is insufficient to keep daughters in control and almost such daughters become sexually polluted or lose their virginity before their marriage. If such a mother remarries then her daughter lives a happy life with the stepfather and this situation does not alter for her if stepfather too has his own children from his ex-wife or in-future, has child from her mother. If stepfather is of strong character then that doesn't matter whether the daughter accepts him easily or not but this is assured that her future and safety is sure and such daughter gets right guidance from her stepfather. If mother dies in the childhood of the daughter and father does not remarry then such daughter becomes gentle, polite and of high ethics. If such father of a girl remarries then if the stepmother already has child or in future she gives birth to child from her new husband then in both the cases the life of girl is made hell by stepmother. Such stepmothers never behave equally to the step daughters and their own children are often found harassing the step daughters of their mother in the absence of their real fathers. Again the situations become worst if the stepmother has a girl child of her own either from her ex-husband or from the father of step daughter whom with she remarried. It is also found that in most of such instances fathers observe and realize that their daughters from their ex-wives are in trouble because of harsh and partial behavior of new wives but are helpless in front of them. If stepmother does not have any child in past and even does not attain in future then only she behaves normally with the kids of the second husband and in such matters only, a daughter gets the actual love of mother from her stepmother. Almost women in the roll of mother differentiate or perform favoritism between their own children and the step children by giving preference to own children.

One incident of the *Kanpur* city is important to be mentioned here. A girl of four years was adopted by her female relative after the demise of her parents. That lady was already having her young daughters. She and her daughters mentally as well physically harass the adopted little girl and made her work day and night. Fortunately one day that little girl could come out of the house then people came to know about her. When this case was brought in the knowledge of administration, the girl was made free from that slavery provided by her step-mother and step-sisters. That underage girl was having numerous marks of brutality on her body gifted to her by the ladies who were supposed to be her legal guardians. Again such situations are found only in those houses where a lady adopting a daughter has her own daughters or gives birth to daughters in future. It is very rarely found that a lady owing her own daughter, behaves appropriately and equally with an adopted daughter. The most disgusting fact sorted out by the surveys of the small orphan girls and other small poor girls was that in ninety-seven percent of such cases, the sexual, moral, physical harassment of small girls is done by ladies and men were unaware of this while in the rest of three percent of such cases, the harassment was done by men also.

Thirty matters were searched where men remarried with their real sisters-in-law after the death of their wives. In twenty-eight matters, new wives behaved like servant to their step sons, who were in fact the children of their demised real sisters. When deep scrutiny was done then it is found that in seven instances, ladies were having illicit sexual relations with their real sisters' husbands and hence they advised their brothers-in-law to kill their wives. In all of such seven instances, wives were killed by their husbands and real sisters and after that, they married. In an instance, wife caught red handed her husband and real sister while making copulation then both of them burned her alive. When the instance came into the knowledge of administration then lady perjured that her sister was mentally sick and was several times caught making illicit sexual relations with other men hence she committed suicide.

The menstruation cycle and the initial physical development of genital organs make a girl irritated and anxious. Generally mothers inform their daughters about the menstruation discharge earlier. Most of the schoolgirls experience their first menstruation in classrooms. Most of the poor working girls or the rural girls involved in agricultural work also experience their first menstruation out of the house. In many customs, the first menstruation of a girl is considered to be an auspicious symptom and hence celebrated by the family because it is a symbol of her femininity. The starting of menstruation in a girl and the related secret guidance given to her by her mother provide the tendency of concealing her own world and making it mystical for others. If a mother does not inform her daughter on this subject earlier then the situation becomes quite difficult for her. If a mother is not able to catch the spot of the first menstruation of her daughter by looking at her lower garment then daughter becomes frightened and herself informs her mother or the female friends about this. Though girls also get familiar about this from their schoolmates or friends who have already experienced this and somewhere they come to know about this by the advertisements shown in television, which publicly promotes the sanitary napkins or the pads manufactured to be used by girls to absorb the menstruation discharge. Thus the girls watching such stuff in the advertisements themselves ask their mothers or friends on this subject. The girls of this age group often ask each other about the starting of menstruation cycle. Such sanitary napkins are easily available at the shops hence it facilitates girls. Again the process of discharge of the fluid and the appearance of stains on lower cloths make the girls embarrassed with the sense of modesty and doubt about it and the girls, who are not aware about menstruation discharge because of lack of the information, consider it as a symptom of some diseases.

In rural areas, girls use long strip of cloth torn from some worn-out or useless garment like some old *Sari* instead of pads during their menstruation cycle. They cut long pieces out of some old garment and put that in between the thighs and fold it upon the vagina by wrapping it around the thighs in many layers. They keep such few pieces of cloth and reuse them after washing instead of throwing. Many ladies experience ultimate pain at the lower sides of stomach before or during the menstruation. Many girls rub their thighs while having the menstruation discharge to make lesser their awkwardness and irritation of the moment and the expression of detestation can be seen on their faces through which it can be deduced that they are undergoing menstruation.

Menstruation is an indication that the girl is now grown-up and with this, it also indicates the inclusion of femininity in her. During the initial stage of being menstruated, girls are often found to be under mental strain because of myths and lack of knowledge about menstruation discharge. It restricts their freedom or their unconstrained behavior. In the beginning, they feel shyness, fear and hesitation to step out due to the probable menstruation. They do not admit this truth instantly that they have to go through menstruation each month throughout the stage of youth till the age of forty to fifty. Gradually they accept it and learn to live with this thought. They try at most not to avoid their work due to menstruation rather they prevent the interference made by this in their daily routine of the life by taking precautions. During the time of periods, they are made realized by their mother or other old aged ladies of the family of being impure. They are asked not to enter synagogues and somewhere even in the premises of kitchen while they are menstruating. Girls gradually understand that some days of the month they have to lead an impure life though such impurity provides the existence to all the male-female creatures by giving them birth and also give entirety to the masculinity of men. Girls are told by the aged ladies that their own bodies become polluted and sinful during the periods. If anyhow they are asked to visit religious place or in the areas which are prohibited for menstruating ladies, they have to reveal that they are unable to go because of going through menstruations. On one side, menstruation makes the girls mature by converting them in to actual maiden stage of women hence making them more responsible for chastity and morality while on the other side it invokes a kind of religious impurity in them. For being a complete lady, the starting as well as the regular occurrence of menstruation is very essential while hiding the occurrence of menstruation from others along with religious restrictions put on them during this period, creates a contradiction or mental dilemma in them. Girls are more troubled by the restrictions imposed upon them during the menstruation period rather than the physical disturbances caused by the menstruation. Hence as per their opinion, the pain of menstruation or it's occurrence is less disgusting and distressing than the feelings which arise when they are made realized to be impure because of menstruation.

The early age, at which girls have the entire knowledge of sexual relations and sexual sensitivity, boys are almost untouched by this. A girl living in the society grabs the sexual knowledge from practical world and friends. Though now the media and movies have been the primary mode to promote the knowledge of sex still mothers are often found providing the sense of realizing the intentions of a man's touch to their growing-up girls. Young daughters are informed by the mothers to strictly resist the men who touch at their untouchable body parts as on thighs, buttocks, breasts

17

and pubic zone. Again they are taught to understand the malicious sexual intentions of men just by looking at their eyes or by sensing the single touch done by them. The indecent sexual conversations done with the same age girls, obscene comments done by men and the attempts done by men to touch them with malicious sexual intentions provide them verbal knowledge of sexual relations and invoke a desire in them to experience pleasure of sexual union. They are often touched indecently to attain sexual pleasure by sexually perverted tutors and incest relatives. At this age, girls learn to differentiate between moral and immoral touching done by men through their consciousness and basic cognizance. Young school girls are often sexually seduced by the tutors appointed to teach them personally. Personal tutors are arranged by the parents for their children when they are weak in some particular subject. Such tutors, who personally teach young girls of the age group of twelve to eighteen, are found to be involved sexually with their minor female students in more than eighty-eight percent cases. Though such under age girls contribute willingly in making sexual plays still it is said to be sexual molestation of them because as per the laws, they are minor in this age group. Sometimes this way of considering a girl as an adult or minor, appears to be questionable and ridiculous because in a wide survey done among teenage brothers and sisters living in same premises, it is found that almost girls of under eighteen or even under sixteen possess the entire knowledge of sex related stuff and are even found to be involved in illicit sexual relations in favorable situations while the sexual awareness or knowledge in the boys even of the age group of nineteen to twenty is found to be very limited. Very few percent of the minor boys have sexual knowledge and this too is because of indecent scenes shown in the movies. Wise parents never keep some male personnel tutor for their daughters instead they send them to attend the mass-classes in the form of private coaching institutes where number of students study together. They knew that minor girls are very fascinated towards the strange world of men at this age group and desire for the safe physical or a kind of sexual proximity of some male elder to them. Some parents think that if they arrange a male tutor to come to house to teach their daughters then their minor daughters will be safe but again this is not true because it is seen that more than ninety-five percent of such tutors molest the young female pupils even more easily because of the overconfident parents. Many young teachers can be seen marrying with their female students because almost of them are pressurized by them whom with they were keeping sexual relations. Though all of them know that the sexual relations between the teacher and the student are considered to be worst kind of relations because nowhere religion allows this and it is still assumed that one, who keeps sexual relation with his female student, is incest because Gurus and students have the relation of fathers and children.

In many residences, where both of the parents are working, minor daughters are sexually exploited or achieve practical sexual knowledge from family servants, distant relatives and tutors. In all of such matters, underage girls readily perform oral sex and other kind of sexual plays with their male sexual associates because they are extremely curious to know about the penis or men's sexual behavior. In some cases, girls are found to be indecently touched while sleeping by their ignorant elder cousins or real brothers, who do not have knowledge about sex but because of curiosity they do such attempts. Again if a teenage boy and his sister attaining the age of adolescence sleep at the same bed then somewhere elder brother due to his curiosity indecently touches his sister with sexual thoughts. This can never be said as sexual exploitation because in fact in almost of such instances, younger girl is more mature in context of sexual awareness and knowledge than her just elder brother. Such situations seldom occur between real brothers and sisters but can be frequently seen in-between real cousins. Teenage girls often put their one leg upon the person sleeping next to them or on a pillow and slowly push themselves towards it like performing sexual pushups whenever they are sexually excited while sleeping. This tendency remains in them till they marry.

It can be seen that some girls of the age around fourteen to twenty-six years often take medicines to reduce the fat of the body or to maintain their figure. Such habit of taking medicines to become slim and attractive is always harmful for the physique and psychology of girls. Few girls regularly take medicines to reduce anxiety or depression while few are addict to pain killers. Girls of this age group can often be seen taking sleeping-pills. Parents are so careless that they never keep an eye on their children. Few guys at this age group usually take strong pain killers and medicines to reduce anxiety. Such guys usually drink the whole bottle of some strong cough syrup and then take some sweat edible item or tea so as to feel the pleasure of being drugged. The most popular cough syrup used by such guys was *phensedyl* but now they take *corex* etc. Few guys intake *iodex*, which is used externally to remove body pain. Smelling with a deep breath through nostrils is done by such guys to intake the flavor of ink-removers as this also provides them pleasure. Well, there is big list of such intoxicants used by girls and boys and perhaps in every country, some youngsters are addicted of such drowsy products. Almost fathers are busy in earning money for the welfare of their wives and children hence this is the duty of mothers to keep an eye and strict control over their children. Unfortunately mothers are very busy with accomplishing their immoral desires hence they seldom take care of this. If an underage girl or a girl up to the age group of twenty-two years is taking such pills or medicines then her mother is the only responsible person for that. Often such girls can be seen involved in illicit sexual relations because of the lack of care and affection that should be provided to them by their mothers. Again if any kind of sexual involvement or harassment is seen with such girls then their mothers are responsible for that.

A girl up to the age group of thirteen to fifteen, if touched indecently by some relative or other person living in her surrounding, feels embarrassing and does not speak about this to others while sometimes warns the respective person that if he does not stop, she may inform about this to mother. In a survey taken fourteen times on different hundred underage girls, it is found that thirty-seven percent of them achieved first experience of sexual touch or such embarrassment by their teachers, forty-three percent of them by the nearby relatives and neighbors and three percent by the strangers. The rest percent denied disclosing the facts. Up to the age group of nineteen years, a big percentage of girls were found to be involved in partial sexual plays or complete sexual course with their boyfriends. In ninety-five percent of such cases, the underage girls were having their lovers or basically sex partners, who were quite elder to them. Though such girls have boyfriends obviously of the same age group but they were not having sexual relations with them instead they have their sex-companions, quite elder to them, in parallel to boyfriends. Hence seldom they are found sexually involved with the guys of same age group. The reason behind this is keeping relations with the boys of same age group means an equal involvement as well as responsibility of both while keeping sexual relations with comparatively quite elder or adult persons means the responsibility goes to one who is not minor. The fact which was revealed by those so-called underage girls was quite shocking. They said, "The guys of our age group are stupid, coward and sexually impotent because they undergo fear when we ask them to play. Contrary to this, the senior men can afford to spend money on us as well as they are experienced hence we need not worry about any probable unsafe situations. If we are caught red handed by parents or something wrong happens then we can easily prove that we were being sexually molested by the senior men and in fact, we say that we were not aware of the intentions of those specific men. Hence we are always safe because of being minor. We can always say that we have been sexually molested or raped." Thus such girls of the age group of fifteen to eighteen are found to be very smart and experienced.

After a certain age, parents do not allow their daughters to engage themselves in sports with boys. If a girl herself is interested in a particular game then hardly any parents allow her to move further in that activity of sport by choosing it as a career. Almost parents advise their sons to take interest in studies instead of sports. A child, who is not interested in games or sports, is never obligated by his parents rather all parents become happy with this tendency of their children. If any person, whether a girl or a boy, becomes a national or international player in future then that is in fact because of his or her intense interest, hardcore labor and rebellion tendency for parents if they obstruct him or her while spending more time in practice. Though almost such successful personalities declare that their parents are behind their success but this is also true that until the parents are assured about the bright future of their children in some sport activity, they never appreciate them. The exception to this is only found in the very rich families or in the families where the head is also having his profession in sports or having keen interest in some particular game.

Parents worry for the health of their sons if they go out of station for sport purpose or for some other reason while in the same situations for daughters, they are more worried for there virginity instead of health. Almost mothers find themselves to be helpless to instruct their growing daughters regarding the proper selection of wearing and are always unable to make them follow the codes of conduct and decency. The keen interest of a daughter to wear indecent improper cloths, which are almost insufficient to hide the body parts, makes the mother anxious. Mother becomes worried by looking her growing daughter's beauty and attitude. Up to this age, girls have come to know that how much beauty they have been provided by the God. They know that their original and precious wealth is their beauty and sexual capabilities which they get without doing any special efforts. Every girl wants to look beautiful and attractive because these are the primary ambitions of her. Beauty, attractiveness and sexual appeal have always been the strong factors deciding the future or destiny of girls. In contrary to this, beauty has almost no role in deciding the future of guys. Every girl knows whether she is beautiful and attractive or ugly and unappealing but even an ugly looking girl never admits that she is not beautiful. In spite of not having the natural beauty, she keeps on grooming herself and uses the adornments and dressing as per her complexion and figure. Most of such less attractive girls are more oriented towards studies than other girls. They often hide their complex by rarely conversing to boys and always pretending to be serious. Girls, who are not glamorous and have dark complexion, also look attractive if they have good figure as well as sharp features and such girls are often found to be brilliant and erudite.

After realizing their beauty level, girls become busy in the experiments regarding choosing the suitable dresses for themselves. From this stage of being a maiden till the aged life, they have to represent themselves in a form of beautiful alluring body by utilizing their God gifted physical glory and ill qualities of women psychology. This is the stage when they have to mature their physical properties like beauty and figure as well as behavioral qualities like feminine nature and make coordination in-between these two, in which they almost give preference to physical beauty and immoral qualities. During this stage of young girls, it is the responsibility of their parents to invoke moral and ethical qualities in them but seldom parents perform this duty. As per the opinion of parents, virginity is the foremost attitude that daughters should maintain till their marriage but unfortunately such attempts done by parents to maintain the virginity of their daughters till their marriage go in vain because of the absence of definite criteria for deciding the chastity of a lady or the purity-impurity status of vagina. Under such attempts done by parents, young girls are restricted in making close relations or friendship with guys and they are not allowed to go out of the residence at odd hours without any proper cause.

By this time, girls come to know the importance and value of their vagina or being a female. Girls keep on hearing from the elder ladies of the house that vagina or *Yoni* is the symbol of helplessness, slavery and innocence while penis is the symbol of ruling, atrocity and brutality. They start utilizing such kind of rumors, spread by their own women society, for their benefits. Sometimes to prove themselves innocent and sinless, they put false blames upon known or unknown men for sexual molestation and experience that the sexual blames put by women on men are always considered to be true by the society without verifying the authenticity of such blames. They also falsely blame men of their surroundings for sexual molestation in order to hide their sexual relations with their favorite men. This is the first experiment done by them in the laboratory of women psychology in which they always succeed. At this age group, they have understood properly that the penis as a symbol of mannishness and the society of men, about which women often pretend to be fearful and unsafe nowhere exist in front of the mercilessness, brutality, false ego and ruling tendency of women. They understand that this is the biggest lie spread by hypocrite women that the society is men based or is ruled by men because in actual, no men can rule over women and in almost families, women are dominating over men. They often ignore the lustful indecent comments and gestures done by lustful men even when they too are having sexual feelings. They become well familiar with the fact that men can never dare to behave indecently to women unless they give their silent permission or open consent. Though somewhere the exceptions to this are found in mob like in a religious or secular fair and in public conveyances or in the places where girls become alone among number of notorious guys. Such instances also appear when some girl with her parents goes in a crowded place where she feels perplexing to resist guy touching her indecently at the back. It is found in a survey that in almost of the festivals of Hindus, which are celebrated publicly and where a big crowd appears, young underage girls are often sexually touched at their backs and breasts by around ten percent Hindu guys visiting there and around thirty percent uninvited Islamic guys, who become a part of mob. Such situations can be easily seen in *Durga Puja, Ravan Dahan, Janmashtami* and other religious gatherings of Hindus. Again this all happens because of the negligence and lethargic attitude of the dumb parents of such minor girls.

The sensitivity of the vaginal route itself decreases if a girl undergoes illicit sexual mating during the age group of fourteen to eighteen years while such decrement in the sensitivity is not seen in the girls who properly marry and perform sex even during this age group. The basic reason is that while making illicit sexual courses in this age group, the fear of probable social pressure and defame psychologically reduces the sensitivity of the vaginal route. In this case the sensitivity again increases and reaches at the hike at around the age group of thirty years. That is why it is said that almost of the underage girls make illicit sexual relations because of their curiosities or financial benefits not because of their sexual desires. Most of such underage girls can be often seen saying that they feel least sexual sensation while making sexual courses.

To know the sexual advancement of an area or locality or city, one has to thoroughly look at the advancement of the size of breasts of young or underage girls and their way of wearing. Though doctors say that the size of breasts depends on the feminine hormones but in fact this is mostly governed by the factor that from which age group, a girl is being touched at her breasts with sexual intentions. Again it seems to be rubbish but is true that wherever the girls of around thirteen to seventeen are having heavy breasts, there the rate of sexual advancement is quite high. One can see in the rural areas that the underage girls are having extraordinary breasts and this is only because people of such villages are more sex oriented and the level of sexual debauchment is much high at family level in such localities.

Young girls are often informed by the elder ladies, who correlate the penis and men's ego, that the presence of penis is itself an indication of the harassment or molestation of vagina or decent women. Such false rumors spread by corrupt elder women invoke natural curiosity or sexual attraction along with detestation in them for men. They want to experience the veracity of the typical descriptions done by aged women about the fear of penis and behavior of men. Thus, such hatred descriptions done with malicious intentions regarding men's psychology invoke a kind of sexual attraction in them for men and persuade them for keeping illicit sexual relations.

If a girl has to go out of the house for some work then parents generally send some other person with her to escort her. It appears that going out of the house alone is itself a challenge to her existence in society. Fear of men is inherited by her. Girls of every age group are forced by decent parents to be accompanied by a man as younger brother etc while going out of the house. Almost of such parents send their small sons of four to five years with their maiden daughters with the intention that perhaps the boy might protect his elder sister in adverse situations. Though somewhere, the safety of younger brother becomes problematic for young girl still as per the opinion of her, the presence of even a small brother provides her a moral support during difficult situations and it helps her in avoiding the indecent comments passed by bad guys. Girls reaching the state of adolescence with the arising feminine symptoms like upcoming of breasts and hips, become the centre of attraction for young guys to aged men. Staring at a girl done by a young man is a normal behavior but if the same attitude is seen in aged people then this is a symbol of excessive amorousness in them. Initially a girl, noticing a man staring her breasts, becomes embarrassed. She knows that lustful men are continuously watching the sequential rhythmic movement of her hips produced when she walks. Initially she feels her breasts as a kind of burden which she hides from men with the help of a shawl or some book. She starts walking briskly as she reaches near the crowd of guys. Gradually she feels pleasure and satisfaction in becoming the centre of attraction for boys. She becomes habitual of the peculiar sight given to her by men. Now she walks in an easy pace as if walking on a ramp by producing attractive movement of hips instead of walking rapidly near the group of guys. Now she considers her upcoming breasts as a symbol of her beauty and sexual appeal and walks with keeping the body straight to expose the breasts as possible instead of considering it as a burden and hiding from men. If men do not give a sight to her breasts or body figure then it invokes a kind of complex feelings in her and she watches herself in mirror for hours thereby giving more time in decorating herself. She achieves the natural quality of women that is realizing the internal sexual feelings of men for her just by looking at their faces and she becomes capable to notice the shine which appears in the eyes of men by looking her beauty. The moment she comes to know that men are fascinated by her beauty, she realizes the significance of her existence. She is not overlooked by men even when she is accompanied with parents or brothers. A brother, while providing social security to his sister by accompanying her, makes believe to be very decent or sometime pretends unaffected or detached from the surrounding but in actual could not avoid looking other beautiful girls. Young girls, accompanied by some male as their brothers, comprehend this and present themselves to be innocent and unaware of this fact.

In future, the after-marriage behavior of girls and boys with their respective spouse is very influenced by the family life of their parents. In the situation where a father is very busy with his business or job and loves his children a lot while mother shows a robust kind of behavior and unnecessarily scolds her children, there such tendency of mothers make girls violent by nature. Again in this situation, most of the mothers keep a sort of rivalry for their daughters as well as for husbands. Such daughters, when get married, are found to be worthy wives but keep a tendency of sexual flirtations. In above situations, fathers are seldom found to be sexually corrupt while mothers are often involved in extra marital affairs or adultery. If mothers are of high morals and never commit illicit sexual relations then daughters are seldom found to be involved in such sexual relations. In the families, where a mother does not fulfill her responsibilities towards her daughters and is often involved in the activities for her own pleasure, there the responsibilities of children come upon father. Again in this situation, if a father is fulfilling the responsibilities and is very much caring for his daughters then this gives rise to stubbornness and violent tendency in daughters for their mothers. Such daughters always seek the image of their respective father in their boy-friends, fiancé and spouse. If a mother performs her all family duties and cares the daughter while father keeps the ladies of the family in strict discipline and performs earning to fulfill their necessary requirements then such daughter becomes a decent and noble wife in future and respects her husband's or father-in-law's rule over the family. If anywhere the different situations from the above are found then in almost of the instances daughters get diverted from the right path. Thus children are highly affected by the factor that who is governing the family. It may be their mother or father or both or none of them. More than eighty-eight percent children find their mothers to be ruling in the family while around three percent families are governed by father or a male. In only two percent families, the actual concept of marriage is seen where both of husband and wife sacrifice for the sake of each other. If a girl seeks the rule of mother in her family then the position of father is just like a tamed animal or a pawn of chess. The rule of the father of a girl in the family provides her mother proper respect and rights while the rule of her mother always humiliates, harasses and disrespects to her father and stimulates the girl or the daughter to perform illicit sexual relations. The in-future behavior of girl, who finds her father to be scolded and harassed by her mother, depends on the fact that who among them is right and what type of behavior they keep with the daughter. If mother is quarrelsome natured involved in illicit activities and behave indecently to father as well as to daughter while father is of decent and calm personality and performs his all duties then she favors her father by assisting him and speaks against of her mother. Such resistance done by the girl for her mother becomes stronger as she grows. Girls having this kind of family background are always in the favor of the rule of men in the family and after marriage also they accept the rule of either of their husband or father-in-law but not of mother-in-law. If in such cases, the cruel mother keeps her daughter under her control wisely then both of them harass the man of the family together. In such families, the life of the father becomes hell by the contribution of wicked mother and daughter. If father of the girl does nothing to earn or acts just like bovine then again he is physically as well as mentally tortured by the ladies of the family and such girls are almost seen to be involved making illicit sexual relations. Most of such freedom seeker girls, who are involved in immoral acts willingly or by the help of their mothers, take the favor of women rule in the family and ruin the dignity as well as the social life of their would-be husbands in future.

In opposite to aforementioned situations, if mother is of very simple and generous nature but father keeps strict discipline in the house then daughter takes supports her father and always respects her mother. Such girls are always found favoring the man's rule in the family and in future after marriage; they are proved to be worthy and faithful wives. In the same situation, if father performs indecent behavior and keeps inhuman attitude for the mother then such daughter takes the side of mother while she always fears with the rule of men. Such girls live a peaceful and sexually unadulterated life and are always proved to be good housewives by obeying and respecting their husbands. It is normally seen that strictness of mother keeps the sons under control while the strictness of father is essential to control over the daughters. If both of the mother and father are of simple nature with decent temperament then either the daughter becomes very generous and of commendable character or she is found to be entirely involved in illicit sexual activities depending on whether she is having elder brother or sister to have a control over her or she herself is eldest. When both of the mother and father are of quarrelsome nature and not caring then such daughters live a painful life. If a daughter seeks affection from either of her father or mother and does not get that then she tries to find that emotional love elsewhere. Such attempts, done by her, to search for the pious love and patronage, shove her in the unfathomable dark chasm of debauchment.

Adolescence and Women Psychology

A girl, who has become youth in the near past, recognizes the intentions of the way of staring done by men. When girls move round and watch their desired or normal youth or just move their head while keeping the body straight, men think that they are fascinated towards them. Girls can not move around to see an attractive man in the presence of family members or known people but they are unable to restrain their feelings. Thus in such aberrant situations, they do not express physical retaliation by moving their bodies or head to look at the men of their liking instead they move eyeballs right and left swiftly. Gradually they become expertise in this activity and men are not able to make out that they looked them. Eyeballs of ladies touch the corners of eyes for fraction of seconds and they are able to watch their desired man. This kind of tendency is often found in young girls. The fear of society is negligible in such kind of gazing as a girl shows herself morally high and unaffected by men while she had got sexual pleasure by viewing at handsome guys. When married ladies are with their husbands, they use this technique of quick movement of eye balls to see other men for the sake of sexual pleasure while show their husbands that they are unaffected by other men.

Due to the revolution that took place in almost all of the fields, the living standard of human has been increased in present environment. The changes or fashion took place in the trends of wearing hence quality and designs are improved in the cloths of both men and women. The dressing sense evoked which changed the basic aim of wearing in women. The extraordinary changes in the garments that took place because of the revolutions did personality enhancement and provided decency to men whereas to ladies it imparted sexual glamour and made them mere objects of demonstration or showpieces. Though ladies also have become free in selection of garments but conflict of uncertainty is always seen in them. Dilemma in thoughts always confused their minds like whether to wear or not with the intention of revealing unseen attraction of their body. It was their opinion that if they wear normal cloths meant for ladies then there would be no meaning of their beauty while if they discard wearing entirely thereby being nude then there would be no concealed attraction left in them. Such state of agitation in thoughts, regarding choosing the extent of nudity by revealing body, came in women mind since the very beginning and would-be carried out till the end.

In the present, ladies have opted the medium way but in this also they have been bifurcated in two groups. The ladies of first group give preference to the traditional dresses due to fear or honor of the opinion of society and family and do not reveal their body publicly. Such class consists of rural ladies because they are given strict instructions from their elders for moral attires. Parents, who are of strong morals and are the follower of the traditions, also take care of their daughters regarding their proper apparel. For such traditional parents, their living standards or backgrounds do not make an obstacle to their ethics. The ladies belonging to other group prefer vulgar clothes which partly or hardly cover their bodies. They go for traditional dresses also which can help them on revealing their bodies. Such kind of ladies keep the opinions that the ladies who opt and support traditional dresses are physically ugly with no body charm hence do not have any body part like breasts and buttocks being attractive to reveal or are backwards or mentally sick. This constitutes of the ladies who belong to urban areas or are with sufficiently rich backgrounds, modern prostitutes, ladies who belong to traditional families but reside apart from joint families, rural ladies living in urban areas and the ladies who or whose families were middleclass or lower class but have become rich in the recent past years. This is also not found perfectly true in present society because ugly or unattractive girls are also revealing their bodies as per their body figure and such vulgarity is defined by them as their dressing sense and it has become a trend for ladies but again unfortunately almost of such ladies are sexually corrupt.

The main part of the traditional Indian wearing of ladies *Salwar-Suit* is *Dupatta* or stroll which is used by them to hide the shape of breasts and protect the breasts from revealing while they bent for any reason. Ladies who are the supporter of vulgarity in wearing or who are against dressing code or who want to reveal their bodies, wear sleeveless and deep neck suits by justifying that they feel free and comfortable in such incomplete wearing. They wrap their *Dupatta* around the neck instead of properly using it for hiding their breasts. Such ladies pretend to adjust their stroll while conversing to youths and try to draw their attention towards their breasts. They have a tendency to allure men and sexually invoke them to commit something immoral, by presenting themselves in the body form. In the same way, girls wearing short skirts while walking or conversing to men, perform failure attempts to stretch it downwards to hide their thighs in order to attract men. They know that by stretching the skirt downwards its length is not going to increase and to hide their thighs, they may wear long skirts but they are ever unaffected by this because of their innocence as a front of their alluring tendencies or sex appeals and always try to play with their garments in order to attract men.

During nights, ladies sleep more soundly or unconsciously in comparison to men. Often their skirts or night wearing, which they wear while sleeping, get folded towards upsides thereby making their lower body almost naked. When they are instructed by parents to wear proper and complete dress in nights, they overlook their statement by replying that they feel comfortable in such kinds of open dresses. Such tendency is found in almost girls irrespective of their physical beauty level. It is found practically being true in very wide surveys that comparatively ugly ladies or ladies with least physical charm pretend more with a typical mannerism where they always appear to be anxious for maintaining their virginity and express more pseudo aversion if they are inadvertently even touched my a man but they are also comparatively more soon found to be ready to accept the love requests or sex proposals done by men. Such ladies get more readily managed for the sexual intercourse even on the little attempt done by men hence one can get their consent more easily in comparison to beautiful ladies. In the families of equivalent financial status, the ego problem is more in unattractive ladies comparatively to pretty ones because they pretend more. This is a pure contradiction found in the nature of such ladies which can be easily seen in their behavior. Again this is usually seen that if a beautiful lady is unintentionally touched by a man then the situation remains normal while if the same happens with an unattractive lady then she immediately protests and blames him for an offense committed deliberately by touching her and pretends her virginity to be ruined. Ladies of normal features, who are easily available for sexual plays or love making, are often seen letting people know about their good character even after having illicit sexual relations with number of lovers or with other men.

Every lady has a self-built sphere of influence around her. A lady loves everyone residing within the circumference of that typical sphere doesn't matter whether he is a maimed or a crippled man, ugly, mentally retarded, under age, familiar or non-familiar like a stranger, any blood relative or an animal like dog etc. Unfortunately this kind of encirclement made by women for themselves is of their sexual lust and passion for love hence it has nothing to do with emotions or spiritual love. As a lady is most close to herself in this typical invisible sphere therefore she is more attracted towards her own beauty and physical attributes than that of anyone else. This unprecedented affection stimulates the feelings and nature of homosexuality, self-satisfaction, self-dedication, subjectivity, self-torment, self-deception, self-praise, self-infatuation and self-assassination in them. A lady can neither see nor listen anything against herself. The beauty of other ladies seems to be a challenge to her for her own beauty. She always keeps a kind of abhorrence for the ladies who are more beautiful in comparison to herself but as she can never accept anyone to be more beautiful than her hence generally she does not express her feelings of detestations for such ladies. She scolds those ladies behind them who are in actual more beautiful than her or with whom she keeps a complex and often abuses them by blaming them of being adulterated character. Again she always keeps enmity with the ladies who are more beautiful than her doesn't matter whether they includes even her mother, real sisters or daughters. She keeps a desire of sexual proximity with every entity residing within the invisible distinctive sphere of her thoughts but she seldom feels sexual attraction with the one residing outside of that globe. It is easy for her to drag someone inside the globe from outside, but she feels embarrassing to throw out someone who is one of the members of her globe only when she does not have any substitute of that member to drag inside. This is the very important part of her women-psychology because this quality helps her in making break-ups in the love affairs by keeping some other boyfriend inside the globe as a substitute of ex-lover thereby forgetting the ex one and living happily with the new one. Though the ex-boyfriend is never able to visualize that what's wrong had happened to her and often ruins his future as well as life. If she has a lady in the vicinity of her within the globe then she becomes a lesbian because of having sexual charm with her. Similarly if some of her servant resides within the periphery of that globe, she keeps sexual relations with him. If she keeps her pet dog within the sphere then that also becomes a toy to provide unnatural sexual pleasure to her. If a lady keeps her father or real brother inside that globe then she tries to sexually allure them pretending herself to be ignorant though in very seldom of such instances she gets succeeded. Very less percentage of married ladies keep their husbands inside that globe hence mostly of them perform copulation with their husband unwillingly and with the lack of their own consent. Such ladies while performing the sexual course with their husbands always bear the thought that as if they were sexually molested by a dog or are being raped. This is the only reason that almost ladies say that they are raped by their husbands. This is an astonishing fact that such ladies are always ready and eager to perform sexual plays with the men and even animals dwelling inside of their globe and this is a very usual course for them but they blame their husbands, who spend their whole of wealth, emotions and life on them, for sexually harassing them because they are residing outside of their globe though they have been authorized by the religion, society and laws to have sexual course with them. It is found in a survey that if a wife denies performing sexual course with her husband without any genuine cause then in all of such matters, husbands remain outside of the specific globe of their wives and other men reside inside as a replacement of them.

A girl becoming youth from childhood, gradually gets acquainted with the art of hiding her real gestures or face expressions and behavior as per the place and time. She pretends to be unaffected and neutral by the presence of guys in her surroundings in front of parents while out of the house, in the proximity of her lover, she performs sexual plays. In every situation, she wears a different mask of gestures on her face. The parents are never ever able to think that their lovingly decent and studious daughter invites her boyfriend in the house and performs sexual plays with him when they go to office. Almost young girls wear the mask of decency, innocence and helplessness to betray their parents and keep illicit sexual relations. Some husbands think that they are quite adjusted with their wives and know every thing about each other but in actual they are dumb and unaware about the fact that a man can never know about the actual temperament and character of his wife even after spending a sufficient big span of years with her on the same bed. Again the reason behind is that almost ladies wear a natural looking artificial mask of lies and deception in front of every person including their husbands. The actual expressions can only be seen in their faces when they are alone. If a man minutely observes the activities and gestures of his wife then he will find that his wife was having different expressions and behavior early in the morning, while talking to other men, while having indecent sexual conversations with ladies and in her behavior with the in-laws. He can observe that the wife was having different appearance in the evening time when he comes back from office. The face expressions and behavior of wife can be keenly observed by him to be entirely different while taking supper, talking to children, talking with pre-marriage relatives and performing the sexual course. When ladies awake in the morning, they rub their eyes from the nail side of finger like cats while men do the same from the inner side of finger. A lot of other gestures of ladies can be seen to be very similar to cats.

All ladies have an invisible layer of nature which could be said as their behavior limit. All the good and bad properties of ladies are present at both sides of this layer. The moral and immoral properties, which lie above this layer, are alive or active or influential and hence can be seen in the behavior of ladies whereas the properties staying below that invisible layer of behavioral limit are in dormant or inactive state and reside to be in hibernation. Such ethical or iniquitous hibernated properties of a lady are not seen in her nature. A lady takes few seconds to transfer an active or visible property into hibernated or hidden state and vice versa. This is the only reason which makes it difficult to judge about peculiar nature, character and psychology of women. This perfection achieved by them to alter their feelings and attitude suddenly through interchanging the qualities by making them below or above the behavior-layer, makes their persona unpredictable. That is why some author with the extraordinary awareness of women psychology, say that women are mysterious by nature. The whole life of a lady is a sequence of making fluctuations by herself in the temperament by interchanging her qualities. Before describing the bad qualities of a lady, it is necessary to understand that no lady can be said to be of good or bad nature because all of such properties dwell in her permanently. The actual behavior of a lady is in fact the illustration of her effective properties i.e. the properties which lie above the behavior-layer. Again all kind of changing of behavior is entirely in her control as this only depends on which property she makes effective and which ineffective and this gives birth to the profound women psychology.

It has been seen mostly that a lady, who is living a peaceful and moderate life, when comes in the propinquity with a lady who is of iniquitous, cruel, quarrelsome and indolent nature, adopts her such awful nature and propensities. Even a husband devotee decent lady starts performing adultery by keeping illicit sexual relations if she gets the imminence with the ladies involved in sexual debauchment. In fact she does not adopt the awful qualities of such illicit character ladies instead the moment she finds those ladies to be excessively self-interested or self-centered hence achieving their own sensual contentment through their awful properties and living just to satisfy their ego, she gets influenced by their immoral way of living and just makes such awful properties of herself to be prominent by making them above the behavior limit. An officer of Government's custom department told that his wife was extremely careless, cantankerous and lethargic. Once he shifted from his apartment to a new colony where one of his very close friends was living with his family. The wife of that friend was of very decent nature and was very attentive in performing house-jobs. He said," My wicked wife became mix-up with that lady and in few months, she entirely changed the attitude of my friend's wife." Friend complained to him that his wife has been of rude nature and she has given up taking care of house-jobs. Such situations can be seen in almost every residence. Again as the properties staying above the invisible layer are visible in the behavior of ladies and said to be their women nature hence we say that some specific lady has been adulterated by her nature by adopting the appalling properties of an ill-character lady of her proximity. The bad property of self-centeredness or being self-interested is perpetually effective in all the ladies and forms the background of all the upright and immoral deeds performed by them. Any good or bad property, which comes above the behavioral layer and gets effective by being exposed in the behavior of a lady, the antonym or opposite of that automatically becomes inactive. The only exception of this is seen when the gender governing properties in female go below the behavior-layer and never come above the layer because of getting eloped permanently. In such cases, even the opposite properties of those can be shifted by ladies up and down but the properties governing the gender never get affected. This situation produces sexual or gender disorder in male and female.

There are eight sections of three hours in a day and ladies possess eight awful properties in every such section. Out of this, four bad properties are same during all of the eight sections while the remaining four are different. The four bad properties which are ever effective in women are sexual desire, jealousy, laziness and egoism. Jealousy and egoism give birth to absence of conscience or lack of discretion which becomes the prime cause behind other bad properties. The remaining bad properties or awful attributes of ladies are rashness or presumption, lamenting, quarrelsomeness, causing distress to others or sadistic nature, covetousness, vanity, insanity, harsh speaking, lying or betraying, garrulousness, tale-bearing or habit of informing about one to others, despotism, cruelty or bestiality, intolerance, captious criticism or reproaching others, unbeliever or performing against religion, possessiveness, physical and behavioral impurity, uncontrollable senses, negative attitude governed by pessimism, retaliation or tendency of taking revenge, self-torment with the extreme of suicidal nature, unreasonable insistence or stubbornness, selfishness, kleptomania or habit to theft, capriciousness, annihilative tendency, false doctrine, hypocrisy or self applause or self deceit, causing dispute, parasite nature or lack of self assurance and depression. Out of these thirty-two, four different awful properties are always active in the eight spans of the day comprising three hours in each. Hence the total awful properties in women are thirty-six out of which eight appalling properties including four common described earlier, are always active because of staying above the behavioral limit.

Depression is the only property which is produced as well as carried by women hence they pretend themselves to be depressed thereby depressing their relatives and well wishers. Besides the eight active properties of any period, rest of the twenty-eight are ineffective or hibernated for the span of three hours but can be made active any moment whenever women need so.

Women possess thirty-two good qualities in parallel to their awful properties which includes purity, mercy or forgiveness, melodious voice or polite speaking, coyness, motherhood, abstemiousness or moderate diet, sexual skills, reverential belief or devoutness, endurance or tolerance, simplicity, virginity or chastity, impartiality, conscience, satisfaction, affection, loyalty or faithfulness or intentness, pacific nature or modesty or politeness, eloquence, habit of saving or frugality, constancy or determination, asceticism, innocence, agility, physical attractiveness, ruling tendency, repentance, presence of mind or deliberateness, honesty, constructive nature, foreboding or premonition of danger or sixth sense, knowledge and moral conduct. Above qualities form eight groups comprising of four different qualities. The qualities of such formed groups are interrelated with each other and are complementary to each other. Such eight groups are purity-repentance-abstemiousness-chastity, loyalty-constructiveness-affection-impartiality, pacific nature-simplicity-tolerance-moral conduct, melodious voice-mercy-innocence-honesty, asceticism-devoutness-eloquence-conscience, constancy-ruling tendency-knowledge-deliberateness, sixth sense-agility-physical attractiveness-frugality and motherhood-coyness-sexual skills-satisfaction.

Mannish qualities includes of forgiveness, moderate speaking, abstemiousness, endurance, gentleness, conscience, religious conductor devoutness, affection, discipline, constancy, intentness, deliberateness or presence of mind, physical strength, gumption, knowledge, assiduousness, masculinity, strictness, confidence, impartiality, asceticism, respect for women, ruling tendency, moral conduct and eloquence. These twenty-five properties as well as their respective opposite awful qualities form the men nature.

In ladies, the melodious and sweet voice is praiseworthy while in gents, moderate speaking includes of the heaviness of voice, clarity and decency. Behavioral politeness of women is termed as gentleness in men. The common properties possessed by both of the genders are abstemiousness, affection, impartiality, moral conduct, forgiveness, endurance, ruling tendency, devoutness, asceticism, conscience, eloquence, deliberateness, knowledge, intentness and constancy hence these fifteen properties do not influence the gender. The rest of the seventeen good properties in women govern their feminine nature. Again the appearance of these seventeen properties or their unavailability in the women nature entirely depends on whether they stay above or below the behavioral line. When any one or more of these properties are below the behavioral line or are absent in the behavior of a woman then the reverse quality of that automatically gets effective and can be seen in the nature of that lady. These seventeen properties, which are not considered to be mannish qualities, decide the gender limit in ladies.

Sometimes when the one or more properties deciding the gender often kept by ladies below the gender boundary then gradually they become permanently ineffective or get eloped. This makes a drastic change in their behavior and because of invoking a kind of gender disorder, the conduct of such ladies appear to be mannish. Similarly because of hormonal disorder or some other internal physical changes, some properties of ladies always stay below the gender boundary which ultimately makes their nature as man-like. Thus the women nature going through the elope of more and more aforementioned feminine properties approaches towards gender limit and hence achieves the appearance of middle stage of men and women that is of an eunuch. Again in such gender governing seventeen properties, the more they are eloped, the more women nature looks like the nature of eunuchs. When such properties are entirely eloped, the nature of women gets completely converted in to nature of eunuchs. Now this starts providing physical disorder in various forms. If a very beautiful lady is harsh and bitter speaking with piercing voice or her voice is of low pitch with heaviness of the voice of men then her such symptom resembles to be of eunuch because being a woman she keeps mannish gender governing quality hence suffers with internal contradiction. Ugly looking and bitter speaking women are even closer to the nature of eunuchs. Similarly in case of men, the fifteen common properties have nothing to do with gender while remaining ten properties decide their gender appearance. If some or more properties out of these ten elope then it provides them an appearance of feminine nature but again while approaching to the nature of women they have to cross the gender limit where they actually adopt the appearances of eunuchs. A man, who speaks like women by showing feminine gestures, having the voice like women and walks in an easy pace by giving harmonious movement to his back, in fact looks like eunuch. Almost of such men are of homosexual nature and found to be involved in sodomy. They even keep sexual relations with number of ladies but prefer anal sex and oral sex instead of normal intercourse with them. They are often seen performing oral sex and anal sex with men. Generally if a man keeps long hair like girls then the basic disorders of women psychology are inherited by him. Almost such men live abnormal marital and sexual lives. Some of them are easily attracted towards ladies while most of them keep feminine attitude. They can be seen involved in homosexuality. Often call boys and pimp can be seen keeping long hair.

The changes could be seen in the normal activities of a lady when her gender deciding attributes dissolve. The basic peculiarity seen in these ladies while they walk is that they keep their hands parallel to body and bend their elbows a bit and hold the palm from ribs in such a way as to make palm to be parallel to earth. Such kind of gait is even found in men who possess the same eunuch like behavior. As the lips and anus hole of eunuchs are extraordinary sensitive because of the imperfect sexual organs hence if a man performs unnatural sexual course with some eunuch then he achieves the pleasure by doing anal sex to him or by the oral sex done by eunuch with him. Similarly when the gender deciding properties elope in women, they reach towards the gender boundary which differentiates between the nature of a woman and eunuch, and hence they become more sensitive for oral-sex or sexual plays done through lips and tongue and anal sex. Such ladies prefer to perform oral sex with their husbands and they want their husbands to do anal sex with them as well as lick their anus hole like an animal. As such ladies experience more sexual excitation while they perform the above mentioned two sexual plays hence their respective husbands perform the same finding them more inclined for that. The men, whose masculine behavioral properties get eloped and hence behave like ladies but in actual keep the tendencies of eunuchs, perform oral sex with friends and under age boys and prefer to do oral sex as well as anal sex with their wives. Men of middle age are often found to be involved in sodomy with young guys and under age boys because of the suppression of their masculine gender governing qualities due to the presence of their dominating wives. Though the religiously abstemious men appointed as priests in different religions are often found performing oral sex and sodomy with underage guys, who are sheltered in the synagogues as orphans but in such matters, their sexual activities have nothing to do with gender limit and they do it because of the unavailability of women.

Eunuchs, who possess the looks and appearances of women because of having women like properties as feminine attitude and looking, are in fact more close to women's side in the behavior-limit. Such eunuchs have more percentage of the feminine character and hence can be termed as female-eunuchs. Similarly the eunuchs having more behavioral properties like men stay near the men's side in the gender-limit and can be considered as male-eunuchs. This becomes the base of unnatural or beyond-normal sexual course which is performed among eunuchs. Thus eunuchs have their behavioral-limit but they too are unable to play with their properties like men. Due to aforementioned reason some eunuchs having qualities of women possess the natural beauty and attractive body figure like women and if they do not talk, one can never guess about them being eunuchs.

Through the figures calculated by different surveys, it is found that due to elope of some gender governing properties, the asperity arises in the behavior and conduct of women and hence such women do not look or appear to have feminine nature even after giving birth to children. Almost harsh or roughly speaking women, with piercing voice and possessing iniquitous attributes, stay in this category. The husbands to such ladies live a horrible and painful life because they are bound to reside in the hell made for them by their wives and this includes of the hell before the sexual mating, hell during sexual mating and hell after sexual mating.

It is often heard that the working ladies undergo sexual harassments done by male colleagues or the male officers. Often ladies blame men of their profession for sexual molestation or an attempt of that. Seventy such matters were surveyed thoroughly and it was found that in only one matter, the sexual harassment of an innocent lady was done. In fifty-two matters men were falsely blamed by ladies. In the rest of the seventeen matters, the women themselves were responsible for their so-called sexual molestation. Before going in deep of such matters, a sufficiently long discussion was made with a middle aged lady working in a government office, who had seen one of such matter in the premises of her office. She said, "Almost ladies working in the government offices or banking sectors or in any job related to public dealing, are very practical and are smart enough to be capable to protect them. Such ladies can never be sexually molested or abused as they always dominate over men and this can be easily seen in their family life. If a man wants to be unaffected or secure after having any kind of hot argument with such ladies then this is quite impossible because they follow the aphorism of "neither forgive nor forget". If a man of their surroundings keeps any type of professional or personal rivalry with them then he always has to face false blames put upon him by such ladies. This category of ladies includes of the ladies who visit their office regularly from their residence situated at a distant place. Such ladies have to go their office through rails or buses and these regular journeys make them highly robust and practical. They achieve a tendency of subjugating over men and hence they never become under pressure and do not accept their mistakes. Such ladies, who make their journey through monthly-seasonal-tickets of the public conveyances of traveling, are expert in scolding and conversing in abusive language. To even assume about the sexual, moral or physical harassment of such ladies in the offices is ridiculous. Such ladies spoil the life of many youngsters of their surroundings and of their colleagues by falsely blaming them for the sexual assaults. Very few percent of such instances regarding sexual harassment of working ladies are factual." The innocent girls of the age group of nineteen to twenty-four, working in offices, initially enjoy when sexually seduced by lustful men and in future they become inseparable part of the chaos of illicit sexual relations. Such girls, pretending being bold, are misused by their cunning bosses of private offices or franchises to sexually allure clients and in making fake commitments with the male clients. This can be often seen in the sectors involved in the business of providing holyday-trips in other cities by taking a sufficiently good package.

In the survey of seventy such cases, it was found that in only one matter a lady suffered sexual harassment. In fifty-two matters, the friends and colleagues of the ladies, who were blaming for their sexual harassment, told that so called culprit men did not do anything but they falsely blamed them because of their personnel or official disputes and spoiled the character of those men. Out of such seventy ladies concerned with aforementioned seventy matters, who were blaming men of their official premises, thirty-one widows and twenty-three married ladies were already having illicit sexual relations with the other colleagues and outsiders. Hence out of seventy such ladies, fifty-four were already sexually adulterated and were having immoral sexual relations with number of men. Twenty-three of them were even already defamed for their being easy to lay for sexual plays. In few matters, such false blaming was done by the ladies with the intention to make their virtuous image in the views of other colleagues and husbands. Except the fifty-two cases discussed above, in ten matters, the ladies were already having long time sexual relations with men whom they blamed later because of not achieving some specific purpose like financial profit etc from them. In rest of the seven matters, such false blaming was done by ladies just to become the center of attraction by highlighting themselves. Many working ladies, who keep illicit sexual relations willingly with their colleagues while later blame them for the so-called sexual harassment, are found threatening and abusing the wives of such men by telephone and even disclose their illicit relations with their husbands thereby compelling them to divorce their husbands. In such legal matters, a wide conversation was done with the authorities affiliated to judiciary and administration. The higher administrative authorities and the judiciary members admitted that they were aware of this fact about the false blaming done by almost women but unable to give judgment against such women because accused men could never proof the illicit character of such ladies and their involvement in harlotry. It is very difficult for a man to prove that some lady, who is now sexually blaming him, was voluntarily having sexual relations with him from earlier. Behind this, a very basic fact lays and that is after performing illicit sexual intercourse with a man, a lady can morally degrade herself up to unlimited extent to blame or harass that man while such degradation is seldom found in a man and when he performs copulation, he rarely discloses such relations for harassing that lady. Exceptions of this are rarely found in ladies but often in men who are sexually perverted.

The society and judiciary have made an assumption that men can not suffer from sexual harassments. This is quite deceiving because a man can proof himself to be sexually molested by some lady only when he is underage. As per the figures collected from the numerous surveys, up to the fourteen years age, thirty-five percent males are sexually harassed and fifty-seven percent are physically or morally harassed while twelve percent of girls are sexually abused and three percent are physically or morally molested. The forty-one percent of the male of the age group of fourteen to twenty-one years are sexually harassed and thirty-two percent of them are physically or morally humiliated while sixty-three percent of girls are sexually harassed and twelve percent of them are physically or morally harassed. The thirteen percent male of the age group of twenty-one to thirty-five are sexually molested and seventy-one percent are physically or morally harassed while eight percent female of the same age group are sexually humiliated and two percent of them are physically or morally harassed. The one percent men are sexually harassed during the age group of thirty-five to fifty and fifty-two percent are physically or morally harassed while three percent of the ladies are sexually harassed and seven percent are physically or morally harassed. At the age group of above fifty, thirteen percent men are physically or morally harassed while twenty-six percent of ladies are physically or morally harassed. Such physical and moral harassments, faced by the men or women of the age group of above thirty, was done by ladies in ninety-seven percent of cases while only three percent by men. If a young boy blames a lady for his sexual harassment then his relatives and society consider him as an impotent. Again this is assumed that only females undergo sexual harassment which is entirely wrong because men are sexually, physically and morally more harassed in comparison to women. Most of the young guys achieve the sexual knowledge when they are sexually abused by widows, unmarried ladies and aged ladies but unfortunately such instances are seldom disclosed. A renowned doctor told that his son was weak in mathematics hence he arranged a widow teacher for him. One day, the son informed him weeping that the widow teacher makes him nude and performs oral sex with him. The father was shocked to hear this and hence he dismissed the female teacher by appointing a male. He said that if the same incident would have happened with his young daughter by some male teacher then he would have ruined teacher's life but if a lady is blamed for doing such immoral act, she would falsely blame the father of the minor boy for her sexual harassment. The reason behind this is that the virginity or chastity of men has no value in the opinion of the society and law but the virginity of a lady, who is not virgin because of her regular involvement in illicit sexual relations or adultery, has a lot importance. He said that by the time he will prove that the widow has done sexual harassment of his minor son, before that she will proof with the help of some shrewd advocate that she was being sexually abused or forcefully raped by the father and now father is falsely blaming her to mislead the court so that she may not put the actual matter of her sexually harassment in front of the judiciary. In such circumstances, the judiciary, media and the society will consider that harlot to be innocent and true.

A very peculiar behavior of making brother to some guys is often seen in the girls. Some girls choose lethargic guys and keep the relation of brother-sister with them. Often girls are found making brothers to guys who are very active and involved in making nuisances so as to protect themselves from other guys. In contrary to this, guys make such relations of brother and sister with the girls who are very active and are beyond their capacity of being handled or are the friends of the girls with whom they are desirous to carry love affairs. Again guys often make such relations of sisters with girls with the intention to influence their desired girls while such relations are kept by girls just to take help of guys in their normal or some peculiar works.

Women have their own interpretations and definitions of the terms related to them and such descriptions done by them with their peculiar opinion are quite different from the descriptions done by society and judiciary. They impose their own social definitions on society and mostly their descriptions look like proper. A lady, who is involved in adultery or sexual relations with her boyfriend or with other man, never admits that such physical relations made by her are illicit and defines that to be true love while if she finds some other lady performing such sexual relations, she describes that to be harlotry. While performing illicit sexual relations with her lover, if she becomes pregnant then she insists him for marriage. In some of such instances, guys keep the opinion that their girlfriends disrobed themselves and did copulation with them without any hesitation in spite of being familiar with the fact that such before-marriage sexual relations are illicit hence there is no assurance that they would not have kept such relations in previous affairs and would not keep the same after marriage with other men. The girl, as a lover, finds herself to be skeptical for her own behavior regarding this. If because of any reason, a guy denies marrying then the woman inside the lady awakes and now she finds the definition of her sexual relations with him to be altered in her opinion. She informs her relatives and society that she has been sexually molested and harassed by that man. Though she herself has allured and motivated her lover for sexual plays but now she explains herself and the society that she was sexually raped by him. Suddenly her parents remember that they mentioned their daughter's age three to four years less than the actual one in the birth certificate, who is in fact of more than twenty-one years. Now that lady involved in illicit sexual relations since past many years, becomes underage and as per the laws, the lover had forcefully motivated her to perform mating to make her virginity lost. She becomes innocent and it is assumed by the society that she was sexually molested. Again the lady, who is involved readily in sexual plays with different men, is now considered to be novice in sexual knowledge because she is underage. If she gets pregnant then she willingly go for abortion and afterwards says that the boyfriend forced her for going through abortion or her abortion was done deceitfully without informing her. Such examples are frequently seen in the society. Thirty-five such instances were thoroughly observed where such blames were put upon the men and it was seen that in twenty-three of that, the girls were not under age but their date of birth were mentioned three to four years lesser in their birth certificates by the parents, who were blaming the men for the sexual harassment of their so-called minor daughters. In thirty one such matters, fathers of the ladies confessed during very personnel conversation that they were familiar with the fact that their daughters were guilty and this was not the first time when they were found involved in such incidents. They confessed that their daughters were of loose character and they were fed-up and became helpless with the attitude of them. When a renowned criminal lawyer was personally interviewed regarding this situation, he said that whenever a girl is found to be involved in some illicit sexual activity or in any other crime, her name is always hided from the society. Even news papers never disclose the name of such girls with the intention that the girls might get defamed. Our society and law never admits that a lady can commit any offense. The ladies always take advantage of this and commit social crimes. Unfortunately this is very true in context of a country like India that such ladies get moral support to perform sexual crimes because they knew that their names will never be disclosed by the media and the society as well as the judiciary will always favor them. If an underage girl is found to be involved in sexual relations then her parents and she herself should be punished because in almost of such instances, she does it willingly and her parents are only responsible for that because of not giving proper attentions to their daughter. Again to stop the so called sexual crimes, this is the best way that if the girl is minor then her parents should be punished equally as the offender while if lady is not minor then she should get more severe punishment if her involvement is proved because she is committing double crime, one as her sexual involvement thereby committing harlotry and the second by misleading judiciary. Again unfortunately this is not possible in India because if a minor boy riding motorbike faces an accident because of his being unskilled and gets wounded or dies then the driver of other vehicle is punished and this happens usually in India. Society or judiciary never blames rich parents for providing vehicle to their underage children, who are not authorized to drive. These all circumstances appear because of prejudiced society and incompetent channel of judiciary.

Somewhere ladies suddenly disclose about their sexual relations with specific men. In almost of such instances, the blamed men are renowned ministers or businessmen or high ranked officers. A lady, who is considered to be virgin because of being unmarried, when declares about her illicit sexual relations with such a celebrity or falsely blames him for her so called sexual harassment then society and media consider that lady to be innocent and destitute and show sympathy with her by starting a mission to destroy the dignity of the celebrity. It is the biggest misconception spread in the society that unmarried Indian ladies are virgin or they do not loose their virginity before marriage. In such instances, parents of the lady compel the accused man through legal channel to intimidate him so that they may get money from him and may prove their characterless daughter to be of virtuous character. Media is very familiar with the fact that nobody wants to see the news against a lady but everyone is willing to see such sexual blames put upon some popular personality hence such media persons start scanning the past of that man. Nobody is interested to know that why that lady is now blaming a reputed person for her sexual harassment with whom she has kept illicit relations willingly and is more or less like a concubine of him. If a destitute lady is compelled to keep illicit sexual relations then this is certainly her sexual harassment but if a lady keeps sexual relations with number of men for the sake of financial gain or to achieve her utterly high ambitions by financially rising rapidly and now blames a man for her sexual molestation with whom even she had kept such illicit sexual relations in past then this can never be considered as her sexual harassment. Such instances can be seen in the society where a lady discloses the secret by blaming someone for her pregnancy. Sometimes they disclose this even when their so called illegitimate children have been young. It is usually found that in such false blames of sexual harassment, initially ladies are involved willingly and get the sexual pleasure as well as financial gain from the men but suddenly blame men if get pregnant while abortion is dangerous for their life or if do not get their excessive demands of either money or some other assets to be fulfilled or to prove themselves of virtuous character, if find being defamed because of such illicit sexual relations. In many countries, it is prohibited for unmarried women to get pregnant because it is considered to be a social crime and is treated with the sight of hatred. Unfortunately in spite of that, such characterless ladies accept the hatred possessed by the society for them voluntarily just for the sake of socially harassing a renowned man. Again in this situation, our prejudiced society and judiciary assume that the unmarried mother or unmarried pregnant lady is struggling for the existence of her born or unborn child. In actuality, a lady who has faced abortions in past and is involved in illicit sexual relations, has no meaning of the motherhood because for her, aborting or killing the child is just like slaying an insect of gutter. A lady, who is involved in any kind of illicit sexual relations or adultery, blames a man for sexual harassment only to satisfy her false ego and sadistic nature as well as to achieve financial gain. Again some ladies put such blames on wealthy and renowned celebrities just because of popularity stunt. It is found in the surveys that in more than ninety percent of such matters, the direct or indirect initiatives to keep unlawful sexual relations are taken by ladies by representing themselves as a purchasable item or appraising themselves to provide sexual services. In spite of this fact, such blaming is always done by ladies never by men. To perform prostitution or living like a concubine of some wealthy renowned man for the sake of sexual pleasure, popularity, financial gain, social power and political status, is a wrong way or unethical shortcut to achieve the ambitions. Such ladies can be seen everywhere who adopted such shortcuts to accomplish their unlimited ambitions. Often ladies can be seen providing their sexual skills and services to higher political leaders to make their own political backgrounds or to make an entry in politics. Now if such a lady, who has ruined the family of other innocent married ladies by detaching their husbands with them, dies or is killed then this is not a very shocking matter because it has to happen. Parents of such ladies blame some peculiar man for the death of their daughter in spite of knowing that their daughter was living a life of harlotry. Such parents never stop their daughters when they keep illicit sexual relations with numerous men. They know that not only a lady publicly available to anyone for her sexual skills is a prostitute instead a lady who keeps illicit sexual relations with a married man for the sake of pleasure or any kind of gain is also a prostitute still they announce that their demised daughters were of high ethics and morals while men affiliated to them were sexually corrupt. Parents are not underage or innocent that they can not understand about few hours' day or night duties of their daughters by which they achieve plenty of facilities and unlimited money.

Astonishing facts have come up from different surveys done regarding this. The public view for a man becomes negative when he is blamed by some lady for sexual molestation or when he is blamed by the relatives of such a lady after her death, for sexually harassing her and causing her death. In twenty-one such matters out of twenty-two, where such ladies died or killed, they were also having sexual relations with other men. Nineteen of such ladies were known prostitutes of their social circle charging ten times more for providing their sexual services in comparison to a normal social prostitute. Seventeen of them started asking for more money or permits for government contracts or immovable assets like a piece of land etc. When concerned men refused to fulfill their excessive demands, they start warning them about disclosing their sexual relations in public. In fourteen matters, men were aware with the sexual relations of their concubines with other men though they were taking their asking-price from them on behalf of being their personal keeps. In five matters, such ladies were compelling men to leave their wives and children. When such endless desires of them were not satisfied by the men, they start blaming them for their sexual harassment. Attributes like self-respect, patience, love and morality were entirely absent in such ladies. They were just living their life for the sake of sexual pleasure, financial gain, making high contacts with authorities and self satisfaction and these were the ground of their blaming to renowned and decent men. It is genuine to call such men as decent because though they were having amorous desires and were betraying their families by keeping illicit sexual relations, the initiatives for such sexual relations were taken by ladies in sixteen matters out of twenty-two. In Nineteen matters, men were puzzled by the behavior and attitude of their wives hence got attracted towards such ladies to seek emotional affection while such ladies took the advantage of this situation and provoked them for sexual relations. Ladies, who are well familiar with men psychology, are often found to be seeking their self interests by sexually tempting men. In almost of such instances, men, who are in distress because of inhuman attitude and immoral behavior of their wives, get trapped in the snares of the illusory world of adultery made by such women. As the sexual appetite troubles men similar to the hunger for food hence the teenage girls and ladies, who are expertise in sexual skills as well as having perfection in expressing women's psychology, offer themselves as a lustful body or a medium to accomplish sexual pleasure to rich and powerful men in order to achieve their unending ambitions of wealth and power. In all of such disclosed matters, society and judiciary keep the opinion that the innocent helpless ladies are sexually and morally harassed by the men but in actual, men are being harassed and sexually seduced by such ladies.

Somewhere such relationship between a man and his keep lasts long and a typical sequence of give and take goes on but as such ladies, who are by nature utter greedy, are eager to achieve self benefit and ready to quickly earn money by any means, possess a keen desire to develop higher contacts and approach to the political lane hence she starts demanding such facilities and benefits which are against the law and are unfair. Again when the concerned man refuses to fulfill her demands, the lady who is in fact a prostitute, threatens him to disclose the sexual relationship in public. The renowned man gets worried because he knows that though such relations were built by the consent of her and even she took the initiatives but she will say that he took the advantage of her helplessness and she was compelled by him to make such relations. This all leads an argument and hence a violent situation arises between them in which lady appears with her most aggressive temperament to hide her own faults. During such conflicts, almost ladies keep the tendency to distress others hence somewhere they commit suicide or somewhere are accidentally killed in the violence that takes place between them and their men. It is necessary to understand that in such situations, if a lady is unfortunately killed by the psychologically depressed or mentally puzzled man then this had to happen otherwise he would have been killed by that lady. This is in fact not a murder instead this is self protection done by man to defend himself. If such a lady performs the same then she takes the help of men with whom she is having sexual relations in parallel hence it becomes a conspiracy or cold blooded murder and can not be considered being done as self-defense. Few incidents are disclosed where professional female media persons, doctors, engineers and ladies studying in the management colleges or other professional colleges died in the same circumstances because at present scenario, a sufficiently big percentages of such professional ladies are involved in earning wealth by providing their sexual skills. When such a lady dies then the accused person gets punishment from the judiciary, though usually it takes a long span but ultimately his social image and family gets affected. This is a subject of analysis that who is the actual culprit. A man who was tempted by the sexual services provided by a lustful lady or the lady herself because ultimately she was behind this so called sexual play but unfortunately died or the society and judiciary members, who are living under the fear of the women of their own families in the form of their mothers, sisters, daughters or wives, but are not able to make a proper assumption to give fair decision against women even when they know that women are wrong. Such liberty provided to women and the laws by which women are made powerful to falsely blame and harass men, have done nothing except making them sexually corrupt and mentally prepare to harass in-laws as well as husbands thereby increasing the growth of social as well as family crimes.

Such a matter happened in India became well highlighted where a lady blamed a renowned political leader for keeping sexual relations with her. In another case, a leader was found involved in a sexual scandal and his video recording was made during sting operation done against him. In a popular instance, a lady declared that the father of her son was a renowned political leader and her motherhood was compelling her to allow her illegitimate son to get the right on the property of his so-called father. Everyone said that the affiliated ladies in aforementioned matters were live deities and should be worshipped but no one could dare to say that why they were keeping illicit sexual relations when they knew that a lady keeping such relations is said to be a prostitute. A renowned advocate said that prostitution is not a legally accepted profession in a country like India. Hence if a lady says that she was having illicit sexual relations and her illegitimate son should get his right or she should get any kind of compensation from the man with whom she was having illicit sexual relations then this is ridiculous. Any mature lady keeping illicit sexual relations is only responsible for her such ill deeds no one else because she utilizes and enjoys the money as well as the facilities she gets from her illegal profession of prostitution hence if she faces some trouble in her profession then law should not take her favor. Whenever a man having a good stock of prohibited drugs for misuse, is caught, he is severely punished while a man purchasing a little amount of that from him for his personal use is least punished or not punished. Then why the rules are just reverse of it in case of prostitution because prostitutes are seldom punished while the men taking their services are severely punished in a country like India. Such instances are often seen in almost every country where men involved in taking the services of prostitutes, when caught red handed, face social menace, degradation of their seniority in offices as a punishment or permanent suspension from their jobs and family-boycott etc. Unfortunately we never hear about even a single instance in which a lady involved in illegal relations faces such situations. Even their names are not disclosed to protect them from probable defame. Shockingly, involvement in prostitution provides men degradation and loss in almost all the fields while the same involvement provides affluent wealth, social status, political future and numerous other facilities to ladies. In all of such matters, the dignity and social status of the so called offender ruins before any judgment is given against him. As such instances are a sort of weapon of the opposite parties against the blamed leader and his party hence the opposition demands for the dismissal of that leader or his ruling party. Such matters are often seen in the political lane. As the opinion of public is in fact an unthinking imitation on the part of a group like a group of sheep hence almost in such instances, the so called liable man is defamed and publicly menaced. Society never considers the present temperament and life styles of such ladies and always assumes that man to be blameworthy. One such personality blamed by a lady said, "It is not difficult for us to take the sexual services of high leveled call-girls or even of beautiful ladies who are newcomer in harlotry because at present, almost young girls and ladies are eager to disrobe themselves for the sake of earning money. Almost ladies are ready for providing sexual services if one is capable to pay them. Ladies normally prefer to adopt the shortcut of harlotry to rise instead of struggling and dedicating themselves towards the righteous path of success. This is the factual image of nowadays Indian culture. If any lady says that she is virtuous and never had illicit relations to rise in the career then this is only because she must not be having any appropriate offer from a man or she may not be worthy by appearance for getting paid. If suppose any lady does not give her consent for sexual union then we never pursue her because multiple times more beautiful ladies than that lady are available just we have to throw money." This is true that the high class society always suffers from the fear of probable defame that can be put upon them because of illicit sexual relations or extramarital affairs while ladies of immoral character with normal financial backgrounds are found to be eager to expose such relations as a popularity stunt because their would-be probable defame becomes a source of fame and wealth for them in future. Hence almost of such blames put by such ladies are fabricated. More than ninety percent of such ladies, who cry publicly for the safety of their virginity and proclaim by the beat of drum about their sexual harassment, tell lies because they have already sexually molested themselves number of times by keeping illicit sexual relations with their desired men. A lady, who voluntarily performs such immoral sexual relations, when seeks that she is not getting appropriate price for that, starts blaming the concerned man for her sexual harassment.

In context of a female colleague, an account manager of a local firm told that during the conversations, teasingly she used to hit on the back and thighs of male colleagues. Once while joking, a man did the same with her then she got furious and complained against him blaming him for indecent touching with malicious sexual intentions. If a lady touches a man then this is her right or a sort of favor to that man because such touches done by her are considered to be done with healthy feeling while if the same is done by a man then it is assumed that his act is an indication of sexual perversion in him. Again the main reason behind this is that, like a custom, it is still assumed that there is no preface of men's virginity hence men can never be sexually molested or harassed by ladies while ladies, even when they keep illicit sexual relations with numerous men, are always considered to be virgin and it is assumed that they are always sexually molested and harassed by men. Another reason is that almost Indian ladies, who have blindly adopted nudity and have been skilled in physical and moral harlotry, though seems to be educated and decent and are well versed with foreign languages, but in fact their cheap mentality is not worth of more than two cowries. A lady blamed a man for her sexual rape and the man was punished by the judiciary for imprisonment. When that man was interviewed personally, he told that the lady, who blamed him, was a prostitute and he was in love with her. He insisted her to marry but she denied and when he compelled her, she blamed her for sexual harassment. The very next day, the same lady was approached for her sexual services just to check the truth of the statement of the culprit. She was ready for providing sexual entertainment by charging two thousand rupees. Unfortunately the judiciary never considers the background of the sexual life of such ladies. How can a single man rape a harlot without hitting her or making her unconscious? We can consider men and women as fishes in a pond. As a single fish pollutes the whole of the pond similarly the nature of twenty-two percent men, who are of illicit character and immoral, is imposed upon the image of rest of the seventy-eight percent virtuous men while the exact reverse way of judging the behavior is done in the case of women and twenty percent virtuous women's behavior is considered to be the behavior of rest of the eighty percent sexually corrupt women. That is why in any legal or social matter, men are almost considered to be wrong while women are always considered to be right and almost immoral ladies take the advantage of this to falsely blame men.

The faithfulness of married ladies has nothing to do with their physique or mental level. Once a lady involved in adultery told that if a man, possessing strong penis and extraordinary sexual power, makes sexual relations with a lady then such lady always seeks him for copulation. Often young virgin girls possess different kind of physical illness including physical weakness, body pain, mental weakness and fits etc. Such girls possess hundreds of disease and when they go to take medical treatment, they seldom get relief. The basic reason is that all of such girls need sexual intercourse and astonishingly, it is found that the moment they are involved in copulation, either after marriage with their husbands or with their boyfriends, they get cured. The aged or middle aged men possess strong sexual power therefore young ladies are more attracted towards them. The young generation is not having that much sexual stamina hence nowadays, ladies go for adultery. Women's temperament is gradually being superimposed over men's disposition which is ultimately invoking a kind of impotency in men. Hence the percentage of infertility in men has been increased. The quality as well as quantity of chromosomes of men is continuously decreasing. A popular lady doctor told that such decrement in masculinity of men is only because psychologically they are suppressed by their ladies. If the situations of women dominating over men in the society are continued then perhaps after few decades, almost men will face infertility. The anxiety of men, regarding the chastity of their ladies, ill-effects their sexual capabilities. Again the over sexual capabilities and stamina of senior citizens can be imagined by this that almost young girls are sexually attracted towards them. Such a school girl told that she could never achieve that much sexual pleasure with her five years elder boyfriend that she got from an aged man. A driver of a middle aged I.A.S. officer told that he had been fed-up with the officer because everyday he has to seek new girls for him. He told that almost everyday his boss demands for two to four girls for sexual pleasure. Though he was earning from all such prostitutes by taking his commission but still he has been puzzled because his boss demands for newcomer girls. A retired I.A.S. officer, living near to that officer, was having sexual relations with his step daughter. The lady doctor said that if the situations remain the same then after around twenty years, all ladies will get involved in adultery because a single man will not be able to calm down continuously increasing sexual craving of a single lady. If a lady is sexually hot then she is always winner in sexual plays and a man can never satisfy her while If she is sexually cold or possesses less sexual excitation then also she is a winner in sexual plays and needs number of men to achieve sexual satisfaction. In contrary to this, a man is impotent if he is having less sexual excitation or is unable to satisfy his bed-mate. This situation is rapidly arising with the guys of present generation. Then what is the solution to this? The only solution is that ladies have to live like ladies. Presently women in India have no fear of their elder relatives, society and judiciary hence they are being despotic thereby suppressing masculinity of men. A renowned female criminal lawyer said that it is good to provide reservation in different fields to women as this is a healthy approach but judiciary has to be unbiased in the matters related to ladies and hence women should get severe punishments on their involvement in ill-activities. If this is not done and judiciary does not become strict on women then certainly in future, ladies will deny obeying or accepting the decisions given by judiciary and this is in fact going to happen in India. If Indian ladies are desirous to adopt ill attributes by performing harlotry and living a self-indulged life declaring it to be life style of American ladies then they should get the equal punishments on their misdeeds by judiciary as men get because that is what happens in America. Unrestrained life style of ladies is an inseparable part of Christianity and it seems to be very normal in their religion because Christian ladies never impose their sexual craving and other women's ill-qualities upon their society and men while such abandoned behavior is not meant for Hinduism as Indian ladies do not know the actual definition of unrestrained life and hence for them, unrestrained life-style starts from making illicit sexual relations and ends on suppressing men of their society.

In the present scenario, in fact the changes which ladies have adopted in the blind race of modernism, calling it westernization thereby blaming western countries, and about which they say essential qualities as an indication of new generation or modernity are nudity, sexual debauchment and false doctrine. As the disastrous thunderstorm of the fashion behind modernity mostly affected the wearing or cloths hence ladies naturally got influenced by that and to reveal the body parts being almost naked, justifying it by calling it to be latest fashion, became an identity of them. They start decorating their nudity by defining it as their dressing sense. Such ladies deceitfully scold the men or virtuous ladies by addressing them backward, barbarous and uneducated orthodox who oppose them for their indecency of the wearing done by excessively exposing the body parts.

In context of this, some young female models were very personally interviewed then before speaking almost of them took the assurance that their names shall not be disclosed. One of those models said that if God puts a layer of skin on the women body just to hide their teats, vagina and the curve of buttocks then every lady will come out naked. Second model said that ladies never keep the feeling of shyness and all ladies are shameless because in fact ladies possess a virtual boundary-line of bashfulness and once they cross that limit, they become shameless. In such case, it hardly matters for them whether they are wearing cloths or are entirely nude because the basic necessity is that they should get money or perverted pleasure for that. Third model said that during the very initial period of her modeling profession, she was frightened that while walking on the stage with sexually alluring wearing, she might get indecently abused or sexually approached by the young guys but gradually she came to know that men society is bounded to live like an eunuch or an impotent even after having mannish qualities. She again explained her statement by saying that when some male actors, singers, players or some other male celebrities are performing on stage or are on the stage then sometimes young girls come over the stage and kiss them publicly and the celebrities become shocked. In a popular case recently happened in India, a lady did the same and even she scratched the celebrity by her nails. Female media persons announced this shameless act as her enthusiasm and guts. One female lady from a channel said that now women are awaking and this is a start of new era entirely governed by women. She declared that this was a symbol that women are being aware for their rights. If the same act is done by a man with a female celebrity then the female media persons describe it a sexual assault or an attempt to rape and the so called offender would have faced legal punishment as well as would have been brutally beaten by the public. If we ask to that lady announcer that suppose her daughter performs such immoral act then what she will say. She will definitely say that she would have supported her daughter. The reason behind this is that such nudity can be done voluntarily by professional female only and almost such ladies possess a keen desire that their daughters should perform any kind of sexually or socially immoral act to achieve popularity which they could not achieve in their life time. Such indecent rigidity arising in women is an indication of the devastation of the society and codes of morals, in coming future. The fourth model said that she did unlimited efforts to become a model as she belonged to a rural area. Whatever she heard about the sexual or physical molestation done in the field of modeling, situations were very better than that. Sexual harassment of a model in modeling profession happens only when she gives her consent hence in actual it is absolutely wrong to call it harassment. Almost models are eager to disrobe themselves or make sexual relations on the directions of the promoters because they want to get success quickly by adopting any kind of immoral shortcuts. The worst situations are in the villages or rural areas where the girls of even fourteen to fifteen years, voluntarily keep illicit sexual relations. She said that one of her friend was pregnant at the time of marriage ceremony. When the bridegroom's side came to know about this at the eleventh hour, they denied for marriage. In order to hide their daughter's fault, the bride's side falsely blamed groom's side for asking dowry and filed police complaint against them. The groom and his parents were immediately arrested by the local police. Groom's side insisted to the police officer that the bride was pregnant and anyone can judge this just by looking at her abdominal portion but police officer said that he is helpless because he has to follow the laws. Next day, it became the hot news that a bold and virtuous lady denied to marry at the last moment because groom asked for dowry. Women organizations praised that lady by saying that all ladies should learn a lesson from that lady. It was mentioned nowhere that the virgin bride was pregnant at the time of her marriage. She said that the parents and relatives of that lady were aware of the fact that their girl was pregnant and when the groom's side denied for marriage then parents of bride requested to her and some other friends of their daughter to falsely blame the groom's side youngsters for sexual teasing so that they may get a point to blame and quarrel with groom's side and deny for marriage. Hence in cities, the situations are much better than the villages.

The statements given by models were very normal but the fourth model highlighted the new information. As she was from a rural area hence she told that she has gone through such incidents where on the occasion of marriage, girls' side refuse to marry and falsely blame the grooms' side for asking dowry in order to hide their own faults. To get the veracity of the statement said by the fourth model, such incidents were investigated in some rural areas of the country. Out of such eleven incidents that came to know through the investigations done in only six villages, two were in the knowledge of administration and were highlighted and three were managed by the local village court while rest of the six were settled through the mutual consent of the aged men of the villages. In all of eleven such matters, the brides were having illicit sexual relations and even six of them were pregnant at time of marriage. In such six matters, the parents of the bride were familiar with the fact that their daughters were pregnant therefore they arranged their marriage immediately with the men of their community and did not inform the grooms' side about this with the thought that once marriage is done, grooms would not be able to raise their objections because of one sided laws favoring all illicit women's community and brides' side. When parents of the grooms' side came to know about the pregnancy of their would-be daughters-in-law, they refused for marriage hence the brides' side immediately falsely blamed them for asking dowry. In three matters, the brides ran away with their lovers at the time of marriage and parents of them blamed grooms' side for dowry demand instead of accepting the truth. In two matters, would-be grooms came to know about the illicit sexual involvement of their would-be brides through their friends, who were invited in the marriage ceremony and hence they denied for marriage. These two guys were sent to prison because they were falsely charged for asking dowry. Five tremendous matters were sorted out in the same villages where after the marriage, grooms came to know that their brides were already pregnant but they were helpless to take any step because they were threatened by the brides' side. In two separate instances, the brides' side denied to give the dowry about which they promised at the time of betrothal to give at the time of marriage. When the earlier decided dowry was demanded by grooms' side, the parents of bride boldly denied giving that and instead of expressing their helplessness, they pressurized for marriage. They deceitfully invited grooms' side and rescued them with the help of other villagers to compel them for marriage. When still grooms' side did not give consent for marriage, they were beaten by the villagers and were blamed for asking dowry. In all of the aforementioned instances, the grooms and their family members had to face imprisonment and social defame and the blind media made such morally corrupt ladies popular by highlighting their names as virtuous heroines. The ladies involved in social services or women organizations and women psychologists praised such ladies and declared that now revolution is taking place in women. Indeed, the revolution is taking place in women but in the field of making illicit sexual relations and harlotry.

This is true that awful properties of women are utilized in the society on very wide scale and almost women are sufficiently paid for this. Ladies, who are ready to disrobe or reveal their body, have good opportunities in modeling and film industry. Eloquent ladies with indecent short temperament have good opportunities in the field of marketing, private-banking sectors and in other fields of public dealing. Merciless ladies have good future in nursing profession. Sexually corrupt ladies have wonderful opportunities in all of the fields. Innocent looking wicked ladies are helpful in carrying prohibited drugs or other illegal items. Again sexually corrupt ladies are used as bribes to finalize big deals. People take the help of aggressive temperament of ladies in making agitations or strikes. Women are extensively utilized in spreading rumors. Women are utilized to vilify decent men. Often it is seen that during agitations, people blocking the road to jam the traffic put ladies in the middle of the road. When some men on vehicle request them to clear the route so that they may go ahead, ladies strictly deny. When men argue to them then they start shouting. If the same act of blocking the road is done by men then some passengers or policemen by pressure make the road clear by physically opposing them but in case of ladies, policemen say that they are helpless. Often men facing such situation say," We can do nothing as this is the era of ladies dominating over men." In such a jam, when policemen try to clear the road, ladies start disrobing themselves on the road and policemen run away. In a traffic jam deliberately made by ladies, a sixteen year school girl requested them to let her rickshaw go but ladies did not permit her even after knowing that she was going to appear in her exam. The school girl said to them," Before shouting on the beat of drum regarding your rights, first of all learn to be a woman." Then that schoolgirl went back to take another route to her school. They did not allow an ambulance carrying an injured man to go to hospital. When some decent ladies stood-up against them then they started shouting. In another traffic-jam made by ladies, some decent ladies tried to stop them and requested them to let vehicles go then they started abusing. A lady, who was protesting such ladies when asked about this, said," Brother, nobody dares to fight or argue with such ladies because they have already crossed all the boundary-lines of morality. We have to tolerate such ladies at most for five to ten minutes but just think about their husbands and children, who are bound to live with them. Professional prostitutes get ashamed in front of such ladies. This is an entirely different category of ladies whose count in increasing very rapidly. They never listen to anyone, neither to their parents nor to their husbands. Whatever logic is settled in their dumb conscience, they follow that doesn't matter if someone lives or dies." A popular religious saint following Hinduism, when asked about such changed temperament of ladies, said," This was the biggest mistake of Hinduism giving the simile and status of deities to ladies. Our religion is flexible and unfortunately our religious priests and men could not keep control over ladies that is why almost ladies have been sexually and morally corrupt." A Muslim advocate told that interfere of judiciary in Islamic family codes have started spreading adultery and wickedness in Muslim women. Almost Muslim women are incest as they perform adultery or illicit sexual relations only with nearby close relatives or Muslim men and that is why their ill-sexual relations are hidden from the people of other religions but now they are spreading sexual chaos outside and keeping such forbidden relations with the men of other religions. Muslim men have no problem if their ladies keep such relations within the community but they can never tolerate if the ladies keep the same with the men of other religions. In a matter happened in Uttar Pradesh, two Muslim girls killed their brother because he saw both of them making illicit sexual relations. The elder sister was married while younger was unmarried and both were having such immoral relations. The brother tried to explain his sisters that they were going against Islamic culture then they killed him as he was being an impediment in making their ill-deeds. Later they falsely blamed their brother that he was corrupt and often used to abuse religious scripture holy *Quran.* He again said," Such shrewdness is taking place in women only because of excessive support that they are getting from incapable and absurd judiciary. All Islamic men should get united to oppose judiciary interfering in Islamic family matters otherwise we too will face the worst situations caused by our ladies in future that is at present Hindu men are facing."

Ladies involved in women welfare societies or women organizations seldom give proper guidelines to other ladies instead they advise newly married ladies to struggle for the legal rights of women and such legal rights are performing sexual debauchment and harassing the in-laws. They seldom advise newly married ladies to improve themselves. One such newly married lady told that once she misbehaved with a guest and her mother-in-law put objection on her fault publicly then she herself retorted her. When her husband tried to make her understand, she got furious instead of accepting her fault and went to her father's residence. The mother of her was working in some women organization and was of very arrogant temperament. When husband came to convince his wife at her home, mother of the lady scolded him and sent him alone by not permitting her daughter to go with son-in-law. After some days, lady realized that in whole of the incident she was wrong while her husband and mother-in-law were right. She told her mother that she wants to go back to husband's place but her mother did not allow her. To pass her time, she started visiting to mother's office of "Freedom seekers women". There she realized after hearing the problems of newly married ladies that in almost of such instances, the problems arise only because of the false ego of such ladies. Ladies never admit their mistakes and enhance the complications by wrong arguments. Almost of such organizations look for such ladies and provide them unethical guidance, who are already misguided. They are provided the shrewd advices of lawyers and are taught numerous ways to harass husbands and in-laws. They are taught how they can prove their husbands to be sexually impotent and how they can trap their in-laws in the false blames of asking dowry. Such morally corrupt ladies are taught there the ways by which they can force their husbands to live separately with them by isolating other family members. They are told to keep their desires in front of husbands at the time of sexual intercourse and should allow them to touch only when they assure to fulfill such immoral desires. Every kind of false blames that can be imposed upon husbands, are taught there. Again such ladies, who are in problem because of the troubles produced by themselves, are never advised to improve themselves. Though such wicked advices which are provided in almost of such organizations, are very helpful for those newly married ladies whose in-laws are of disgusting nature and harass physically as well as mentally to them but in reality the percentage of such instances is very less in comparison to the matters where new brides are responsible. Almost of such instances, which in actual happens in very less ratio, where new brides are harassed, seldom come in the knowledge of administration. It was horrible to see the ladies of the organization misguiding to young ladies approaching for the advices thereby ultimately making their family life hell. Very few of such organizations give proper guidelines to such ladies and they are ever succeeded to settle the family matters in real sense. Ultimately, one day, that lady silently left the home of her parents and went to husband's place. She said, "My own mother behaves indecently and keeps inhuman behavior for my brother's wife, who is her daughter-in-law, then how can she give proper advice to other misguided ladies, I could never understand." This is the biggest example of the dual identity of women as they desire their daughters to rule in their husband's residences while they never allow their daughters-in-law to live freely. All young ladies are desirous to rule in their family by dominating husbands and in-laws while they never allow their brothers' wives to rule in the similar way.

Is it so that women have no conscience to differentiate among virtuous and immoral deeds and why do they consider all the immoral deeds done by them as virtuous and the good deeds done by others as immoral, to understand all of this, it is essential to know the perspective of women. Every lady keeps dual opinions or perspectives for any incident or behavior shown by one. We can call these two perspectives as pretentious perspective and actual perspective. We can comprehend this as some aged ladies are discussing about some another lady, who mentally and physically harasses her daughter-in-law. They all scold that lady for her misbehavior and this is their pretentious perspective while almost of them keep ill feelings with their own daughters-in-law and do not leave any chance to harass them hence this is their actual perspective regarding the behavior that should be done with daughters-in-law. It is also found that as much a lady proclaims by beat of drum about her pretentious perspective, her actual perspective on that subject becomes negative and disgusting up to same extent. Women express their actual perspective only when their opinion gets very affected by jealousy and egoism. For example if a lady is in love with a man then her female friends never say that she is in love instead they say that she has trapped that guy or she has been trapped by that guy. They often say about their friend, who is in love, that she is having passion for sexual cravings etc. This is their actual perspective which is disclosed by them publicly at a very low level because their other properties have been subjugated by jealousy and egoism. Suppose they all are in love and had kept sexual relations unlimited times with their respective boyfriends then also they call their own love to be passionless spiritual love or a kind of love that has never been done by any other couple. This is their pretentious perspective about themselves. All of the ladies, who start shouting while discussions or unnecessarily become aggressive or speak in indecent manner, are familiar with the fact that they are wrong. They behave in this manner just to hide their faults and weaknesses. Suppose it is said that a husband physically harasses his wife and the matter has been disclosed to all through the humble assistance of media for example we take the latest matter happened in past month in India, where a male celebrity performed sort of *Swayamber* for getting married. His wife blamed on him after one month from the marriage for her physical harassment and even earlier he was blamed the same by his previous wife. Now what are the reflections of the ladies on this are significant to mention here. Again here the reflections of the ladies are affected by their dispositions and the differences in between their statements can be easily understood if we are able to differentiate in between their pretentious perspectives and actual perspectives. A female contestant of his so called marriage ceremony or *Swayamber*, who was definitely willing to marry him, said that she was fortunate that she was out from the list in very initial round and perhaps God saved her life from that man. This is her pretentious perspective because in fact she was thinking of being his wife and was thrown out in the initial stage but was not having any kind of rivalry with the lady who won the contest and became the wife of that celebrity. Another lady said that she was not going to believe that a guy extremely gentle like our celebrity could do such indecent behavior with his wife and the wife was lying because she herself was culpable. This is her actual perspective because she was extremely jealous with the wife of the celebrity. A lady, who was quite familiar with the celebrity from a show, where both of them worked together, was having a sort of moral relation of brother and sister with that fellow said that she can not believe that the accused did inhuman behavior with his wife because he was a very gentle guy. She again said that the concerned man or her so called brother has been blamed by two different ladies as his wives but in fact he is very decent hence something was wrong which was still hidden. She said that may be they are blaming on each other for the sake of some kind of popularity stunt or something else was there behind this. It should be noticed here that "perhaps something else" could be something related to sexual relations or a peculiar kind of demand of sexual plays done by the celebrity. A lady, who was supposed to be responsible for the divorce of the celebrity from his first wife and was found involved in making conflicts in between the celebrity and his second wife, said that he speaks to her regularly and says that he will suicide if she does not response him in positive way. She said that she becomes very anxious when she hears that he is depressed and thinking for suicide. This is her pretentious perspective because she is in fact just desirous of making conflicts in between the celebrity and his wife and to make the social life of the so called celebrity hell. She was succeeded in her initial attempts of separating him from his first wife now she is doing the same with his next wife. Why she is doing all of this? The answer is perhaps she is having extreme hatred feelings for the celebrity and hence through the emotions, she is taking a kind of revenge from him or his wife. As per the psychology, such temperament of ladies is said to be their internal sexual perversion. No one is authorized for intervening or making complications in between a pair of husband and wife then why that lady is doing so. If a lady says that celebrity makes phone calls to her in odd hours and says that he will commit suicide then she should let him do so. Who is she for that man and why she is supposed to be worried for a man of other lady?

For women, possessing the audacity, braveness and presence of mind have different meanings. For men, audacity means not being ill-influenced in adverse situations, braveness means performing moral duties without hesitations and presence of mind means keeping the skill of diplomatic conversations while for ladies, audacity means disrobing themselves without any hesitations, braveness means not caring the social or ethical codes and presence of mind means perfection in indecent conversations as well as being capable to prove their bad deeds as virtuous by wrong arguments. Unfortunately such distorted definitions of aforementioned qualities are made by women for other women. That is why ladies, who are eager to disrobe their wearing or ladies in the field of modeling or acting, are said to be bold while ladies who commit harlotry and publicly blame men are said to be brave.

A model performing modeling on the stage charges ten times more when she has to reveal her body part for a moment by letting her cloth slipped off on the stage, while pretending that it all happened accidentally. For that little span, she becomes almost naked and it enhances the curiosity of the audiences as well as the popularity of the show. Such incidents never happen accidentally because they are always pre-decided. One model, on the assurance of not disclosing her name, told that usually organizers provide more money to some specific model to perform this mistake for the sake of popularity of the stage program and some models perform it just to achieve publicity by their nudity. If such incidents are accidents then it should affect the character or personality of that model but instead of that, she adjusts her garments without any symptoms of shyness or embarrassment on her face, continues her cat-walk and goes back to again perform such nudity. She considers such act done by her as a positive step for making her career bright. Female organizers define it as her self-confidence and boldness. That model again said that very few ladies are sexually molested in modeling because almost ladies give their consent to denude themselves and to keep sexual relations when they are offered reasonable price. Though the exceptions to this are the ladies belonging to very rich families and the ladies who are already having their guardians in the same field still they too become ready to perform any immoral act because to prove themselves independent and hence adopt the shortcuts of indecency to achieve success quickly. Why do the ladies adopt such specific fields like modeling etc as their profession about which they usually say that they are sexually harassed there. One other model confidentially told that if models are asked to perform any kind of indecency on stage or are requested for sexual relations then usually they give their consent because such offers are very alluring and exciting. Female models or even all ladies are always safe because they can blame the person who offered them if they feel that they are not paid well for some specific job of such kind. Few models told that they are often instructed by the organizers not to wear brassiere while wearing typical dresses made by designers so as to make sure the visibility of their breasts from outside of the transparent upper wearing. Such instructions are given to models by some female designer or organizer. Somewhere it looks like huge brothels, where the organizers are ladies, called as aunties, not men. It is also found that modeling in not very different from high level prostitution.

Ladies can often be seen seeking or achieving a peculiar pleasure termed as pleasure of perversion. It includes of pleasure of sexual perversion, pleasure of moral perversion and pleasure of sadistic perversion. Almost ladies seek such pleasure of sexual perversion in making illicit sexual relations. The pleasure of moral perversion is felt by them when they humiliate and harass others. The pleasure of sadistic perversion is almost secretly achieved by ladies but the satisfaction on achieving such pleasure can be seen in their face expressions. Ladies feel pleasure even when they buy their undergarments including bras and panties from the shops of male shopkeepers. Almost ladies prefer purchasing their undergarments from male shopkeepers. A male shopkeeper exclusively told that when he asks the size from the ladies who visit to purchase undergarments then most of them barefacedly say," Can't you guess?" while few say, "watch yourself" etc. Some ladies literally disrobe their outer garments to show the size and make of their undergarments to the male shopkeepers. Astonishingly the ladies visiting the female shopkeepers of undergarment's shops never behave like this.

Ladies have their own theory of virginity which is termed as virginity-concept by them. According to the scholars, breaking of virgin knot or hymen is considered to be as losing virginity and as per medical science, first sexual intercourse is the symptom of losing the virginity but women's concept of virginity reveals new theory of it. Should breaking of virgin knot because of masturbation be considered as loss of virginity or not, is a controversial subject. The virginity-concept of the women psychology states that every woman considers herself to be virgin with respect to the men with whom she has not performed copulation. Hence breaking of hymen or virgin knot, through illicit sexual intercourses performed before marriage, has no importance to ladies and it gives no sorrow or repents to them. The psychology of women makes such assumptions regarding sexual relations and their virginity, governed by their virginity-concept. As virginity has actually no means for ladies hence expressing themselves to be fearful regarding the safety of virginity is their pretentious perspective while as per their actual perspective, they want to lose their virginity as soon as possible. Because of this virginity-concept, more than eighty percent ladies, who have been involved in illicit sexual relations before marriage, assume and express themselves as virgin in front of their husbands in the first night and hence never confess about their before marriage involvement in sexual activities. Ladies never hesitate to perform illicit sexual intercourses with their lovers and when they quit from such affairs thereby making new sex partners, they assume and pretend themselves to be untouched in front of their latest lovers. Hence till marriage ladies consider themselves to be ever virgin and after that, while performing extramarital sexual affair, they again consider themselves to be virgin in context other men even after being married. In fact ladies follow the concept of pseudo virginity. According to this theory, the ladies who are always eager and conscious to protect their virginity, in fact never possess virginity because they had already lost it through illicit sexual relations. A virgin lady behaves very normally and even at the time of marriage, she acts very naturally. The percentage of unmarried non-virgin ladies who have performed sexual relations, is comparatively very high than the percentage of unmarried virgin ladies. Such ladies with immoral character can often be seen to be very conscious regarding their virginity which actually exists nowhere. Hence a lady always considers and presents herself as a virgin during her first night of marriage, hardly matters whether she is in actual a virgin or a harlot. This type of mental situations and negative thinking is so powerful in ladies that they assume awful deeds done by them to be virtuous for the sake of their self-centeredness while the virtuous deeds done by other ladies seem to be an unpardonable transgression to them. This is the primary reason that ladies never accept their faults. Often poets and authors say that the chastity of women is sold in the market or brutally ruined by men uncountable times. The reason behind this is that ladies never consider themselves being sexually polluted and every time they keep such sexual relations, they assume that they are performing this first time and when they do not get the required price of their sexual skills, they blame that they were sexually molested. Again because of such contradiction in the opinion, a lady living a life of prostitute also considers herself to be pure virgin. This also creates a difference in thoughts of men and women regarding such relations. A lady, living happily with her husband, when sexually intercourses with other man then during that period, all of her attributes are superimposed by her sexual lust while after that she again considers herself to be husband devotee. Hence even married ladies involved in adultery never feel guilty conscious. Once a lady performs illicit sexual plays or sexual debauchment, she gets ever ready and eager for such relations in her lifetime and this has nothing to do with her marital status. In this situation, society, family and ethical codes become secondary for her. Sexual lust for performing illicit sexual relations arises in ladies because of their curiosity, excitement and greedy nature. This curiosity in them is produced by other ladies while the cause of excitement is their own flickering nature.

Almost women adopt the concept of nudity which is entirely based on the concept of the fear of nudity. We can define the concept of the fear of nudity as almost men are desirous to see young women naked but all of them also fear from the naked form of them. All men are fearful of the nudity and indecent behavior, publicly shown by ladies. Men become uncomfortable just with the thoughts of the probable nudity of their mothers, sisters and daughters. A man is even frightened from the physical and mental nudity of his own wife with whom he is authorized to keep sexual relations. Now according to the concept of nudity, ladies always favor nudity in context of their physical and mental state and becoming naked by disrobing themselves is the desire that always remains in them. The main reason behind their accepting the concept of nudity is that while attaining the maturity, they all understand that men keep the desire of watching them naked but at the same time on peculiar circumstances, they are afraid from the nudity shown by ladies deliberately. The second reason behind this is that almost women want to become the center of attraction for the familiar men, lovers and the society and for this they consider the concept of nudity to be very successful for diverting men's attraction from other ladies by certifying those other ladies existing nowhere in front of their beauty. Again the concept of the fear of nudity can be understood by this way as ladies, who have crossed the age group of forty-five, desires to live almost naked in their own residences, in front of their husbands, sons and daughters. Such tendency increases in women with the increase in their age. By this, they directly and indirectly put the fear of their nudity in the subconscious or conscious mind of their family members. Such ladies do not close the door while taking bath and if they have only daughters then these tendencies are increased in them. With the help of such nudity like changing cloths in front of other family members, taking bath being entirely naked, wearing indecently while sleeping and to sit anywhere to excrete urine instead of going to lavatories, they create mutual brazenness among their husbands and children and keep them frightened. Young girls realize the anxiety, consciousness and fearful mental state or disposition of their parents and brothers on their probable nudity hence they often play with their dressing styles to create such situations. More than eighty percent married men live under the fear of their wives' physical and ideological nudity. Men of comparatively beautiful wives are always perplexed, anxious and dubious by the thoughts of their wives having sexual relationship with other men. Somewhere men coming back from offices produce some sound or ring the bell even when the door is already opened or call some family member's name loudly before entering the house so as to avoid seeing their wives in some objectionable situation with some male relative. Again this is the fear of the nudity of their wives which puzzle them therefore they indicate about their arrival by producing some sound so that wives or other ladies may become conscious. Ideological nudity or the nudity of thoughts and attributes means the shameless behavior. When a husband attempts to make his wife realize about her fault then instead of accepting her mistake, she starts shouting on husband loudly. No husband wants his parents, relatives and neighbors to get familiar with the rude and indecent behavior of his wife hence he is frightened by such nudity shown by his wife and stops arguing by asking pardon from her. Almost ladies know it very well hence they often perform the same to harass their husbands and in-laws thereby keeping them in psychological pressure. Again after a peculiar age, almost ladies change the cloths in front of their children. They just pull their lower garment and sit in open space like courtyard to excrete urine even in the presence of their children. When the children raise their objections then mothers brazenly say that why should they feel shyness with their own kids. The habit of wearing lower undergarment reduces in ladies as they grew old. More than sixty-five percent ladies of the age group of fifty to sixty years avoid wearing lower undergarment or panties. More than eighty percent ladies of the age group of above sixty years avoid wearing panties.

The concept of the fear of nudity is so effective that when a father finds his unmarried daughter in the arms of her lover, he becomes violent and sometimes even physically scolds his daughter publicly. Such instances are seldom seen because girls take utmost precautions while visiting their boyfriends or sex-companions. Though such instances, when a father becomes violent, are only seen seldom in middleclass families and mostly in lower class families still these become a kind of precedent for other parents who watch such incidents happening. Even after this, middleclass parents find themselves to be helpless in making their daughters following the moral and behavioral codes because they regard for the opinion of society and the relatives and hence accept their defeat in front of their daughters of immoral character instead of making a scene by scolding them publicly. The other reason behind the so called helplessness of the middleclass parents, which has been discussed earlier, is that at present, almost middleclass men have been utterly rich because of their involvement in earning money through illegal sources or bribes. More than ninety percent of such people hide their financial status and income from the government taxation department and hence they are always busy in earning money and concealing that therefore seldom give time to provide proper guidance to their daughters. As low class and very low class families rarely care for the opinion of society hence they never hesitate to physically punish their daughters publicly if they find them involved in such sexual affairs. Again middleclass families live an ostentatious and deceptive life hence they prefer to hide the sexual debauchment performed by their daughters instead of strictly giving them ethical guidance. In the higher class families, parents can not prove themselves backward or conservative by compelling their daughters to follow the codes of conducts hence if the ladies of such families are involved in illicit sexual relations then they do it openly. The sexual nudity performed by ladies of higher class family is decorated by the phrases like modernity and broad thinking. Parents belonging to all of these three major categories usually perform different behavior with their daughters still none of them succeeds to keep the ladies of the family within the boundary of decency and moral codes and hence almost ladies of all of three categories are found to be involved in making illicit sexual relations. Here comes the most contradictory legal matter of honor killing. It literally means by the killing of someone arranged or done to protect the honor of the family or the dignity of someone closely affiliated. It happens on sufficiently large scale in the country like India where the codes of conduct are strictly followed by some so called orthodox families to maintain their ethical family backgrounds. Often such incidents can be seen in the society where some boy kills his sister when she is caught red handed while making illicit sexual relations. Somewhere fathers kill their daughters when they find them in some objectionable obscene posture with guys. Husbands kill their wives when they find them performing adultery. Similarly young guys kill their fathers or mothers or sisters or other very close relatives when they find them involved in sexual debauchment. The significant truth of such matters of honor killing happening in India is that the causes behind almost all of such incidents are illicit sexual relations. The most popular and perhaps unsolved mystery happened in *Noida*, where a young underage girl was brutally murdered, was the matter of honor killing. The matters of honor killing can be divided in three sub categories. The first one is that in which the person keeping illicit sexual relations or the one who is guilty is killed by some of the family member. The second is where the blameworthy person kills the one who becomes witness of his ill deeds. The third is that in which illicit sexual relations has nothing to do with killing and the person is killed by the family member or by someone emotionally very close when he goes or acts beyond the expectation of the family. Again the base of the honor killing is the fear of nudity as men can never see their sisters, mothers, wives and daughters involved in illicit sexual relations. Numbers of instances, where girls are killed by their lovers or are injured by acids or physical torture, are the examples of honor punishment. The extreme of honor punishment is honor killing. The second kind of honor killing is indeed a severe crime but almost of the examples of first or third kind of honor killings can not be considered to be unpardonable criminal acts. The Government as well as judiciary is proved unable to keep social and ethical codes hence such attempts of honor killing, to protect the honor and customs, are done by families at family level. In fact if all men get familiar with the illicit sexual relations of the ladies of their houses then the incident of honor killing will happen in almost every residence. This is an accurate assumption that out of all the families, where one or more than one ladies are involved in illicit sexual relations, gents are aware of such facts only in around less than 0.0005 percent families. That is out of ten thousand families where ladies are sexually corrupt, in at most two families, gents are aware of this. Now suppose if the men of all such families would come to know about the illicit relations of the ladies of their families than what will become the ratio of probable honor killing matters, need not to explain here. This is the incapability of government body and judiciary as they have always been proved to be incompetent in controlling over the sexual crimes done by ladies and this will definitely cause a social chaos in future. The ratio by which the involvement of ladies in illicit sexual relations is increasing, it can be easily said that by 2020 to 2030, all of the ladies will get sexually adulterated and this situation will take disastrous form till 2040. At that period, either the blood relatives like real brothers and sisters will start keeping sexual relations with each other or they will keep illicit sexual relations in different rooms of the same residences with their respective lovers or the percentage of the incidents of honor killing will increase abruptly. It can be said that a situation of sexual compromise will appear which will enhance the wife slopping unexpectedly and unmarried brothers and sisters will make a sexual compromise of keeping illicit sexual relations in the knowledge of each other.

This is an unbelievable fact that almost of the killings in a country like India are the examples of honor killing. The only difference is that girls are killed because they are caught red handed in making illicit sexual relations while guys are killed because either they are witness to such illicit sexual relations or they oppose their female relatives as their wives or sisters in making such illicit sexual relations. Almost family and social level crimes are because of active participation of ladies but unfortunately judicial and administration are not ready to accept this fact. Again in fact in a country like Indian subcontinent, girls become sexually mature at the age of fourteen to sixteen years while guys become mature at the age of around twenty-four years. A father involved in the honor killing of his daughter said that both of his daughters were involved in illicit sexual relations. He married his elder daughter in a decent family with the thought that perhaps she will change herself but unfortunately instead of adopting decent attitude, she ruined whole of her husband's family. She misguided her sisters-in-law and involved them in keeping illicit sexual relations. The father said that when he caught his younger unmarried daughter making sexual relations, he killed her at the spot because his conscience did not allow him to let her ruin the future of young guys and would-be in-laws. This is true that if judiciary and government keep strict control over sexual debauchment done by ladies than happening of such incidents will automatically get controlled. Again whatever the figures disclosed by the government departments or institutions involved in surveys state but this is true that almost of the killings happened in India are the example of honor killing. More than ninety-eight percent of the dowry instances, where young brides die, are either the example of honor killings of first category or suicidal matters.

A young guy involved in honor killing of his real sister told that his father searched number of marriageable guys for his sister but she denied to marry and rejected all of them. Father thought that perhaps she was willing to get higher studies hence he let her complete her studies. Once he saw his daughter with a guy in some objectionable posture then he said to his son to get the truth. The son, on the permission of his father, chased his sister and once found her making illicit sexual relation with her lover. He told his father and father warned the daughter to stay away from such relations. The daughter cut her veins and threatened her father that she will commit suicide if she is not permitted to marry with her lover. She said to her father that she is authorized to live her own life by her own way as per the laws of the country. Father allowed her to live her life as she was desirous to live. Next time the brother caught his sister with some other guy then father permitted him to kill her. Father said that he was having three daughters and the eldest was involved in illicit sexual relations. To protect the honor of the family and to save the morals of rest of the daughters, he permitted his son to kill the eldest daughter. This is the law of the country which permits ladies to commit harlotry and when a family member takes care of the honor of the family, society and ethics by punishing the lady of his family than he is punished by the biased judiciary. There is no incident of honor killing where a father compelled his daughter to marry with some specific guy of own community because if a girl rejects one then she is provided the options of other guys of own community. Right of selection of the bridegroom is always given to ladies but unfortunately almost of them misuse it. This is a perfect rumor that honor killing has a correlation with the difference in the upper and lower castes because almost of the examples of honor killing done to prevent inter-category or inter-religion marriages are seen in the families of lower caste.

Almost ladies are pertinacious and never accept the right decisions of elders. Young ladies often cut their veins, take excessive dosages of medicines and burn themselves by cigarettes or by some other burning object to threaten the parents and husbands. They use such techniques when they are prohibited to do something or to take some decision of their choice by elders. Some girls lit the candle and pour the melted wax on their arms and other body parts so as to remove their depression.

Changes in the behavior of ladies appear very gradually because of the changes made by them in the stage of their properties by making them either active or inactive but it is seen sometimes that such changes take place suddenly and persist lifelong. To understand the cause of such permanent changes, we have to understand the concept of changing of internal disposition and the theory of changing the stage of the properties together. When a lady gets very confused or experiences excessive bashfulness or extremely humiliated by someone or experiences extreme hesitation or becomes very frightened, she adopts escaping tendency and achieves dual personality. In fact such situation occurs when she faces some peculiar incident or some accident and hence sudden changes in the stages of her properties take place. In this, either her active awful properties decreases to be three to four thereby making her very generous and full of virtuous qualities or the count of awful properties increases to be twelve or even more than that thereby making her of very rude behavior with full of awful qualities. Such changes persist in her for whole of her lifespan and the number of awful properties in her varies from the normal count eight. Now again in such matters, few properties suddenly achieve active or inactive stage hence such effected properties become either permanently visible or eloped from her behavior thereby making sharp changes in the internal disposition of her and persist life long in her. Such changes make an unrecoverable image on her conscious, subconscious and unconscious mind hence sometimes she is never able to realize or accept the occurrence of such changes in her while the nature of her in the views of her familiar persons has been changed entirely. Somewhere very introvert ladies become extreme loquacious after their marriage while somewhere introvert unmarried virgin girls become loquacious and ill-mannered when they approach to the age of thirty years. Similar changes can be seen in introvert men, who are sexually and mentally puzzled by their wives or whose wives keep excessive sexual demands.

It is the assessment of many scholars that men are afraid of the gender of women. This is mostly seen in the form of a husband frightened from his wife where wife disrespects her husband as well as her in-laws publicly. The one sided laws favoring young women have increased the percentage of occurrences of such complications in-between husbands and wives. Almost husbands are physically and morally tortured by their wives. In some families, wives adopt a peculiar method to harass their husbands by disrobing themselves and going in front of in-laws or outsiders being almost naked. One of a man told in an exclusive talk that his wife misbehaved with his mother hence he had an argument with her then suddenly during the conversation, wife torn all of her cloths and went outside of the house being almost naked. The man was shocked to see this peculiar way of blackmailing done by the wife. Such ways of threatening to husbands or suppressing them, adopted by ladies, are often seen in the families. Some ladies start shouting when they are mistaken while some start beating the children. All of such methods are applied by ladies just to make their husbands frightened. Again as a normal husband hides the faults of his wife from rest of the family members or relatives hence he avoids these kinds of situations just by patiently tolerating such misbehavior of his wife. Marriage is the end of roving life and flirtatiousness as it invokes the family concept in men and provides moral guidelines for their sexual life while it provides freedom from moral constraints and uncontrollable sexually corrupt nature to women. Married ladies are free to carry illicit intercourses with other men thereby committing adultery because they do not have to answer about their probable pregnancies anymore and they have no fear of losing their so called virginity. They know that other men keeping sexual relations with them will never bound them for marriage because they are already married. In the unmarried life, they have to answer on being pregnant hence in such situations they silently go through abortions to prove their virginity and chastity while after marriage they do not have to worry for such burdens because it is obviously considered that the children in wombs are of their poor husbands. A lustful married lady, having complete right to perform sexual course with her husband, never leave any chance to sexually allure other men and committing adultery. This tendency of ladies has nothing to do with their peculiar liking about a man. A lady, during her initial period of fourteen to twenty-three years age, prefers to perform copulations with aged men expertise in the skills of sexual plays while at the age of around twenty-three to thirty-two, she prefers to have sexual relations with the man of almost equivalent age to justify her arrogance. At the age group of above this, she prefers to sexually rape young boys who are not familiar with mating and are quite younger to her. Such contradiction in choosing the sex partners can be seen in almost women. A renowned lady gynecologist while joking said that the level of adultery in women has crossed the limit and if a general D.N.A testing of the children and their fathers is performed then sufficiently big count of the families will face the complications because a disgusting truth will come out that fathers are taking care of the children who are in fact not their children. This situation can be easily seen in the Asian countries. She said that suppose like the pregnancy test strip, some strip or other medical test is invented by which it can be verified that a lady did intercourse in her previous life or not, then either ladies will become united to put objection on the authenticity of such test or government of India will prohibit that test. Why? The only answer is that all of us know that almost Indian ladies lose their virginity before marriage. A renowned advocate told that gender informatory test through Ultrasound is prohibited in the country similarly in future, D.N.A. testing, to get the actual originator of a child, will be made forbidden by the judiciary.

Every man is fearful from the nudity shown by ladies hence without silent or open consent of a lady, no man can influence her or seduce her or make sexual relations with her. Though if a lady is desirous of a man then he can never be unaffected by her sexual delusion. When a lady is willing,

71

she pretends to be innocent, unaware and helpless in front of desired man and such dumb man considers this all as his ability to allure ladies. The men, who are in love, often found to be happy with the thought that their girlfriends emotionally love them while in actual, almost ladies just love the sexual pleasure and the wealth. A wide survey done regarding love-affairs and the objectives of such affairs disclosed tremendous facts. Less than five percent ladies keep emotional love and attachment with their lovers while rest of around ninety-five percent are attached in such affairs for the sake of bright future, financial gain, sexual pleasure and other benefits. In contrary to this, sixty-five percent men keep emotional love with their lovers while thirty percent are attached for their passion for sexual pleasure and five percent for the probable financial gain. Again as per women's opinion, the worthiness of men is decided by their sexual capability and wealth. Therefore very brilliant scholars of psychology mentioned that women are only responsible for their good or bad regarding sexual relations and this all has nothing to do with the existence of men. Men go to office or for earning outside the residences almost every day leaving behind their wives and how many wives maintain the dignity of the trust done by their husbands by not performing adultery, is hard to say. Such trust bestowed by men upon their wives itself provides them fear from the nudity of their wives. A Man always explains and makes believe himself that his wife is faithful to him and the only reason behind this is his fear. When a wide survey is done regarding the men and women who are involved in extra-marital illicit sexual relations and the basic reasons for performing such relations, the shocking results revealed. Out of the total count of married ladies performing adultery, twenty-five percent were involved in such act to achieve financial gain, fifty-five percent for their passion for sexual love, six percent because of their extra-marital affairs, seven percent because of their curiosity and excitement. Out of the remaining seven percent, four percent were usually send by their husbands to provide sexual services to their senior officers and rest of the three percent were involved in such relations because of sexual incapability of their husbands. Out of the married men affiliated in such illicit sexual relations, two percent were sexually perverted and were eager to perform sex even with animals or cadaver, twenty-three percent were in emotional love, and seventy-five percent were involved in such relations to fulfill their sexual desire and to get rid of the frustration given to them by their wives of quarrelsome and ill temperament. Again out of aforementioned ninety-eight percent normal men keeping illicit extra-marital sexual relations, sixteen percent were of over lustful nature, twenty-one percent performed this because of the unsupportive tendency of their wives for sexual course or denying for mating while rest of the sixty-one percent were inclined towards such relations because of the ignorance, inhuman behavior and violence done by their wives.

A father, who sends his daughters to distant places for achieving higher education, always becomes fearful regarding the virginity of his daughters. As a father is well familiar with the sexual relationships and knows about the flickering tendency, lustful nature and lack of conscience in women hence he is always perturbed to think about the safety of the chastity of his unmarried daughters and therefore he becomes fearful of the probable nudity of his daughters. Every man is frightened with even the thought of his daughter performing sexual relations before marriage and his mother performing adultery. He can never even imagine his wife keeping sexual relations with other man. Hence he is afraid of the vaginal or sexual nudity of women and such fear essentially needs the presence of society because men only get frightened when such nudity of the concerned ladies gets public or disclosed. A woman can never fright a man by her naked behavior or attitude if the family, relatives and society are absent. Hence when there are no probable hindrances of involvement of family, relatives and society, women are always frightened from men because they are wrong. The moment ladies come in society or family, they wear the veil of shamelessness to frighten their husbands, brothers, parents and other relatives. Such nudity shown by ladies to frighten men never affects other ladies because they too are familiar with the women psychology and have done or performed the same to harass the men of their surroundings.

The families of lower class and below lower class do not have toilets at their residences thus for excretion, they go to some lone place like fields, sides of highways and near the railway tracks. Because of the unavailability of the lavatories, people of even middleclass on emergency, perform excretion at the side of road. Men passing urine publicly when find some lady approaching towards them, turns away to hide the genital organ. When the similar situation happens with ladies who are excreting in sitting posture, they hide their face with some cloth or hands. In such situation, if a man comes more near to them then they pretend to hide their genital organs or stand up hiding their face. Such reaction of ladies is sufficient to describe their actual disposition. If a lady is assured that her identity will not be disclosed then she never hesitates to entirely disrobe herself even in front of men. This is the basic reason that ladies involved in prostitution, lower class bar services, cheap dancing and in the businesses where in fact they are committing harlotry, never reveal their actual name and identity in front of their customers.

If the girls are given proper family environment and guidance then it can be seen that their capacity of memory is twice in comparison to guys. Their grasping power is five times more while the imagination power is infinite. Their tendency to do hard work or their dedication for the work is four times more than men. If their efficiency to work is built in the age group of fourteen to nineteen years age then they are proved to be very assiduous in their jobs during later period of their lives but if they are made indolent in this age group then they are proved to be extreme lethargic at the later age. In the same age group, girls are around three times more talented than boys. Their sexual power is around seven to eight times more than that of men. When the internal qualities of girls are not utilized properly because of lack of genuine guidance and restrictions then almost of them get diverted towards sexual perversion. Let us visualize the concept of dissipation of internal energy in ladies. Normally internal energy of ladies is released through five ways. These include of release of energy through physical labor, verbal conversation, sexual involvement, thoughts and eating. Energy release by physical efforts takes place by roaming here and there, performing house jobs, official works and general activeness. Energy release through verbal conversations takes place while making arguments, unnecessary quarrelling, lying, scolding and reproaching others. Energy release through sexual involvements takes place while performing sexual course, during pregnancy, giving birth to child and breast feeding. Energy is also released in ladies who are fond of eating and are voracious eater or gluttonous. Energy release through thoughts can be seen in the ladies who are great philosopher or affiliated to literature or are in politics. In a normal lady, the major portion of energy dissipation or consumption takes place by at least three of the above mentioned ways out of which energy release through copulations is common. Hence total combinations made by two out of four are six. One combination can be seen in ladies who are sexually inactive or rarely perform sexual course and are childless. Hence total groups are seven and all the ladies fall in these seven categories. If the balance in the amount of energy released through the two ways, except the one through sexual relations, is not maintained then such energy imbalance psychologically diverts the ladies towards making excessive copulations with their husbands and illicit sexual courses. This is the reason that in the ladies, in which most of the energy dissipation takes place through their excessive eating habit and verbally, if any one of such source to release energy becomes weak, they demand for more sexual pleasure. Balanced energy release is seen in rare ladies. When some lady is of very arrogant nature and does not perform any house jobs properly then wise husband to such a lady makes her pregnant so that she may give birth number of children and her energy may release. Energy release through physical efforts also takes place in ladies when they are physically harassed or beaten by their husbands. That is why most of the ladies finding excessive lust or arrogance in them desire to be beaten by their husbands regularly.

A lady respects a particular man till the moment she has not made any sexual relation with him. Once a lady becomes naked in front of a man and performs sexual course with him then the respect for that man in her views decreases and gradually she starts behaving shamelessly with him. A lady even starts keeping brazen attitude for an erudite scholar if he has performed sexual intercourse with her. This is the reason that ladies never respect their husbands who are elder and more knowledgeable to them. Fifteen percent of the ladies become barefaced and indecent natured at their youth, forty-seven percent get shameless after marriage, thirty-one percent ladies become brazen after giving birth to children and seven percent adopt such unabashed nature at their middle age. Hence a lady spending whole life span certainly becomes shameless regarding sexual relations in context of her husband or other men at some stage of life. Big gentry of ladies at present do not follow the concept of respecting the men with whom they do not have any sexual relations. This is again a disorder in them caused because of the awful properties concerned with the short-temperament or aggressiveness, like quarrelsome nature or causing distress to others or harsh speaking or resentment or tendency to retaliate, of their nature being active in them during their sleeping hours. Hence such ladies carry the indirect reflection of such ill-properties in their behavior in the form of hidden frustration. Such ladies are mostly found to be talented and prefer to join fields of public dealing as their career. They can often be seen working in the private banks in the loan sanctioning division where they release their frustration by abusing clients who are unable to pay back the bank loans. They can also be seen working as marketing agents or medical representatives or working in the private or governments offices where they perform public dealing. Almost such ladies face excessive bleeding during their menses and they achieve the same pleasure while indecently talking or scolding to men as a normal lady achieves during sexual course. Hence such ladies do not follow the concept of respecting men with whom they do not have sexual relations.   A lady never respects other ladies but she always wants to be honored by other ladies. If a lady appears respecting another lady or she says that she respects some other lady then this is mere her ostentatious disposition not real. A lady always fears from her beautiful real sisters and friends in context of her boyfriend and husband. Again in context of her husband, she even keeps such fear from her mother if she is attractive and lustful. Hence in such situations, she is almost frightened from the sexual nudity of her female relatives because she feels that attractive females of her surrounding may seduce her lover or husband. In this situation, she never respects her beautiful female blood relatives and even her beautiful looking mother but same time she desires her husband or boyfriend to respect them. She knows very well that in peculiar relations between a male and a female, respect gained by a man from a lady as the outcome of the respect which he bestows upon that lady makes the possibility of sexual relations in between that lady and man to be nil. Again this is because in general, a lady keeps the feeling of respect for a man unless she performs sexual relations with him. If husband respects and obeys his own mother and other blood relatives then the wife becomes distressed as she knows that there is no possibility for sexual relations in such relations.

It is very normal behavior of a lady to look other ladies with disgusting views but in some ladies, changes can be seen in this tendency which is because of lesbian nature of them. A lady with homosexual lust keeps mixed feelings for her companion lady. Seventy-eight percent ladies do not hesitate in changing cloths in front of other ladies. The twenty-two percent ladies, who hesitate to change cloths in front of other ladies, behave like this least because of coyness and mostly because of having inferiority complex regarding their figure and body look. Such hesitation or inferiority complex does not exist in ladies with homosexual liking. Two lesbians performing homosexual plays perform the feminine role because they are filled with such homosexual feelings while the moment, one of them performs the role of a man and uses artificial penis to do unnatural sex or masturbation of other, they do not possess homosexual feelings even after performing homosexual play. Similarly the homosexual relations among two guys includes of oral sex while the moment they commit sodomy or anal sex, the homosexual feelings ends because the one who performs anal sex, considers the other man as woman-body though they are in fact performing homosexual relations.

Hence the moment a homosexual male pair or a lesbian pair performs the anal sex or artificial penetration, the lady whose vaginal path experiences such penetration of artificial penis done by other lady and the boy who penetrates his penis inside the anus hole of the other guy, get free from the feelings of homosexuality because such lady and man see their sex partner imagining them to be of opposite gender. Now if such penetration is not done then both of that boy and lady keep homosexual feelings in such homosexual plays. In men, if homosexual feelings arise till the age of seventeen years then it continues for life long in them while if such feelings do not arise till the age of seventeen years then it is never seen in them. Exception to this is only seen in the middle aged and over aged men who do not find some female for their sexual hunger. If such homosexual feelings do not arise in women till the age of twenty-one then it is never seen in them in future. Exceptions to this are found rarely. Though the homosexual feelings reside in all ladies because of the necessity of breastfeeding and embracing done by their mothers to them in the initial childhood but properties governing such homosexual nature are mostly active during their sleeping hours hence normally they are not homosexual. We can say that all ladies possess homosexual feelings but in practical life, they become lesbians only when such tendencies superimpose their behavior. We can imagine this through the result of surveys done in context of this which revealed the fact that if a lesbian offers for homosexual plays to her closest friends then out of ten ladies, eight give their consent for this while if the same request is done by a homosexual boy with his close friends then out of ten guys, none permits him.

Out of the men who perform anal sex with their wives, more than twelve percent possess homosexual tendencies. The children of the lustful ladies, who possess very rude and indecent nature and inhuman behavior for their husbands, mostly possess homosexual tendencies. A guy who seeks his mother's rule in the family while his father is comparatively calm and decent and further his mother keeps excessive sexual lust then a part of gender deciding qualities elopes in him hence he seems to be having feminine characteristics and achieves homosexual nature. Such men usually perform anal sex with their wives. This kind of homosexual nature or tendency of committing sodomy makes them coward. Such men, who seem to be very sharp in speaking, are always found frightened during personal conversations and sexual courses with their wives. They are found interested in performing sodomy and other hatred unnatural sexual activities with minor boys. Such examples can be seen in some Bengali men.

A man, who seeks the masculine nature caused by eloping of feminine qualities in his mother and other female relatives, achieves inbuilt homosexual tendencies in him. In such families, mothers possess masculine attitude like fathers. Again such elope of gender deciding properties in the mothers contrive the features of eunuchs in them. Such ladies prefer to do oral sex with their husbands and give preference to anal sex to be done with them and always keep such sexual desires from their husbands. As the husband to such a lady has already faced such eloping of feminine qualities in the ladies of his surrounding hence his sexual feelings least depend on gender of the mating partner and he too prefer performing such unnatural sex with his wife. Such examples can be seen in some Punjabi families. Such men can be seen performing unnatural sexual activities with eunuchs in coaches of engineless trains, lavatories and narrow lanes. In against of the early described homosexual's category, these are not coward by nature hence seldom perform sodomy with minor.

Sharp nature and quick temper of women invoke impotency in the thoughts and attitude of concerned men. This kind of impotency can be seen in the behavior and sexual performances of men. All of the men facing this situation get internally depressed and outcome of this in their attitude make them cruel and merciless for the destitute of the society. Almost men, engaged in earning money by taking bribe as government officers or who are earning money from illegal way, release their family frustration by following such negative ways of earning money. Such men compensate the sexual and behavioral perversion of their wives by expressing themselves capable to earn money by illegal ways and harassing poor people of the society. Almost men behaving rudely or harassing other poor men, in fact attempt to prove them capable in front of themselves and their ladies. It seems that by harassing poor and needy of the society, they are trying to console themselves that they are having mannish qualities even after regularly getting abused and harassed by their wives. In an extensive survey, it was disclosed that the tendency of taking bribes, harassing or scolding others and inhuman attitude appears in a man only because of the direct or indirect impact of the ladies of his surrounding including his wife or mother or lovers. This kind of frustration mostly caused by wives is never confessed by men but the degradation in the relations with parents and blood relatives that occurs after marriage, is the direct impact of that. This is also because of women's peculiar family-concept discussed later.

Feelings or tendencies, to perform unnatural and perverted sex with other ladies or prostitutes, in men are almost generated because of the inhuman behavior of their wives. It is also found that tendency to perform sodomy or unnatural sex in men if invoked after marriage then the basic cause of this is the excessive lust in their wives. The religions in which men are permitted to marry with more than one lady, all wives demand for sexual course and when such a husband finds him to be incapable to sexually satisfy all the wives, he demands for anal sex and oral sex with them. These kind of peculiar demands are refused by the wives then the husband gets time-being relaxation from the burden of performing sexual courses. That is why the wives in this situation, performs lesbian plays among them or seek the other family members to fulfill their sexual desires thereby producing crossbreeds. This is the main reason that ladies belonging to such environments never compel their husband for isolation from the joint family. Because a man in aforementioned circumstances demands such sexual activities from his wives which are unnatural hence wives too express them to be unwilling to perform sexual courses while perform adultery by making sexual relations with the nearest male family member. This attitude of asking for anal sex gradually becomes permanent in the nature of such men which ultimately diverts them towards sodomy. The religious priests of such religions are strictly prohibited to perform sexual courses and hence they are often found performing sodomy with minor orphan boys sheltered in the synagogues under their guidance.

Homosexual relations or sodomy or lesbian plays are immoral because such relations are unnatural. Though the supporters of homosexuality of many countries described such relations to be ethical by giving false reasoning and took the shelter of judiciary to prove them legally right and unfortunately judiciary, in almost of such instances, ultimately took the favor of them. Now such judgments are right or wrong is a subject of conflict. We are least concerned with the culture of other countries when we know that we too are losing our ethics and culture rapidly. A tourist interested in Indian culture, who came to India on a visit, was asked the same question that whether homosexuality should be permitted or not. The tourist said, "Almost of us come to visit India to know the country of Lord *Ram, Mahatma Buddha, swami Vivekanand* and *Gandhi*. It is my third visit to India and I have realized a lot of changes in the thinking of Indian public. There was a time when we feel proud to visit India but now it seems that the ancient culture has entirely lost. In our country, it took a very long period for the degradations of moral codes but in India such changes have come very rapidly. Indian gentry are rather confused in differentiating between the advancement or development and ethical codes. Ancient ethical codes can not be upgraded because they are perfect and only degradation in them is possible and that is what happening in India. Indians have intermingled the loosing of morals and advancement and hence they think that nudity is also a sign of social development. We escape from the nudity of our western culture to seek true religion and religious people in Indian subcontinent but unfortunately now situations are worse in India. In our own country, homosexual relations are legally permitted but almost of our people consider such relations to be disgusting. We can consider homosexuality as illicit and perverted sexual relations under the shade of judiciary. This is the most disgusting sexual play and no one with healthy disposition and mentality can ever support this or give consent for this. When in our country, where under the shade of broad mentality and freedom, adultery is performed on a large scale, almost of us are against of homosexuality then in a country like India, where sexual relations are considered to be pious when made after marriage with life partner and strictly illicit when performed with one other than spouse, it is very shameless and shocking when one expresses his or her thoughts publicly in favor of homosexuality." In fact the descriptions done by the judiciary or society regarding a subject and the ethical ascertainment done regarding that subject to be moral or immoral should not possess much difference and if difference is seen in that then it is the indication of mistake in judicial decision. Well, we can justify some decisions just by considering us to be involved in that. For example, one should ask to himself few questions like, Will I permit my daughter or son to keep homosexual relations? Will I permit my daughter to marry with a lady or my son to marry with a man? Will I permit my wife to keep such relations with other ladies? Will my wife permit me to keep homosexual relations? Shockingly, perhaps the answers to all of such questions are "No". A renowned advocate teasingly said that no wonder in future he will send the marriage card of his daughter mentioning that "On the auspicious marriage ceremony of my daughter named ********with the girl named ********". If judiciary allows disgusting act of homosexuality by mentioning such relations to be genuine then this is only a foolish attempt to break the law of nature and almighty God by proving itself more capable to interfere in such natural laws. If homosexual relations performed by mutual consent are legal then performing immoral, perverted and hatred sexual course with animals, mentally retarded or with women cadavers is also legal and authentic because judiciary can never be certain that aforementioned were unwilling. If judiciary says that a man performing sex with cadaver or animals is perverted while one performing homosexuality is of healthy thinking then the decision requires retrospection. Though there are lots of judgments which need reconsiderations and in fact Indian public need to be aware for their social duties instead of their rights. Populace of a backward country or a developing country should definitely take part in the fair race of advancement but they should not involve themselves in the rivalry or battle of advancement because race has the rules and every thing is not fair in that while in battle, every thing is fare as it has no rules.

If the young virgin decent girls or virtuous ladies are sexually molested in actual then seldom of such cases get disclosed because almost women have rumored and disclosed fake cases by blaming men falsely to such an extent that now innocent parents of a decent girl fear to disclose the actual sexual harassment of their daughter. Again the reason behind this is that almost of such instances which get public are forged and imagined by the shrewd women. One of such mother faced sexual harassment of her daughter then she was advised by the well-wishers to file a complaint against that man who tried to molest her daughter. That lady denied and said weeping that almost women have polluted the present social environment for the virtuous ladies just for the sake of publicity stunt and money, through sexual involvement and false blaming, in such disgusting ways that it has been very hard for a innocent morally high lady to state her problem. Now situations are so worse that every lady is familiar with the fact that the lady blaming on a man for sexual harassment is lying. Unfortunately all of the ladies express their ostentatious opinion in front of the media or public to support that lady who is wrong. Why they support a lady who is wrong or is lying, through their public opinion. The answer is almost of them also perform the same ill deeds and are wrong hence they fear that if they will not support such a lady then perhaps in future if they will face the same circumstances then no lady will support them. Again if they have an interest in the blamed lady or man then they oppose that lady, who is blaming, otherwise they all get united to support the unethical conduct of that lady. Actually they all feel insecurity because of being wrong in their personal or social lives and hence they assure themselves by making a false of lady to be converted in a truth. They become united to convert a false into a truth in such a way that perhaps their female society will get sexually molested or ruined if that wrong lady is publicly proved to be wrong.

The men who support ladies on their misconducts do this in three situations. The first category of such men is of blood relatives who are bound to help them even when they know that their ladies are wrong. Second category includes men having the tendencies of eunuchs and the third category is of the men who seek sexual intentions with such ladies. Often it can be seen that when a lady pretends to be in trouble and falsely blame a man then a crowd of men appears to help her. Such men only includes of the men belonging to any of the aforementioned three categories.

Almost of such instances related to the harassment of ladies are false and are perfect conspiracies to harass men. The matters, in which young girls are sexually harassed in actual, seldom get exposed because such instances happen in very organized manner under the shade of police, local mafias and administration. Even now, the selling and purchasing of young or under age girls are performed in organized brothels. The girls who are sold and purchased sometimes never know that for what purpose one is interested to purchase them. Such underage girls are provided by female social workers to higher politicians and bureaucrats. In seventy such instances affiliated to higher government officers and politicians, it is found that in all of the matters, young minor untouched girls are provided for sexual services by experienced ladies hence in all of such instances, few popular ladies were acting as Aunties or pimp not men. One of such lady involved in supplying girls to renowned men said during very personal conversation," It makes such activities safer when conducted through women as women organizations or other societies can blame men but they can never dare to blame us because we too know their actuality." Young girls are also sexually molested on behalf of religion. Somewhere girls coming for repentance are learned different postures of sexual course in the confession chambers by the religious priests. Some girls are made intrepid from the fear of *Dojekh* or hell by massaging their body parts inside the *Burka* or the veil. Somewhere on the name of baptism, young girls are made nude and sexually molested. Though such cases are seldom found happening but it is rather genuine to say that such instances often happens but seldom get disclosed. This was one of the reasons behind not permitting women to enter in the religious premises. Some witch-doctors of all religions remove the cloths of girls and perform sexual course with them to give them spiritual treatment for their problems and the girls find themselves very near to almighty God. Such examples of the peculiar coordination in between sexual pleasure and spiritual pleasure can be seen in the society. Some religious priests perform the role of pimp to offer their ladies as prostitutes to allure the men of other religions to make them converted but in such instances, women give their whole consent.

The freedom of women has always been the primary cause behind the confinement of men and played a vital role in ruining the ancient culture and civilization. Young boys never want to visit the place where their real sisters or mothers go. Husbands to working women avoid visiting the circle of their wives. All men feel embarrassing visiting the places where the ladies of their family visit or roam for entertainment purpose and behind this stands the fear of them. Men never feel comfortable when they seek their mothers or sisters or wives conversing to strangers. Hence to avoid such situations, they try to stay away from the personal or social circle of the ladies of the family. How the freedom given to ladies increases the liability of men and bound them can be understood with the following figures sorted out from various surveys. When girls are provided freedom to study by their parents, twenty-one percent of them get involved in illicit sexual relations. The social freedom or freedom to intermingle among others provided to ladies make twenty-three percent of them diverted towards making illicit sexual relations. The freedom to go outside for earning money diverts forty-one percent of such working ladies to involve in illicit sexual relations. Hence eighty-five percent of the ladies, who achieve aforementioned three kinds of freedom with no strict restrictions, have been involved in sexual debauchment. Rest of the fifteen percent ladies gets involved in such kind of harlotry if they are given complete freedom. This all does not mean that one should not give freedom to ladies instead it means that ladies should be given complete freedom but under strict guidance and control. Uncontrolled ladies directly or indirectly ill-influence the life of their brothers, parents and husbands. Education makes almost men socially and intellectually powerful while keeps behavioral impotency in them by making their obstinacy to be hollow because such men start caring for the opinion of the society. That is why almost of such men are suppressed by their iniquitous wives because they care for the opinion of the society and other family members hence bear silently the misbehavior and ill treatments done by their wives to them. Literacy provides conscience and discretion to men but the moment a lady in the form of lover or wife enters in their life, they lose conscience and forget their actual duties for their parents, younger brothers and sisters. This change appears in men because of the behavioral impotency aroused in them due to their lovers' awful properties and personality superseding their persona. Hence such men find themselves helpless to oppose the indecent behavior and immoral activities of their wives. Again this makes married men not performing their duties for their old parents because of the ill-feelings of wives for parents. In contrary to this education makes ladies immorally strong and shrewd. The immoral sexual relations or adultery is also performed by illiterate ladies on a large scale but such debauchment when performed by literate ladies, is decorated by defining it as an indication of revolution in women. Women never follow the codes of moral conduct because they never face any compulsion for that. For women, following the codes of conduct includes of having decent behavior, virtuous character and the faithfulness or devotion for the husbands and in-laws. A woman who possesses these three qualities, is considered to be worthy of social reverence and considered to be very respectable. Men possessing thousands of qualities never considered being equivalent praiseworthy as of a lady having aforementioned three qualities. Again ladies living happily and following the codes of conduct in their family are respected everywhere and this respect is never given to a man doesn't matter how morally strong he is. Unfortunately such respectable ladies following the almost codes of morality are less than three percent in the country though in general their count is considered to be twenty percent when we include those ladies in this who are having just appraisable temperaments.

Some ladies say that women were kept in confinement of moral and ethical codes from the beginning. They were living the lives of slaves. Men deceitfully decorated them by the alluring terms of deities and provide them utter respect with the intention of making them aloof from the pleasure. They were not allowed to live their lives with their own life styles. If this is true then to whom with men were enjoying by keeping all women in incarceration. If women were restricted to live like slaves then who were ruling in the residences. Even at present scenario, financially poor men can be seen in the society, who do not take meal and remain starved to feed their wives and children. Wives of ancient kings were termed as queens and were respected more than the kings even after not having single quality. Even now a highly qualified successful man's wife is known by the status and the degree of her husband even when she is illiterate. From the first certified battle of human till the last battle till now, were fought because of women. The brain behind the battle of *Mahabharata* was a lady similarly the cause behind the death of the most knowledgeable king *Ravan* was a lady. Doesn't matter what the history says but this is true that almost all of the emperors were killed because of either over-affection or the treacheries and betrays done by their own loving ladies. There are some countries where women killed their blood-relatives to achieve higher rank in the politics. Somewhere ladies kill their blood-relatives who become a kind of hurdle in their political career. Somewhere a worthy minister is killed by a lady and such a lady never gets death sentence in a country like India.

Again whenever a man finds himself very close to death, he transfers or makes a registered will to transfer all of his wealth to his wife. First of all he seeks the safety and security of his wife. When a doctor says that situations are not normal and hence during the delivery of child, either of the wife or child in womb may be saved then a husband always gives preference to the life of his wife. If all of this is a kind of confinement for a woman then there is no meaning of the existence of women on earth.

Women at present can not be considered to be the religious partner of their husbands because of the continuous elopes of good qualities in them. If men would be having any substitute of women for giving birth to children then the women would have eloped from the earth in the very early period and if there would be having some substitute of women in context of sexual pleasure also then perhaps women would have never been on the earth. Women are having these two God gifted attributes because of which men are bound to tolerate their numerous sinful activities. The earth is not of men only as every creature has the right to survive but the most disgusting fact is that woman is the only creation of God who takes advantage of her aforementioned two physical God gifted qualities to rule men. This behavior is found in the female of all the existing creatures. It is found that a witch leaves seven homes of her proximity and does not harm them when she starts devastating the others while a jealous woman possessing awful attributes does not leave her own residence even. Some extraordinary brilliant philosophers have mentioned that a characterless man is like a vulture ready to eat dead or alive while a characterless woman is like a poisonous female snake, ready to devour even her children. A characterless woman is like the running soar as an incurable disease in the society to which the over attraction or aversion shown by men ultimately causes death to them.

Women are considered to be a live symbol of mercy and forgiveness. Women accepted during numerous surveys that they are unable to ignore the incidents or discussions or situations which are against of them and are ever ready to take instant revenge or retaliation. If they find themselves not able to retaliate on some subject because of adverse circumstances then they silently accept that for some duration which is considered as their mercy and tolerance by impotent society of men while in fact they follow the tendency of wait and watch. Actually a lady never forgets even small incidents happening in her life when she bows or is bound to bow or suppresses her desire and she keeps memories of all such so called incidents, in which she could not retaliate, inside her in the form of a kind of vengeance and aversion. Such tendency of taking revenge is distributed inside her in the form of her awful properties resentment, negative attitude and causing distress to others. In future, the moment she finds the situation in her favor she scolds to affiliated men by giving the examples of the previous incidents. If parents give proper advice to her and she feels such suggestions to be against of her freedom or desires then either she immediately retaliates or keeps silent. If she is bound to follow the parents then she does whatever the parents say but again she never forgives her parents and in future, may be after marriage, disrespects the parents by making them remind about that simple incidents happened in-between them in past. She performs the same acts, which were prohibited for her by her parents, while living with husband and waits for her husband to put objections on her such ill acts so that she may relinquish her frustration that she faced in her unmarried life because she could not oppose her parents. Most of the men face this kind of situations with their wives where wives usually take the matter of some incident happened years back and quarrel on that topic thereby making the present life of their husbands like hell. This is a bare fact that almost women make the preface or ground of such quarrels so that they may raise the example of the incidents happened in past. A woman neither forgets nor forgives her opponents and the shocking fact is that mostly such opponents includes of her righteous parents, elders and husband providing her right guidance. Because a lady never accepts the right path of virtuousness and codes of conduct hence she always considers such men as her enemies. In contrary to this, if parents are immoral and teach her to oppose and harass the innocent husband then she considers such parents to be her utmost well-wishers. Women always ruin the life of men who give them proper ethical guidelines and who nourish them by fulfilling their desires that is why they are compared with the devil *Bhasmashur*. Again such attitude brings contradiction in the behavior of women.

The level of the tendency of taking revenge and egoism is continuously increasing in women hence the outcome of this can be seen in them in the form of lack of decency and tolerance power. The increased level of self-obsession made them sadist. The tendency of causing distress to others is also enhanced because of the extreme of self-obsession which ultimately evoked the tendency to suicide in them. Such attempts of suicides are done by the ladies not to end up their lives instead the main cause behind this is to cause distress to others. The bifurcation of joint families, happened because of the false egoism and obstinacy of women, can be seen in the almost families. Ladies can be seen cruelly suppressing and harassing the opponents or in-laws including their husbands. The killing tendency that is seldom seen in men can easily be seen in women. There are numerous families which have been destroyed because of the false ego of women. A journalist female friend told that the men's ego about which often ladies are found to be protesting, in fact does not exist anywhere in front of women's ego. In a broad survey done regarding the joint families, it is found that to maintain the dignity and the integrity of the family, seventy-two percent of the men compromise while nineteen percent women compromise. In rest of the nine percent matters, such compromise is done by both of the husband and wife.

The family concept is bequeathed by the Hindu religion to the entire human race which is now accepted by all the religions. Unfortunately the mentality of almost Indians is peculiar and almost customs or new themes adopted are extensively ill-utilized by the public. These kinds of changes in the mentality of the public took place in past one and half decade and even running at present. Such extensive utilization of any subject ultimately brings devastation in that field. We can understand this by numerous examples though for that we have to go beyond the subject. It is very hard to say that which country is the originator of piracy but now at present, India can be considered under top countries involved in piracy. There are very big markets of piracy and whichever new electronic project is launched, within nine to ten hours, it's exact duplicate is formed in the market. The same situation can be seen in software's piracy. India adopted the piracy concept and used it so extensively that at present, we are nowhere lesser than other countries involved in piracy. Similarly we have broken all the records of making blue films. On the name of providing computer education, the number of institutes available in India has broken all the records. This seems to be very good but in fact this is not because due to the absence of educational standards provided by government, more than seventy percent institutes are bogus. Astonishingly, almost of such institutes allure boys and girls and take big fees for their different modules but educate them in fact nothing. Such bogus institutes can easily be seen near villages, taking the advantage of unawareness of parents and earning a lot of money from them. The shocking factor is that India is again one of the top rankers among the countries possessing such bogus institutes. Again these all factors showing the tendency of a big part of Indian public to earn money by cheating others have risen in past one and half decade. India is top ranker among the countries involved in unhygienic adulteration of edible items. There is a big list of such items because in the country, no edible item is pure. Unfortunately such adulteration is done by mixing unhygienic and harmful elements causing gradual degradation of the health standards of public. It is hard to believe but is truth that such substances which are used for adulteration of edible items include of shit and urine of animals, ash of insects etc. Again every edible item like fruits, vegetables, medicines, oil, honey, milk product and grains etc are polluted or impure. We can say proudly that even most advanced countries are at least hundred years backward in comparison to Indians in the field of different techniques of making adulteration in edible items. No edible item being sold in markets is pure. No branded company is there whose edible product is not made locally by using unpalatable or synthetic components through adulteration by the persons involved in such bogus business of making spurious products. Unfortunately such spurious edible items illegally made by persons involved in such business look very similar to the actual items produced by the renowned companies. There are numerous factories that make same packaging of the products of renowned companies and the adulterated material is filled in that to sell in market. Hence we can summarize this all by saying that almost concepts of technologies are misused or all illegal methods, which can provide money or pleasure, are utilized in very large scale in India and this is happening since one and half decades while government is unable to control over that though judiciary is very strict on such offenses. The same thing occurred regarding the family concept of Indians. Since past decade, a peculiar tendency is seen that men after marriage adopt the family concept in a very typical manner. The definition of family has been so narrow that almost men consider their wives and kids only to be the part of their family by discarding the aged helpless parents and blood relatives. It can be easily seen that when the elder son of a parents gets established and marries, he seldom helps his younger brothers and sisters in achieving financial establishments. The moment a man marries, he considers himself to be separate from the parents and this tendency is very rapidly being adopted by Indian men. Though this all only happens because of iniquitous newly married ladies, who bind their husbands to live separate, but still just by blaming women, men can not get rid from their responsibilities. Thus family concept has become a curse for the joint families and this is happening on very large scale in India because Indian government and judiciary have been proved impotent in front of increasing women's power. In fact, no lady desires her in-laws to be united because in that case, she finds herself enable in making chaos in the family. Family concept adopted by ladies can be easily understood by this that husbands are not allowed to speak anything against wives' parents but wives can abuse or humiliate their in-laws. In contrary to this, wives can abuse or misbehave their own parents while husbands always have to disrespect their own parents. Again, this all doesn't mean that ladies respect their parents but again their husbands have to respect the parents of wives. Hence ladies' family concept is very tentative and it's hard to predict whom they consider as a part of their family. Almost ladies only consider their own parents, husbands and children to be a part of their family.

In few rural parts of India, the village courts are very effective and the judgments given by such arbitrating bodies are followed by the concerned villagers. Such local courts are termed as *Panchayata*. The guidelines provided by such courts are followed from family level to social level, under the premises of villages. Sometimes such courts are so stern on love infatuations and illicit sexual relations that the decision taken by them becomes example in the society. Though superficially, whatever is shown by media and channels, it seems that the dictatorship of such localized courts is increasing and they should be controlled or banned but the actuality is quite different. A lady journalist affiliated to some channel told that if such local arbitrating bodies do not compel villagers to live under codes then in almost residences, adultery will start because illicit sexual relations' chaos spreads in the villages more times rapidly than in the cities. Under one of such decision taken by the local bodies, the pair who was found living the life of debauchery and tried to escape from the village was caught and the boy and girl were sent to their respective residences by declaring such marriage to be void. One such pair of a lady and an underage boy who were involved in illicit sexual relations, were compelled to live like brother and sister. Few pairs were exiled from the villages because they broke the laws of marriage. That lady journalist during very personal conversation said that the families of such boys and girls are living near to each other in the village atmosphere since the time of their grandparents and hence they are very familiar to each other. Behind the shade of such kinship, girls and boys visit to each others place and fell in sexual infatuation with each other. To hide their sexual affection from the parents they even call each other by brothers or sisters. They keep sexual relations and one day, declare that they are going to marry or caught red handed while performing copulation or escape from the village. They leave behind their distressed parents who are shocked to express their thoughts on such shameful matter happened within the premises of the village. Parents familiar with the brother-sister relationship of their offspring feel very embarrassing to inform the relatives that their son escaped with his sister because they were having illicit sexual relations. If concerned parents do not put their objection on such illicit conducts of their sons or daughters then local courts or *Panchayatas* take strict steps against of it so as to ensure such harlotry not to be performed in every residence.

It is very essential to describe the safety factor adopted by all women in their life for their own safety. Any lady, who is involved in illicit sexual relations or adultery, lives under the boundary decided by the safety factor. The moral compulsions, codes of conduct and the physical difference among both genders mould the thinking of the women at the initial period of their life and they establish some safety factors for themselves. Men never keep such safety measures while performing emotional relationships but women never care for such emotional relations. There are no specific codes for such safety factors hence these safety measures vary from woman to woman. Unfortunately ladies apply such safety factors in all matters concerned to them and these are the extreme of their selfishness. They take precautions while keeping affairs or illicit sexual relations so that they may not be blamed. They take utmost precautions as safety factors while fetching money or assets from men by providing their sexual services or by emotionally blackmailing them. Though such safety factors somewhere are directly or indirectly considered by men also but they never give priority to their own safety when they are with their families or wives or lovers. If a lady has to go beyond her self-decided safety measures then she becomes aggressive because of the fear of disclosing her identity and the men, unaware about women psychology, consider this peculiar behavior shown by her as her depression. The same aggressiveness is shown by ladies when their mistakes are disclosed. Expressing negative reactions on some failure, becoming violent to take reprisals and pretending to harm the own body or committing suicides are caused in ladies because of the hostile nature of them. The only intention of such antagonism is to cause distress to others including well-wishers. All such activities performed by ladies in aggressive temperament has nothing to do with depression because they are the originator and the carrier of the depression while such aforementioned performances if found in men are only because of depression.

A familiar lady working in an advertising company and living in a working women's hostel informed that in the girls' hostels or working women's hostels, there are various provisions for the visitors or relatives of the ladies so that they may meet with them. Mostly in such arrangements, a record of the visitors is kept in the register in which the visitors have to write their own names as well the names of the girls they want to meet, purpose of the visit, date-time-duration of visit and their relation with the girls. Almost of such visitors are the boyfriends or the sex partners of ladies. All ladies compel their respective boyfriends to mention their relation with them as cousin brother-sister in the register. If lady warden or even other girls ask about the guests then also they introduce them as cousin brothers. If the visitors, with whom they keep sexual relations, are quite aged in comparison to them then they introduce them as uncle and compel them to write their relationship as uncle. This is the biggest example of adopting safety factor, done by ladies. When such matters informed by the lady friend was thoroughly scrutinized by the surveys then shocking results were revealed. A survey revealed the fact that more than ninety five percent visitors in the ladies hostels are the lovers or sex-partners and all of them mention their relation as cousin or uncle. Numerous girls hostels including the one affiliated to engineering colleges and medical colleges and number of working women's hostels were surveyed for this. When such visitors were interviewed on behalf of the assurance of not disclosing their names, all of them told that their girlfriends or lovers compel to mention the relations as cousin or uncle instead of writing friends. Some ladies are so shrewd that they have warned such friends either to write their names in such a way so that no one can easily read it or just to write the name of any girl but not of them.

A survey disclosed the facts that seventy-three percent educated guys and thirty-nine percent educated girls watch porn sites in the internet cafes while sixty-nine percent boys and eighty-nine percent girls living in hostels watch such porn sites or blue films. The incidents of the ragging of newcomer students in colleges usually happen. Ragging is essential because it is the only way by which junior students get closer and familiar with their seniors. It is found in a survey that the almost students, who do not face ragging in their first year, take vulgar and cruel ragging of newcomers in next year, when become senior. Ragging develops the inner skills and personality of the newcomers if it is done properly and decently. Again all of the students who do not face ragging or the probable fear of ragging, never know the manners to speak their seniors. Even teachers of the professional colleges instruct seniors to take ragging of the junior batch when they found newcomers behaving in uncivilized manner. Nowadays almost complains regarding raging are forged or are the outcome of personal rivalry because again judiciary started taking unnecessary support of newcomers and hence started interfering in ragging matters. Again administration as well as judiciary knows that in India, wherever some kind of biased support is provided to some lobby by judiciary through new laws, the people of that category start taking over-advantages by misusing such laws. Well we are not here to discuss about the decision of the judiciary on ragging because there is another important aspect of ragging to discuss. It is found that the ragging taken by senior girls in the girl's hostels is numerous times more vulgar than that which is taken by boys. Senior girls make the newcomer girls entirely nude and they are asked to crawl like a lizard on the wall of a dark room while some other girl focuses the light of table lamp on them. They are instructed to show the activities they will perform while making sex and for this they are given pillows as their so-called male partners. They are compelled to masturbate with brinjals or candles and somewhere their nude dance is recorded and shown them in front of all the girls. Two groups of such newcomer girls are made and both are said to abuse each other loudly. These activities can be seen in all girls' hostels.

According to the guidelines provided by the religions, a lady can live with a particular man after she marries him. This is a custom that ladies after marriage go to the residence of their husbands and the reverse of this is nowhere mentioned. It is assumed that a lady accepts the residence of husband as her own residence and respects the parents and relatives of husband as her own blood relatives. This custom is based on the assumptions that ladies are merciful and flexible in nature therefore they quickly adopt the changes. Such assumptions are recognized by all the religions. In some countries, as soon as the children become capable to earn, parents separate them so that they may live their lives by their life styles and may become self-sufficient. According to figures, the concept of ladies going to the residences of their husbands after the marriage is most popular and highly recommended. Again it is assumed that the modes of working as well as opinion of women are flexible and because of having politeness and generous thinking, they are easily adjusted in the new environment of the premises of their husbands after marriage. At present, all the ancient assumptions and expectations done regarding the virtuousness of women are broken and hence the actual situation is just reverse of that. In ninety-eight percent of the families in which disputes or quarrelling of the male or female members is seen, the reason behind that is women may be in the form of the mothers or sisters or wives or daughters. It is true that married ladies never get satisfied even when they acquire complete comfort and proper respect in the husband's family. Wives generally complain that they do not get proper respect in the husbands' families which they deserve and mothers-in-law with sisters-in-law always try to humiliate them. To know the veracity of this, such families were observed where husbands were living in the families of their wives. Again the life of such men was like hell because of disputes between the ladies. The difference was that now the disputes and quarrels of the wives, living in their own residences after marriage with their husbands, usually occur with their real mothers and the wives of their real brothers. Ninety-eight percent of such ladies, who are living with their parents after marriage, humiliate their real brothers' wives with the help of mothers. On the basis of the surveys done in such thirty-five families, it is found that in thirty-three matters, husbands were earning but they were bound to perform house jobs in parallel with their jobs. The mothers and sisters-in-law of the wives usually humiliate and scold them and treat them like servants. In the rest of the two matters, husbands were lazy and not willing to perform any earning and were like parasite. In four such instances out of thirty-three, men willingly accepted to live in the premises of their wives because their in-laws were rich and were having plenty of wealth with no male child to take care of that. In two matters, the parents of the wives were physical incapable and financially poor hence men were living with their in-laws to take care of them because in-laws were orthodox and were not ready to live in the premises of their married daughters. In twenty-seven matters, men were bounded by their wives to live with their in-laws thereby leaving their own physically lean aged parents alone. All such men have become of introvert nature and living their lives in depression caused by their wives. They were bound to serve their in-laws even when scolded and humiliated regularly but were unable to visit their own parents because they were frightened with the awful behavior of their wives. They seldom manage even to talk with their parents through telephone because they have to hide their affection with own parents from their wives. Again they seldom are able to manage financially helping parents because they have to do this without being in the knowledge of their wives. Unfortunately there are no strict rules of the society and judiciary to protect married men from their harassment and humiliation done by their immoral wives. Because of the absence of the rules to stop or punish ladies, who isolate husbands with their aged parents, both of the young men and their parents are helpless to take any action against such corrupt ladies. Under the shelter of biased laws, married women have crossed all the limits of cruelty, indecent behavior and humiliation. In context of such ladies, a renowned lady working in a popular women organization told on the assurance of not disclosing her name that out of around hundred ladies approaching to the organization asking for help, only two or at most three are actually harassed and need help while rest of the ladies make the snares of the false and treachery to pretend themselves to be innocent and accept legal guidance from us in fact to harass their husbands and in-laws not to protect themselves. Any kind of harassment of such ninety-eight percent ladies is not possible. They tell lies innocently in such an efficient manner that no one can judge the actuality. All of us know that such ladies are lying and are responsible for every kind of disorders and conflicts happening in their residences but we are bound to help them as per their opinion because of the sake of popularity of our organization and the presence of other female organizations who may become more popular than us if we reject to take such false matters. Almost such organizations are nowhere helping needy ladies because seldom of such matters are true and in fact we all are supporting to women lobby even after knowing that our female clients are wrong in almost matters. We are in fact working like a legal consultant or advocate, who always seeks new customers and has no concern with the culpability of the customers. We have to misguide such ladies because that is what they desire from us and if we truly guide them then they will move to other organization and will never come to us. We can compare iniquitous ladies with a bull who if set free, eats the grass of whole of the ground and if tied with a rope then grazes the circled area of the approach. Wherever an animal eats it used to excrete there and more loosely the rope is tied the more far it goes. The shit of an animal can be cleaned immediately or later but to clean the shit spread by women through their awful properties and illicit sexual relations causing crossbreeds, is a very lengthy process and takes generations.

Let us see what actually happens with the dependent family members of demised soldiers in any war. All the wives of deceased get sufficient financial help and other facilities. A very extensive survey was performed secretly to know the conditions of those widows then extremely shocking facts were disclosed. Almost of such widows marry within one year span from the death of their husbands. Many of them join some organization and start secretly running brothels. In many instances, parents of such demised soldiers are bound to live the life of beggars because they get nothing after the death of their sons. Almost of the widows take all the money and other facilities and escape to their parent's house. Again few of them remarry within three months from the death of their husbands with the men whom with they were having extra-marital affairs. A big crowd of such widows can be seen living alone as a renunciant while regularly involved in illicit sexual relations. Very few of such widows comprehend the dignity of_the sacrifices of their husbands and live peacefully by helping the parents of demised husbands.

The nurses working in hospitals or missionaries told that only women are successful in the field of nursing and men are not fit for this job because men possess mercy feeling. It is only possible for a lady to serve a sick or patient without any feeling of hatred and mercy and to keep patient under adjustable control by applying professional cruelty. In private hospitals, the situations are normal because of the strict control of management though a big amount is charged by them for all the facilities. To judge the actual behavior of the ladies in the form of nurses, the government hospitals' maternity sections or pregnant women's delivery departments were surveyed. There it is found that nurses often scold pregnant ladies and keep indecent attitude for them. All of such nurses were found asking for money as a bribe from the relatives of the pregnant ladies. Female sweepers take money to change the bed-sheets or to sweep the garments of patients. At the time of delivery, they scold indecently to pregnant ladies who are crying because of delivery pain and often say to them that they did sexual courses in different postures and enjoyed in that then who else has to bear the pain of delivery. Almost of such nurses demoralize to the female patients. If such nurses are provided some money then they start behaving properly. Such nurses often change the just born male infant of a lady with the just born female child of other lady by taking money from the mother of female child. As in such hospitals, many kids take birth at the same time hence it becomes easier for nurses to perform such interchanging secretly. In this, they inform the relatives of the lady who gives birth to a male child that she has given birth to a female child. Sometimes they even interchange the dead born infant of one lady with the living infant of another lady. Such interchanging of the kids is usually performed by nurses but seldom gets disclosed. It is also found that when a financially capable lady gives birth to a female child in a nursing home then her mother-in-law takes that child to government hospital and changes the female infant form a male infant of other mother by giving a lot of money as bribe. It is said that the mothers of the newborns are unaware about such interchanging that has been done among their kids but in fact in almost of such matters, the mother of the female child knows about this. Parents of the male infant never come to know about this. Seriousness of such crimes can be imagined by this fact that somewhere mothers or grandmothers of the female child give sufficient money to nurses to slay the female child and the men of the family are informed that the lady gave birth to a dead child but again such incidents happen rarely. In India, the unmarried ladies giving birth to children throw their newborns near sewage lines or in public dustbins where the infants are eaten by pigs and dogs. In very seldom of such instances, some man notices this and the life of infants are saved. Somewhere when the public dare to come to save such child till then pigs have eaten almost of the flesh. Again all of such cruel and inhuman activities are done by women not men. This is often seen in the villages but unfortunately seldom such infants are saved and people never come to know about the parents of such infants. This is shocking that women, the biggest symbol of mercy and generosity, never hesitate in performing such cruel tasks of slaying own children. It is said that when a female infant comes out from womb, a kind of impression and attitude of the surrounding persons is imposed on her, who are present at that time of delivery. Hence a girl child taking birth herself carries the impression of the virtuous or immoral temperament of wet-nurses. Perhaps, that is why the graph of immorality and indecency is continuously increasing in the new generations.

A female advocate said that almost ladies, who are of flickering nature and perform illicit sexual relations, never accept the proper guidance given by men and even after marriage they perform disloyalty and refuse to accept the gravity and honor of the husbands but when caught red handed while aborting their fetus, innocently say that they were bound to do this by husbands or in-laws or lovers. This is the biggest example of the shrewdness and disgusting nature of women. Almost ladies never hesitate to falsely blame on the character of men for the sake of achieving some peculiar objectives. That lady told a very interesting incident that happened in front of her. She said that once for some judicial matter, she visited to a police station. She had an exclusive discussion regarding some matter with the in-charge of that station. Suddenly a young lady with her aged mother arrived there and said to police inspector to file a first information report against a young man. Young lady said that the man living near to her residence tried to sexually rape her. All policemen were shocked and sub-Inspector said to ladies to sit for a while so that he may understand what happened with her and may arrange medical checkup of her. Lady started shouting and insisting for arresting that guy immediately. During the conversation, the young lady torn her blouse and made her breasts naked. The police officers stopped her to do that but unfortunately there were no lady constables hence they could not dare to touch her. Then to control the situation, lady advocate interfered and she saw the fresh cut marks made on the breasts of that lady and blood around that. It seems that she was right. The police station in-charge informed to circle officer and when he found that the lady was becoming aggressive for the little delay, she said to them to locate the house of culprit. They all with the advocate lady went to the culprit's residence. Culprit's mother told them that her son was out of station since two days and she even gave the cell phone number of her son. Police dialed him and said him to reach neatest police station immediately. He did the same and he was right because he was at more than thousand kilometers distance from his house in even different state. Police officer was shocked that how he can perform sexual rape one hour back with the lady when he was not even in that state. He informed to circle officer and then to sort out the matter a female lady inspector, who was very popular for her strict functioning, was sent there. They all came back to police station. The lady inspector went to a separate room with that young victim and the lady advocate. The lady inspector asked the matter with the victim and suddenly gave two slaps on her face. Then victim lady told the truth that she was in love with that man but he was not ready to marry hence her mother gave her this idea. She said her mother to make cut marks on her breasts so that she may blame that guy for sexual molestation. Fortunately those ladies were unaware about the visit of that man to other state hence they arranged that drama on that day. That lady inspector told to advocate that she had managed thousands of such matters of ladies and almost ladies speak lies but male police officers are bound to file their complaints because they do not understand the temperament of ladies. She said that if suppose the so called accused in that matter was caught in his residence then he would have been arrested and beaten by police because no one would have believed his statements. The lady advocate said that she was familiar with this fact that such incidents frequently happen in the Indian society but this was the first live incident that she saw in her life.

It can be seen written in the premises of private hospitals, government hospitals and the clinics or nursing homes of lady gynecologists that to know or to attempt to know the gender of unborn child by ultrasound and to perform abortion of unborn child are criminal acts. Unfortunately performing abortion with the help of renowned gynecologists or nurses is a very usual incident. In India, it is also a crime to know the gender of the unborn baby because it is assumed that people slay their unborn daughters. The pregnant ladies willing to give birth a child are admitted in the private female doctors' nursing homes if they are financially capable otherwise they go to government maternity hospitals. The private doctors' supervision is considered to be better because all the facilities and hygienic environment are available there. At the time of expected delivery, ladies are admitted to such private centers on the advice of the lady doctors. They either give birth to children by normal delivery or the children are birthed by the help of surgery. Lady doctors charge more money if they have to perform caesarean. As lady doctors charge more if they have to do surgery to make the child out hence some of them tell lies to family members or husbands of the pregnant ladies that due to some complications inside the womb, they have to go for surgery. They lie just to earn more money and in this they normally say to a husband to frighten him that umbilical cord of the lady has wrapped around the neck of child or the child is not at proper location hence if they do not allow operation, either of the mother or child will die. At the crucial moment, the anxious husbands give their permission for the surgery and lady doctors perform caesarean even when there were no such complications or urgency as mentioned by them. In many of such instances, the wise husbands give the doctors' fees for doing surgery earlier and ask them to perform normal delivery and in all of such matters, the mothers and the infants both remain physically healthy without the surgery that has been told to be extremely essential by the doctors for the safety of mothers and kids.

According to psychologists and psychiatrics, women are uncountable times more cruel and bestial than men. Men are usually generous, merciful and sensitive to small children, aged people, sick people, helpless ladies, beggars and handicapped but women keep cruel behavior and feelings of hatred for them. Though at a glance, it seems that women are very sensitive for such aforementioned destitute but in fact this is their pompous manifestation because they only pretend so. In the surveys conducted on the persons who help beggars, it is found that out of hundred persons who give some money to beggars, ninety-seven are men while only around three are women. While giving money to such beggars, the gestures of hatred can be seen on the face of ladies while men keep the expressions of mercy. Is has been observed in the various experiments that if the charge of criminals and prisons is given to ladies then the level of cruelty done for prisoners increases rapidly. In such situations the female prisoners face more ill-treatment than male prisoners and such harassment or ill-treatment of lady prisoners by female staff mostly includes sexual tortures. A female author once told that women, who are considered to be the symbol of mercy and politeness, in fact never possess these qualities. She further said that the poets or authors, who write or express their thoughts on women in literary form, actually never get succeeded to touch even the shade of the actual form of women. Ladies will never accept if some male author illustrates the actual form of them but if a lady author writes on the actual disposition and desires of women without making delusion of literature and high flown language then perhaps a widespread disaster will happen in the human society because the present actual form of women is very disgusting just like hell and hell is in fact hell even if it seems to be very attractive from outside.

Women are the masters of the art of exploiting men. They impose their own desires on men in such a marvelous decent way that men consider such desires of women as if they are their own desires. Women are the master of the art of_making men scapegoat. Only a woman can release a man trapped in the snares of treachery of another woman. All women are the master of the art of making conflicts among men but seldom a man is seen being expertise in the art of_keeping women against women. Married ladies often provoke their husbands against their parents and other blood relatives by speaking untruth to them. They incite their husbands to quarrel with the parents. All women achieve a perverted satisfaction when they suppress their husbands and create conflicts among in-laws and husbands. Bringing complexity in family relations, making conflicts between two persons, creating or being an impediment in the rise of other ladies, keeping active enmity with in-laws, imposing own thoughts and opinions upon others including husbands and unnecessary quarreling are the inseparable essential parts of women's temperament and almost women experience a peculiar pleasure in performing these activities. Married ladies, who often complain about the ill-treatment done with them and the harassment of them by husbands and in-laws, blame mothers-in-law and the sisters of the husbands in ninety-eight percent matters. Such ladies blame to their husbands in twenty one percent matters while in three percent matters, they blame to fathers-in-law and brothers-in-law. If such ladies are not supported by their husbands in their iniquitous attributes then they start falsely blaming to them. Most of such ladies complain that husbands never oppose their family members when their wives are harassed by them. Mothers-in-law always blame their daughters-in-law for the ill-treatment done with their sons and other family members. Hence in such instances, either mothers-in-law or daughters-in-law are wrong and men of the family are never responsible for such happenings because in all of such matters, the ladies who are actually wrong make the family men morally impotent. Concerned men become helpless and are bound to see the harassment done by one lady for the other lady and unnecessarily get puzzled because of such senseless conflicts of women. It is not possible for men to work outside for whole day and come back home to solve the conflicts of the ladies. As ladies never accept their faults and hence never do compromises hence the related men get depressed and make their life style very limited. In all such instances, no men are culpable for the harassment of ladies and ladies are the only cause of the distress and harassment of other ladies. A married lady eager to achieve higher education was strictly denied by her mother-in-law. The decision taken by her mother-in-law was right or wrong, is difficult to predict but she said a statement regarding ladies that all ladies are trapped in a deep swamp made by themselves not by a man. If a lady is desirous of her intellectual development in real sense then she is pulled down in the swamp by other ladies because ladies can never bear the progress of other ladies.

Human life is like a game played by ladies and men are the mere pawns in this game. Men are the clay mould vertebrate whom ladies give birth and feel proud and govern them by wearing the veil of mother for the initial life span. Then ladies wear the veil of sisters, lovers, wives or daughters to force their rules upon men. Hence a man is always governed or controlled by ladies. Such possessiveness in a woman for a man destroys his life. In the game of the life, men take the form of a pawn, knight or horse, king, camel and elephant like the game of chess. This is a lady who makes a man king at a moment and a normal pawn at the other moment. The forms which a man is bounded to adopt mostly in his life are of donkey and a dog. From this moment, his life differs from the game of chess. Women always put unnecessary burden of the senseless and useless work in parallel with the essential liabilities or responsibilities upon men just because of their lazy nature and egoism and hence they put physical as well as mental distress upon men thereby making them to perform like donkeys. When women want to satisfy their uncontrollable sexual desire, they compel men to act like dogs and even treat men as they are dogs. Women who are very expertise in sexual practices and are of very lustful temperament often say that men are dog. This is the biggest confession done by women regarding their ever unsatisfied sexual craving. It is said that behind the success of every men there are some ladies as inspiration of them. In present environment, we can say that behind any kind of failure and moral or physical degradation of a man, there is a lady as the only cause. Less than one percent of boys, who have fallen in love in their student life, consider this as an inspiration while more than ninety percent guys ruin their career in such affairs. In more than ninety-three percent of the crimes happening in the society women are directly or indirectly involved out of which in more than seventy-two percent criminal matters, women are directly involved. These figures are the result of the surveys taken in various states of India. The very shocking fact is that the only three percent of the criminal cases, where women are directly involved, their names are disclosed. Again we can understand this from the fact that out of the hundred such cases where women are directly involved, their names are disclosed in around seven matters out of which they are proved to be guilty only in three matters while in rest of four matters, they get the benefit of doubt and judiciary forgives them because they are women and look decent and unaware about crime. This is the prime reason that the count of women prisoners is very less in comparison to the male prisoners even when women have numerous times more involvement in crimes in comparison to men. According to the criminologists, if judiciary starts taking unbiased decision by not expressing mercy for women then the ratio of women prisoners will cross the ratio of male prisoners even in few months. In family crimes, if judiciary considers the direct or indirect involvement of ladies in even a peccadillo to a big crime and does not avoid the involvement of them and becomes neutral towards their feminine character then the ladies of every second house will be eligible for getting accused and being punished. This is an indication of the present condition of the society and the wide involvement of women in crime. The personal conflicts, property disputes and separation of the joint families in the life of an unmarried man can be seen in less than three percent matters while appearing of such circumstances and all other family crimes take place in ninety-seven percent matters when a lady in the form of new bride comes in the life of man because ladies enter in the family of their husbands with the everlasting awful properties of jealous, active enmity and quarrelsome nature. The appearance of a girlfriend or lover in the life of a guy makes him against of his parents. Real brothers, who are eager to sacrifice for the welfare of each other, don't want to even see the faces of each other after their marriage. Why? Before marriage, parents are everything for a son but after marriage, they seem to be an intolerable burden for him. Why a man disrespects and avoids his mother after the marriage? Perhaps this all is because of incompetent judiciary, sexually corrupt politicians and blind society who always favor the young married ladies thereby discarding the rights of aged parents. A wife draws the attention of her husband towards her attractive breasts thereby letting him forget about the debt of the milk of mother's breasts. All wives attempt to divert their husbands from their responsibilities for the aged parents and blood relatives. A man hides his face in-between the breasts of his wife to hide his impotency, depression, distress and repent for not fulfilling his duties for the aged parents. To hide him from himself, such a distressed man tries to insert his whole of the body in the *Yoni* or vagina of wife during intercourse so as to forget that his mother gave birth to him form her vaginal route and he has to respect and serve her. Now he becomes shameless and narrow-minded and considers his wife and kids to be the only member of his family. The *Yoni* of the wife shallows his feelings for the parents and blood relatives thereby making his social and family circle extremely narrow. Sufficiently big gentry of married men blindly follow the immoral guidance provided by their wives and behave like a slave eager to follow the instructions given by them. In such circumstances, men start misbehaving and ill treating to their mothers and they start giving respect to their wives instead of respecting own mothers. Wives make them understand that they should be practical and the very first step to do this is breaking the relations with parents. Such a stupid man immorally guided by the wife never asks his wife that why don't she breaks the relations with her parents. A man forgets his obligations for the parents and ruins his moral life because of the attraction of the *Yoni* of the wife even when he knows that ladies take birth from *Yoni*, with *Yoni* and for *Yoni*. As per the opinion of ladies, *Yoni* is the only wealth of them. They pretend protecting the chastity of *Yoni*. They sell their *Yoni* or gift it to men for the sake of sexual pleasure. They govern the nature from their *Yoni*. Their destiny is decided by their *Yoni*. They rule with the help of their *Yoni*. They destroy the kingdoms by their *Yoni*. They change the governments by utilizing their *Yoni*. They ruin the honor and dignity of the families through their *Yoni*. They perform adultery by the help of their *Yoni* and give birth to *Yoni* from their *Yoni*. They live for *Yoni*, they die for *Yoni*. They achieve another *Yoni* after death and take birth to achieve the same *Yoni* from a *Yoni*. They are cursed to carry the *Yoni* because they perform all iniquitous deeds with the help of their *Yoni*.

Marriage and Initial Married Life

Marriage is a social as well as moral relationship which is accepted by the men and women to live happily with each other by performing the responsibilities towards each other. Marriage is not a moral sexual debauchment consented by the society instead it describes an ethical limit of morality in sexual relations beyond which the sexual relations are considered to be illicit or adultery. Marriage is a great attempt to keep the society free from sexual debauchment by assigning one man for one lady and one lady for one man. Marriage is not a compulsion instead it is a confession done with mutual consent to live a peaceful life devotedly with each other. Marriage is not a custom instead it is a trustful dedication; a dedication which is contentedly expressed by men and women to keep the foundation of future. Marriage can not be defined separately for men and women because neither a man nor a lady can marry in own gender to carry family succession. Marriage is a mutual oath between men and women. Again it is not an organization or institutional body or society because these can comprise of only men or women. Marriage is a stage of human life by achieving which only men and women become physically as well as morally absolute. From the point of view of sexual relations, marriage is a factor which distinguishes human from animals. Marriage is in fact obeying the guidance that has been provided to us by the omnipotent creator God. Marriage is a symbol of an easy and ethical social life. It is sacred tribute to ancestors. It is an indication of family succession or genealogy. It is a religious attempt to provide worthy citizens to the society in future. Marriage is a sacrifice and entrustment of oneself done contentedly by men and women for the sake of the welfare of each other. Marriage is a way of protecting men and women physically as well as morally and it is an assurance of the nurture and security provided to elders. Marriage is a probable solution for achieving the security in the old age. It is a divine remedy to the sore distress of depression caused by solitude which is like an incurable disease. It is an inspiration for performing devotion based obligations hence motivates men and women to perform their duties. Marriage is the very first attempt or an endeavor to maintain the life style following the codes of conduct. It is an assurance to decide the proper *Gotra* of forthcoming generations. Marriage is the identity of men because it helps out the coming progenies to get familiar with their respective fathers. Marriage is an indication of women's chastity and refinement. Marriage is a ritual to provide social as well as legal acceptance to the child in the womb. Marriage is an indication of the death of the parents in the form of coming generations as it assures the eternal truth that older one has to end to provide the life and opportunities to the incoming generations. For men, marriage is in fact performing the moral, ritualistic and materialistic duties while for women this is mere the accomplishing of sanctifying rites and following the codes of conduct. Marriage is not an agreement done on behalf of a legal contract instead it is a complete dedication free from compulsions. Marriage is a sacrifice of personal desires done by men and women for the expectation and welfare of each other. Wherever aforementioned feelings do not exist in the background of the objectives of marriage, there marriage means mere accomplishment of sexual satisfaction and false ego and in this situation marriage is just like a contract which if done by a man with one lady or four ladies, is mere sexual debauchment in the point of view of the morals and ethics.

Though the manifestation of marriage appears to be dissimilar in different religions and communities because of different traditions or customs but the basic ancient assumptions as well as the objectives of marriage are same in all the religions. Almost religions show their consent and acceptance of the above mentioned logics behind marriage and if any religion keeps different approach to this then it is only because of the absurd, confusing and biased interpretations done by the so called holy priests of that religion. In Hindu religion, marriage is considered to be thirteenth sanctifying rite among the total sixteen rites performed by a man in his life. After the betrothal done among the family members of would-be bride and groom, at the day of marriage, the ritual of worshipping lord *Ganesha* is done to materialize the marriage ceremony. In the process of worshipping or paying reverence to Hindu Gods and Goddess, the adoration of Lord *Ganesha*, the lord of nine planets, sixteen *Matrikas* and seven *Ghriti Matrikas* is done. After summoning the religious deities lord *Varun* or the god of air, *Kalash* as the pious Vedic symbol, lord Sun and the principal deities worshipped by that family, the divine process of *Kanyadaan* is done. In the *Kanyadaan*, the father of the bride or her elder brother or otherwise in the absence of male blood relatives, some male family member bestows the bride to the bridegroom and bridegroom holds her hands from palm as a consent as well as an oath of accepting the all possible moral liabilities of the bride from that moment till his own life span. The one end of the garment of bride and bridegroom are tied together as a symbol of family knot and the pair jointly touches the feet of the parents as well as the elders of both the sides to accept their blessings. Bride and bridegroom move around the sacred fire to make encirclement of it and such seven rounds are taken by them. In first four rounds, the bride escorts the groom by walking ahead of him while in the rest of three rounds; the bridegroom guides her by walking before her. In the first four encirclements taken by the pair in which bridegroom walks afterwards, bride throws grains of rice provided by her brother in to sacred fire with the intention that she is leaving the premises of her parents and going to accept the family of her husband. All of the seven encirclements are affiliated to different oaths mutually taken by the bride and groom for the welfare of each other. The objective behind the first encirclement of the holy fire is in the form of an oath taken by both of them jointly to follow the codes of ethics and religion. The objective of second round is in the form of a blessing as well as an instruction to them to live a wealthy and comfortable life by making coordination in the voluptuousness, family duties and charity services. The third round blesses them to live a happy married life by enjoying the sexual pleasure. The fourth round ensures them to achieve the blessings of God or *Moksha* or paradise after death if they live their life by following the codes of moral conduct and chastity. Hence after performing the seven encirclements of the holy fire by making seven promises, they are considered to be prepared to live together as husband and wife.

Thus in these seven encirclements, both of them have to give their joint words or have to make promises. In the first step, the joint promise done by them is for keeping patience thereby being stubborn to live with each other without quitting on finding the difficulties. Second promise is done to fulfill the family responsibilities whole heartedly. Third promise is taken for not carrying sexual relations with other men or other women and never performing polygamy. Fourth promise is done to behave properly with each other and in accordance with each other. Fifth promise is done to live helping each other in good time as well as in bad time. The sixth promise is done to co-operate each other in every genuine, legal and ritualistic performance. Seventh step is regarding the promises done with each other and keeping aforementioned six oaths.

The basic part *Kanyadaan* of a Hindu marriage ceremony is directly or indirectly adopted by all the religions but unfortunately because of religious enmity, other religions hesitate to accept this. In the utter religious ritual *Kanyadaan*, the bride is neither donated nor entrusted to bridegroom. We should know the reason behind calling it a *Daan* or donation as well as about the objectives that stand behind the process of *Kanyadaan* because if those objectives are strictly followed by the family members of both sides irrespective of their religion then it would strongly help in minimizing the crimes against women and it would certainly stop the harassment of bridegrooms and their innocent parents done by the brides in future. In the holy scriptures, donation of cow is described at number of places and it is said that the donation of a young cow capable of producing milk to a poor man who is worthy of accepting that, is the biggest good deed done and is equivalent auspicious for the donator as the *Kanyadaan* or marriage arranged of an orphan and financially poor lady with a suitable man. Hence the very first liability of the parents of bride is that they should never hide the shortfalls of their daughters and should never tell lies about their daughters to grooms' side and should marry their daughters with the men of equivalent social, moral and financial status. After the donation of any living or lifeless object like money etc, the donator loses the rights over the donated item and hence can not even imagine accomplishing any kind of advantage from that. In the similar way the parents of the bride should not accept or even imagine of any kind of profit from their daughters or sons in law. They are not permitted to express any right on the property of their married daughters and are not allowed to interfere in their families. They can only interfere when invited by their sons-in-law or when they find their married daughters in trouble. Now if any complication arises in the family of married daughters then parents should make fare judgment and support only the right person. If they find their married daughters to be wrong that is what normally happens then they should never help their daughters and should never permit daughters to come back to parents' residences without the proper permission of husbands. They should support their sons-in-law if daughters are wrong. Though, in fact, the exact reverse of that attitude in the parents of newly brides is found nowadays. Hence the basic motive behind the term *Kanyadaan* is that the parents of brides' side can not take money or any kind of financial benefit from the married daughters and they can not sell their daughters. This is the moral responsibility of the parents of the brides' side to help their daughters or sons-in-law in future if they are in need but they are not bounded to do this.

There was a time when before marriage a girl was given proper knowledge of ethical conduct by the parents and relatives of her and she was strictly bounded to maintain her virginity till marriage. Such ethical guidance provided by the parents to their daughters helped them in living a peaceful and happy married life. Mothers advised their daughters to live peacefully in the joint family of the husbands without making any bifurcation in the family thereby not isolating husbands from their parents and relatives. They were strictly instructed by the parents to follow the husbands and respect their family members. It was considered that a married lady should live happily with her husband and sons and her body should be lifted from the same house of her husband when she dies. Fathers instruct their just married daughters to enter in the premises of them only with the consent of husband or along with him. If a married lady used to come to the residence of her father without the permission of her husband or after quarrelling with husband or without husband then parents did not allow her to enter in the premises. The parents and the other relatives did not interfere in the family matters of their married daughters. Even the parents did not drink the water of the family of their married daughters. The financially strong parents always found to be helping their needy married daughters on the consent of their husbands but never accept any gift or financial benefit from the families of sons-in-law. A girl, who has lived in the strict discipline and guidance of parents, does not keep quarrelsome nature, enmity and jealousy for the in-laws and husband. Parents instruct her to respect in-laws, obey husband by being a husband devotee and to live maintaining chastity by not even thinking of other man. Hence a girl grown under such moral guidance was never found to isolate husband from his parents or other blood relatives and lived politely being a member of the family. If a girl possessed some disorder or bad attribute then parents intimate about her shortcomings to the family of bridegroom before the verbal commitment of marriage. The foundation of marriage was based on truth and trust not on untruth and disloyalty as in the present scenario.

This is well known that at present, the concept of marriage has changed. The feelings and the emotions behind the marriage or *Kanyadaan* have entirely eloped. The parents of marriageable daughters get exhilarated by taking the help of betray and shrewdness to speak untruth to the parents of marriageable guys in order to marry their daughters in rich families. During the time of selection of the bridegroom, the qualities like morality, assiduous tendency or laboriousness, honesty and idealistic nature are neglected rather the one who is financially rich or possessing government job with the advantage of taking bribe or a good businessman is preferred. Parents feel proud by marrying their daughters with wealthy non-resident Indians residing abroad or with young guys getting good salaries in private companies. They deny by ignoring and reproaching the parents of guys belonging to financially medium class or low class families, who come with marriage proposals on behalf of their sons. Almost no parents of the brides' side give consent for considering a man as their son-in-law who is struggling in career or is financial lower or normal businessman or is a man working at lower level in private company. Almost parents of the girls imagine for rich sons-in-law so that they may fetch financial benefit from them in future. For this they are found to spend money or dowry at the time of daughters' marriage as a bribe or bait to allure such sons-in-law. Again the parents want to marry their daughters with the guys who are the only sons of their parents with the intentions that such guys get whole of the property after the death of parents. Almost parents do not want to marry their daughters in the joint families because as per their opinion in joint families, their daughters have to do more household work essentially. They want their daughters to live in a nuclear family or alone with husband doesn't matter if for this, their daughters have to bifurcate the joint families by quarrelling or making complications. If the daughters are married in joint families then their mothers viciously instruct them to create conflicts and complications in the family so that their husbands get compelled to live separately from the joint families with them. They instruct their daughters to treat the aged parents and blood relatives of husbands as they are servant and such disgusting behavior should be shown towards in-laws in the absence of husbands. As per the surveys conducted, it was found that eighty-seven parents out of per hundred expect financial benefit from their daughters and hence give improper guidance to them thereby making the personal life of sons-in-law like hell. Out of such eighty-seven iniquitous parents, in eighty-four matters such immoral guidance and improper assistance to the married daughters were given by their mothers and fathers were either neutral or against of this but were unable to take any step against of their corrupt wives.

109

As during the marriage ceremony, the bride veils her face with jewelries and other decorating items like diadem etc hence the clear visibility of her face becomes rare therefore few parents change the bride. In this, at the time of betrothal, they show some other beautiful girl as their daughter while at the time of marriage they change that girl by their unworthy daughter. Sometimes it becomes horrible as parents marry their daughters possessing physical or mental disorder to worthy faultless guys thereby making their life hell. Parents hide the shortcomings of their daughters in the marriage as they are well known with the fact that once the marriage is done, the bridegroom and his family members become helpless because of biased laws and the history of the judicial decisions given in past. In all of such matters, a bridegroom betrayed by the family of a bride becomes unable to take any action against such kind of fraud because he can never proof that he has been cheated and if he attempts to appeal to court then the parents of the side of bride blames him for the further demand of dowry and physical as well as mental harassment of their daughter. In almost of such matters, judiciary never considers the veracity of the incidences and troubles of the bridegrooms' side and always gives judgment against them because of being prejudiced that a newly wedded lady is usually harassed by the in-laws. While considering an ideal pair, this is almost everywhere considered that man should be in a proper job or business to earn livings and able to provide other facilities to his spouse while lady should be good in looking with spotless character as well as body. The beautiful features and spotless character of a lady are appraised while the financial status, strong body and masculine nature of a man are considered to be appraisable. No man gives preference to marry with a lady of masculine nature and figure similarly no woman likes to make a man her life-partner if he is of feminine nature and figure and unable to earn his livings. If a married couple is found in which the wife is physically ugly looking or is unattractive and either belongs to very rich family or working in government job or working in some private sector where she is earning a lot while the husband is comparatively more good-looking but belongs to poor family and does nothing special to earn then in all of such matters it is found that husband was purchased at the time of marriage. Such mismatching in the pairs can always be seen in the married couples. Very unattractive looking men marry with the ladies who are extremely good looking while very handsome men can be seen marrying with unattractive ladies. This also happens in the case of love marriages. Almost all of the ladies, who are very good looking in comparison to their husbands, perform adultery and the married life of such husbands is like hell because they live in the fear of the beauty of their wives. Stupid men still consider that the beauty of ladies is a symbol of their chastity. Wherever both of the husband and wife possess attractive features and beauty there almost men seems to be carrying the properties and features of eunuchs. Again more than seventy-eight percent pairs are mismatched by their physical appearance. At present, almost government servants possess beautiful wives because the parents of the beautiful ladies or rich ladies give preference to marry their daughters with men, who are in government jobs. It can be seen that almost of such guys have the ugly and unattractive appearances and stand nowhere in context of beauty of their wives. Similarly very handsome guys are married with the ladies, who are extremely unattractive. The reasons for such mismatching have already been defined.

With such facts, the parents of the girls hide the shortcomings of their daughters like white spots on the body, symptoms of some incurable disease, physical inefficiencies, stinking teeth, pre-marriage illicit sexual involvements, pre-marriage abortions and the shortcomings of nature like excessive aggressiveness or indecent conduct etc. As mentioned earlier, it is also found that few brides are pregnant at the time of their marriage due to pre-marriage sexual relations with other men and parents of them hide that from the family members of grooms. In such a matter the bride was running through the seventh month of her pregnancy and she cleverly hided that by tightly wrapping a piece of cloth around her stomach. After the marriage, at the first night, husband came to know about this then he was shocked and helpless. Ladies, who are regularly involved in harlotry and numerous times have committed abortion, are said to be virtuous and innocent and married by their parents with the worthy and sexually unadulterated men residing at very distant as in other states so that they may never know about the sexually corrupt background of their wives. In all aforementioned situations when a disloyal or unworthy lady is married with a worthy man than the man as her husband and his family members are bound to accept her because of one sided laws in favor of such corrupt ladies and their deceptive parents. Again the ladies, who have been very defamed by their involvement in sexual adultery in the society, are married deceitfully to the men residing abroad or at distant places with the intention that no such husband could ever be able to know about the blemished past of his life partner. Now pre-marriage activities of a wife or some physical fault in her or even her involvement in sexual relations before marriage can be tolerated if we consider the ethics of marriage on behalf of grooms' side because it is said that one should not consider the past of the spouse and should not let the past disturb the present or future but the painful situation creates when such immoral parents mislead virtuous men to marry with their mentally retarded or abnormal daughters. At present, mothers teach their daughters to keep negative and illicit attitude to make the separation of husband from his parents and blood relatives. As mentioned above, parents teach and evoke their married daughters to keep rivalry or antagonism, deceitful intentions, disloyalty, indecency, dishonesty, unnecessary quarrelling to impose own mistakes on others, making conflicts, disrespecting as well as neglecting the in-laws, falsely blaming for the dowry, doing physical as well as mental harassment of in-laws, being malevolent by involving in violence and making frightened to in-laws and husbands to keep them under mental pressure by threatening of committing suicide. Mothers are seldom found to be advising their married daughters to live a peaceful and compromising married life by obeying and respecting husbands and in-laws. It is found in a wide survey done that wherever in the families there are complications among husbands and wives and the wives are of arrogant temperament and are culpable then in the background of such ninety-seven percent cases, the basic factors as well as causes of conflicts were the direct or indirect influence or involvement of the parents of wives. In all of such matters, the parents of the wives as well as wives themselves were behind the complications and were guilty but even after that they were found to be falsely blaming husbands and their parents. Out of the total count of married men, who were not living with the parents, four percent were bound to live with the in-laws thereby leaving behind the helpless parents alone because of the pressure of the wives and in-laws. In half percent cases, men were living with the in-laws willingly by neglecting own parents because of achieving financial benefits from in-laws or being unemployed thereby financially depending on the in-laws. In twenty percent matters, men were living with the wives leaving parents alone because of their source of earning of jobs being at distant places. In four and half percent matters, parents themselves were willing to live alone. In seventy-one percent matters, the wives or in-laws of men bounded them by mentally and physically harassing, to live separately from the parents.

The side of bridegroom visits the place of a girl for the purpose of marriage or with the same intention relatives of the girl go to meet the desired bridegroom. In both of the situations, betrothal is done on the mutual consent of the parents of both sides. In many areas, there is a popular custom that at the time of betrothal or after it but before marriage, some lady of groom's side asks the girl to remove the garments at a secluded room in order to make sure that she is not having any physical disability or white spots probable of being transferable to the incoming progenies or any kind of infectious disease or a symptom of leprosy. This peculiar duty is performed by the sister of the bridegroom's father or mother. After this, a get-together of would-be spouse is arranged by their parents so that they may see each other and have a short conversation with each other. If a girl and boy are in love with each other and they manage their parents to give consent for their marriage then in all of such matters, the girl compels the boy to approach to her parents with his parents for asking of their approval. In this situation, the parents of the guy become upset but girl maintains the pseudo dignity as well as honor of her parents by not sending them first. Before the love-cum-arrange marriage or an arrange marriage, once the date of marriage is decided, both the sides get busy in the arrangements. Usually in the duration before marriage, would-be husband and wife communicate with each other via telephone and sometimes arrange meetings. Such attempts of conversations may be carried out by boy or girl. It is also found in some orthodox families or in some dignified families that after the betrothal, the would-be husband and wife never do any kind of interaction till the marriage but this does not happen in the case of love-cum-arrange marriages. In number of cases, when the parents of a boy visit to some girl's residence but do not give their consent immediately by saying that they will let them know the decision later-on, the girl starts conversing with the guy through telephone etc and insists as well as sexually allures him to say yes as soon as possible. She is even found saying to him that he is a coward and unable to take the decision of his marriage himself hence waiting for the decision taken by the parents. Then that guy, made foolish by the clever girl, informs his parents that he will marry only with that girl. The general discussions that took place in-between would-be bride and groom are of very importance for the girl because in such discussions, she is told by the boy about the behavior and nature of his family members. Thus the lady comes to know about the environment of her would-be husband's house before the marriage. Here she controls over her talkative nature and listens to would-be husband carefully pretending that she is a very peaceful spectator. In fact she does keen observation of the thoughts and the mentality of her would-be husband. Such kind of before-marriage conversations between a boy and a girl become troublesome for the boy in his after-marriage life because now the lady has come to know a lot about the would-be husband and his family members and hence she has already pondered on it for long. Such thinking over the relations done by women is always found to be effected by their negative tendency and by the worst aspect of women psychology. It is also found that for women, having more than just necessary information about any matter or having it before the proper time, is always found to be disastrous for the men who are affiliated with that matter. This is a perfect misconception spread among youngsters that such type of colloquy or conversations done between a bride and groom before marriage help them to understand each other more deeply and even are beneficial for both of them to live a happy and peaceful married life in future. The before-marriage proximity of would-be wife done by a man and the exchange of thoughts done by him with her during this period always make the foundation of probable complications and troubles for him in his married life. The introduction of the would-be husband and his relatives to the lady does not provide her a normal and good approach instead it invokes dominating and deceiving tendency in her. The affection or generous behavior shown by the would-be husband and his relatives for the would-be bride is considered to be a kind of conspiracy by her. Only those married men are found to be living a peaceful married life by their own life style who always pretend themselves to be uninvolved or detached from the attraction of sexual life and willingly perform the only necessary duties for their family. This detachment shown in behavior has different kinds. The men who perform usual sexual courses with their wives but never ever show themselves being allured or impressed by the beauty or sex appeal of wives, their wives can never overrule them or subjugate over them. Such men are almost found to be successful in their married life as they never request to their wives for sexual mating and if they find that their wives are unwilling, they too avoid even touching them. Wives are always ready to catch the behavioral weaknesses of their husbands and they learn to perform only those activities by which they found their husbands being irritated. A man showing excessive emotional or sexual affection for his wife is always harassed by his wife. Hence all the men, who implore their wives for desiring the love, beseech them for love making and are fascinated by the beauty of them thereby never keep their dignity or self respect maintained, are treated by their wives as a pet dog wagging it's tail. It is also found that very gentle, experienced, practical and well-versed men adopt unabashed conduct and frivolous attitude while begging their wives for love making. It is almost found that the imploring done by husbands to their wives for sexual courses and the trivial sexual conversations done by them, are considered to be a reflection of their personality by their wives and such shameless attitude done by them while love making is laid upon the whole life of them by their wives. It can be seen that if a husband peacefully or by love, explains something right or moral to his wife when she performs some immoral deed then wife never accepts her fault and pretends to be unhappy by weeping or carrying a hunger-strike thereby utilizing her deceitful qualities of women psychology. If a husband, in above situation, still attempts to make her happy by gentle speaking then he always remains worried by the attitude of his wife because wife develops a habit of being aggressive and stubborn even when she is mistaken. If it seems that a wife accepts her fault when she is explained by husband then this is a mere delusion because a lady can never be guilty conscious.

When a bride is having sufficient information about the would-be husband's family through him then she becomes very confident and carefree. Such freedom from care diverts her from obligations of married life hence in such situation, the husband as well as the in-laws are ignored by her and she makes a fun of her husband among the other family members. These situations mostly appear when the bride and bridegroom had get-togethers and conversations with each other before marriage. Men are almost unaware about the probable consequences as the outcome of such before-marriage conversations and the probable adverse situations that may appear in their married life because of such discussions done with would-be wives before marriage. They consider themselves to be very smart and forward while conversing with their would-be wives and pretend to be very generous and caring for them. Actually in this situation, they are almost betrayed by their innocent and decent looking would-be wives because ladies come to know about the temperament and level of their would-be grooms and their family members without doing any effort and without putting their queries. Such stupid and dumb men always become happy with the thought that they are guiding their would-be brides but in fact they themselves are directionless and the would-be brides are guiding them very shrewdly.

Sometimes the parents of bridegroom take time to give their decision after seeing a girl for their son. In this situation as mentioned above, the girl remains in touch of the boy through telephonic conversations or love letters or get-togethers and always allures him thereby motivating him to give his consent for marriage. She consistently stimulates the boy by taunting him that a man who is waiting for the decision of parents for marriage can not live a self-dependent life. Further she also comments on him by saying that he is a coward and is having lack of self-assurance because of not deciding to marry and not giving his consent and waiting for parent's decision. Now foolish boy compels his parents to let him marry with the same girl. A man marrying with that lady under such circumstances can never live for long period with his parents after marriage and keeps antagonism with his parents because the lady is already having prejudiced hatred and enmity for her in-laws as they were not ready for the marriage. Such ladies are found to be of very cunning nature and are eloquent hence always rule their husbands by making them mentally impotent.

In some places, the parents of girls take the help of black magic so that their daughters might marry with the desired boys by overpowering them. In such magic, the use of cloves, unbroken rice, the soil beneath the footsteps or a piece of cloth soaked with menstruation discharge of the lady for which groom is needed, is done. People sanctifies the cloves by chanting some specific verses and grind it to mix in some sweat dish so that they may give it to the required boy to eat. It is assumed that the moment a boy eats such sweat dishes; he becomes subjugated because of becoming in complete control of the concerned girl. Somewhere people do the same process with the unbroken rice to create blind affection in the conscious and subconscious mind of the boy for specific girl. Some witch doctors take the photograph of the boy from the mother of the girl and with the help of the skeleton of the reptiles they perform a kind of hypnotism on the boy. Somewhere an iron nail is soaked with the menstruation discharge of the lady and is thrown inside the residence of the required boy which creates disputes in the family and the boy becomes stubborn to marry that specific girl. Though this all seems to be ridiculous and indicates illiteracy level in the public but this is also true that such attempts done by the parents of young girls with the help of incantations are always found to be succeeded and such acts are mostly done by the educated people not by illiterates. Mothers of the boys, in order to protect their sons from such black magic or charms, instruct them to keep a piece of the turmeric under the tongue before going to the residences of the girls with the intention for marriage. Mothers, who are aware of such incantations, warn their sons not to eat any sweet dish of yellow color offered by the parents of the girls. It is also assumed that if the boy wears a ring having embedded turquoise, at the place of the engagement ring, then it protects him from any kind of incantations done to draw his sexual attentions towards a lady.

Boys and girls have different imaginations in context of their probable life partners. Ladies expect their would-be husbands to be high ranked in the job, wealthy and handsome. Apart from this, all ladies desire their monopoly in the families of their would-be husbands. Though mostly parents seek the bridegrooms for their daughters and would-be spouse are introduced with each other by the help of them in some hotels or parks or temples or in the residence of any side but still in context of the dowry, marriage seems to be a mutual contract done among the parents of the bride and bridegroom or his parents. Again in such verbal contract of give and take or dowry, brides are never considered to be a party because all of the decisions are taken by their parents on behalf of them. This becomes very helpful for ladies to ignore or deny about the promises of dowry done by their parents before marriage. If daughters decide to marry with their lovers then parents become almost free from giving dowry or spending money. Few mothers advise their daughters to trap rich men for the purpose of marriage so that they may be free from giving dowry to them and may take financial help from their would-be sons-in-law. In all of such situations where ladies deliberately seek rich guys to trap them for marriage, the husbands chosen are always treated like slaves by their wives and they lack the conscience. All beautiful ladies seek lesser attractive, more educated and more wealthy husbands in comparison to themselves. Wealthy but unattractive ladies desire for good looking husbands belonging to financially medium class so that they may rule over them by providing them financial support from parents. Girls of normal looking with unattractive features, belonging to financially medium class, desire attractive and rich husbands. Wealthy, beautiful and popular ladies like actresses are never seen marrying with financially poor or middleclass men. This is because all beautiful ladies with strong financial background prefer high leveled businessmen or highly ranked government officers and the reason behind this is such renowned men have limited time for their families and they never keep any kind of restrictions over their wives because they have to prove themselves advanced and broad minded. Suppose if such ladies marry with financially middleclass simple men then their marriage will not sustain for even few months because ladies of this category are of extremely dominating and egoistic nature. Hence almost ladies desire for wealthy husbands who should be very active and dexterous in their professions but should follow the instructions given by the wives blindly without applying conscience. Every lady desires unconstrained atmosphere for her after marriage so that she may fulfill her unsatisfied cravings under the shade of the vermilion mark at her forehead as a symbol of her married status. When experienced and virtuous married ladies were interviewed then all of them said that a family runs properly only when the husband is having strict control over his wife because the actual appearance and outcome of the freedom or unrestrained atmosphere that almost married ladies desire for, is very horrible and disgusting. Ladies themselves being the source of sensual pleasure are most affected and allured by sensual pleasures. Again if a girl of rich family marries with a poor man without the consent of her parents then she is seldom financially helped by her parents and in this situation, she experiences distress in her married life because of the lack of luxurious items and hence ultimately she invokes depression and distress in her husband. Increase in the level of the availabilities of the sensual pleasures, wealth, political power and luxurious life makes a lady unrestrained and autocratic while the degradation of the status of aforementioned provides her distress and frustration. Similar depression is faced by the ladies during the period of menopause and at very old age when they are physically incapable to achieve sexual pleasure. Somewhere girls belonging to rich families are married with poor guys because of their physical deficiency or ugly appearance or known adulterated character then in all such instances, men are very greedy and they are in fact purchased by the parents of such girls by giving unlimited money. In such a matter, a renowned government officer proposed a young guy to marry with his ugly looking and sexually corrupt daughter on the assurance that after marriage he would make him selected in the civil services, which are considered to be a gateway of top level government jobs. The guy accepted the proposal and married to that lady and the father-in-law gave a big amount of money to make him pass such high level competition. In one matter, the senior professor refused to give PhD to a student when he refused to marry with her sexually corrupt daughter. Such instances can easily be seen in the influential families. Again in all such instances, where parents purchase the sons-in-law for their daughters having physical disabilities or ugly complexion or known adulterated character or spots on whole of the body, after marriage such husbands are found to be keeping illicit sexual relations with keeps or concubines. Financially very high class men, when marry with the ladies belonging to almost same financial level, are never able to ask their wives for the very personal normal routine work and if they dare to say then conflicts arise while in the same conditions, wives very easily make their husbands to perform such very normal personal tasks. It is found that in such pairs, if the high profiled men are not extreme busy with their work then their personal lives surely become hell. The social as well as personal lives of highly renowned families are seldom hidden from media hence natural form of their relations disappears and the normal attitude shown by them for their spouse in public are mere ostentations. If a man belonging to a high class or very high class family marries with a middle or low class girl then the attitude of the lady in future depends on the behavior of husband. Such ladies, who have seen poverty or living economically before marriage, when achieve plenty of wealth after marriage because of marrying with rich men, become arrogant and lose their conscience and discretion hence behave like an insane. If such a rich husband is wise and keeps his wife away from the glory of wealth or luxury thereby fulfilling only requirements of her which are essential and keeps her away from the sexually corrupt ladies of his society then his family life runs smoothly but such examples are seldom found. More than eighty-five percent ladies, who achieve wealth or fame or both after marriage, pretend to maintain the dignity in their social life while in actual, less than ten percent of them are able to maintain the dignity in their family life and sexual relations.

Young men desire for beautiful ladies as their wives. When a middleclass or lower class suitable man is married with a simple looking girl then in almost of such instances he demands for money as dowry before marriage. For the girls and their parents, a worthy groom means one who is wealthy or appointed at high post hence parents of ladies are eager to gift money or other luxurious items to such grooms in the form of dowry. It is very difficult for a financially lower medium class or low class boy to achieve higher education from renowned institutes and because of the wide corruption spread in government sectors, such guys seldom achieve high post in government sectors. This situation is worse for the financially poor guys belonging to forward caste because they never get any financial or other kind of assistance from the government. Hence it is a hardcore task for such guys of poor financial level to achieve a dignified post and bright future. Most of such students do not achieve success even after spending plenty of money in the coaching institutes. Such coaching institutes teach the students so that they may qualify medical or engineering entrance exams or qualify civil services. The poor parents residing in the villages believe that just by getting the admission in such coaching institutes, their children will achieve a bright future hence they sell their agricultural lands so that they may pay the big amount of fees of such private coaching institutes. Such matters can be seen in the villages where parents give the fees in the coaching institute so that their sons may become doctor but they never know that mere admission in coaching is not any kind of assurance for their sons' even selection in the medical entrance exams. Unaware parents spend money and start saying to their relatives that their son is studying in medical college. This situation is same for the guys belonging to medium class families but they get the advantage for directly getting admission in the private medical or engineering colleges by giving a big amount of money as donation. When guys are unsuccessful to achieve their goals, they join some business or private concern to earn their living. Such unsuccessful or successful guys, when marry, desire for dowry from the parents of the would-be wives. Parents of the brides are eager to give plenty of money as dowry to purchase a professionally successful groom or a wealthy groom but they never want to give any financial assistance in the form of dowry to a boy who is struggling for career and whom with they are going to marry their daughter. The contradictory attitude of the parents of the daughters can be understood by this fact that parents of more than one daughter can be seen giving the sufficient amount of money as dowry to the financially strong and high ranked wealthy husband of one daughter while they give almost nothing to the financially struggling husband of the other daughter. One of such parents, when interviewed personally, said that giving dowry in the marriage of a daughter is just like a stake in a horse-race because all parents desire to give minimum dowry to their sons-in-law but are willing to achieve maximum financial profit from them. In present scenario, parents give dowry to those men who are already rich because they know that such investment is safe and is an open or silent assurance of the return of multiple times more money through the daughters hence dowry is like a money back policy for the parents of the daughters. The moment parents feel that they might not fetch financial help from their sons-in-law through their daughters and their daughters are not having smooth relations with the in-laws and husbands, they motivate daughters to blame on them for asking dowry. It is found in surveys that almost parents of the married daughters usually get financial help from the sons-in-law but never confess about this among relatives or society and such parents always tell lies regarding the amount of money they have given as dowry. Parents who don't give dowry or give limited amount always tell the relatives that they gave unlimited amount as dowry to their sons-in-law. They often tell the dowry amount numerous times more than the actual amount they gave. The parents of a girl willingly give dowry either to show-off in relatives or to maintain psychological pressure on the financially poor groom's side or to influence the financially strong groom's side. The good feelings of the parents of the brides never stand behind giving dowry. Again somewhere dowry is given by the parents with the intention of purchasing a groom for compensating the defects of their daughters like ugly appearance, incurable spots on the skin, physical disability and mental disorder etc. The parents belonging to financially very high class families often found purchasing brilliant grooms, who are recently selected for administrative services, for their beautiful looking characterless daughters. Very shocking but true is that such marriageable girls go with their parents and select the groom among the young administrative officers and like an auction, they ask for the price of such selected grooms. Such bids are mostly made by the influential rich parents during the training period of officers. Sometimes if an officer selected by a lady denies selling himself then he has to face the anger of influential parents of her. Such grooms' market are not very different from sex market because in a sex market, women are purchased every day for a short span for sexual pleasure while in grooms' market, young men are purchased for ever. If the purchaser is not genuine then a prostitute has to tolerate him for at most few hours and then she gets free while when grooms are purchased, they have no choice to quit even when they know that they have sold themselves in the wrong hands. This peculiar kind of *Swayamber* or the publicly choosing of bridegroom by the bride among her assembled suitors, is performed very secretly and when a bride selects the groom then parents make bids and purchase that guy in the form of their son-in-law for the sake of satisfying the sexual craving of their lustful daughter, who is already merged in the marsh of sexual debauchment, and to satisfy her false ego.

The desire to marry daughters with the rich non-resident Indians or the Indians residing abroad is often seen in the parents. Parents can be seen discarding worthy grooms living in the own country and marrying daughters abroad. In such few instances, boys residing abroad tell lies regarding their jobs or salary and the financial status so as to draw the attention of the parents of the daughters living in India but unfortunately the Indian parents are influenced by the snares of the illusory world of the charm of foreign countries hence without any proper inquiry about the trustworthiness of the statements proclaimed by the guys, they arrange the marriage of their daughters with them. Sometimes such guys are already married or divorced but the parents of the girls are told that they are bachelor. Such betrayal is experienced by many parents who marry their daughters abroad. To get the truth of such instances, a survey was conducted in the families living in India who declared that they have been betrayed in such matters. All of such parents confessed that they took wrong decision by neglecting and reproaching the offers of worthy guys and preferred to marry their daughters to the guys living abroad because they could not control over their voracity for the charm of foreign countries. One of such familiar parents told that the attitude and behavior of their daughter was awfully shameless and she was not able to adjust herself in a decent family. She was not eligible for marrying in a ritualistic family following the codes of conduct and was having number of boyfriends. Hence the moment they got an offer of marriage from abroad they immediately decided to marry her there with the thought that perhaps an Indian man residing in America would prefer to marry with such a lady having broad mentality regarding sexual relations because this is a normal culture in Western countries. More than fifty percent parents, who marry their daughters with the guys residing abroad, have the same compulsions and they marry their daughters abroad with the view that the would-be sons-in-law will never come to know the disgusting past of the ladies they marry. Hence most of such parents do not enquire more about the would-be sons-in-law because their own daughters are morally misfit and sexually adulterated. One of such parents clearly told that the non-resident-Indians come to India for selecting the bride with the thought that perhaps they may get a strong character, decent and polite life partner but they are mistaken because when the Indian grooms never get such girls then how the guys residing abroad will get them. The worst condition is of those abroad residing guys who are eligible bachelor and marry with the Indian girls as per the guidance of their innocent parents with the thought that Indian girls are virtuous, virgin and trustworthy but in more than seventy-two percent matters, they get sexually corrupt, indecent and arrogant wives. Again the worst condition is faced by the three percent virtuous girls who are sexually unadulterated and decent but betrayed by some guys residing abroad, who lie about their marital or financial status and are already married or divorced and having illicit sexual relations with prostitutes. It is senseless to mention here about the figures regarding the couples where both of the partners are either immoral or moral.

The concept of *Swayamber* has already been discussed earlier. It is literally made by two words "*Swayam*" and "*Ber*". Here *Swayam* means self and *Ber* means either selection or groom. *Swayamber* is a ritualistic process of ancient period in which a worthy bride chooses her groom among the men who visited to her place considering them to be worthy groom for her.

Somewhere few conditions were supposed to be fulfilled by the participants to prove themselves being worthy. At present, this concept is used for the sake of popularity stunt. As the concept of marriage has almost been demolished hence performing a *Swayamber* is only making a joke of pious rituals of marriage. That is why marriages performed through *Swayamber* are never succeeded at present.

Scholars of psychology go through an aberration in their opinions regarding the disposition or state of mind of the would-be brides and bridegrooms. As per the opinion of such psychologists, a bride is very conscious at the time of her marriage because of mental pressure while groom is like a careless winner for whom every situation seems to be easygoing. In fact a groom does not want his anxiety to be revealed hence he engages himself in essential works and amusements while the bride hides her unlimited carelessness and acts as she is very frightened. If a lady does not apply extensive make up on her face at the time of her wedding then she will not be able to hide her actual expressions for long time. The jewelries, make ups and heavy wearing makes her realize every moment of her marriage that she should keep such false expressions on her face as well as in temperament. Again such make up helps the bride in hiding her expressions though experienced ladies immediately guess about her actual disposition and nature just by looking at the flickering movements of her eye-balls. When the very close friends of the bride ask her about the feelings of just before marriage, she answers that she is very normal because whatever her lovers did with her in past, same will be done by the would-be husband in future hence nothing new is going to happen. This discloses the careless behavior of brides at the moment of their wedding. Though this is not true for every bride still it is found to be true in the context of most of the brides. As per the figures drawn from the surveys, more than eighty percent of the ladies who marry at the age of twenty-four to twenty-six, have already experienced the sexual pleasure before marriage while ninety-three percent of the ladies who marry after reaching the age group of twenty-eight, have already molested their virginity through illicit sexual relations. Thirty-two percent of the ladies who marry before the age of twenty-four years have performed sexual plays before marriage.

The virgin knot or hymen in women body breaks itself when they perform late marriage or play outdoor games, in which physical effort is done, including running, cycling or swimming etc. Normally doctors or scientists impose such illusive opinions in context of the breaking of virgin knot. In a survey conducted among married ladies, who did not face bleeding at first night while making copulation with their husbands, it is found that in less than one percent matters, virgin knots have broken because of reasons aforementioned. In two to three percent matters, the virgin layer broke because of the attempt done by ladies to curiously play with their vagina or masturbating with the help of finger or brinjal or an object of the shape of penis while in remaining more than ninety-six percent instances, it has broken because of illicit sexual relations kept by them before marriage. A girl of seventeen, studying in higher secondary in a convent patterned school of city *Lucknow*, said, "If we consider that all the young Indian ladies are virgin till their marriage then who are the girls visiting with their lovers in romantic roaming places, in defamed hotels and in dark and isolated places popular among youths? Who are those unmarried ladies going through abortions in the clinics of lady doctors or taking contraceptives regularly? The average count of such abortions performed by unmarried ladies is more than thousands in a day in the small city *Lucknow* only. Who are the female hosts meeting with the male visitors to the working women hostels or girls' hostels behind the shade of addressing them as cousin brothers? Who is paying the bills of cellular phones and other luxurious items used by girls when such amount is in thousand rupees? Definitely parents are not giving this much amount to their teenage daughters." She again said that almost girls are involved in sexual affairs and the remaining girls who are not involved in such relations possess multiple times more knowledge of sexual plays than the same aged guys. Again a survey is performed about the decency of the terminology that girls and boys use while having conversations within the friend circle of same gender. Up to the age group of twenty one years, more than ninety percent girls speak indecently while sharing thoughts with their very close friends and the level of such indecency is multiple times higher than the conversations that take place among boys. Around thirty-nine percent guys of this age group speak very vulgarly and twenty-one percent of them use slight indecent language while conversing among close friends.

There was a time when the chastity or virginity of a lady was identified by the virgin knot or hymen situated in the vaginal path. At the moment of first sexual intercourse, bleeding occurred because of the breaking of virgin knot through penis was considered to be the only indication of the virginity of that lady maintained till marriage. Even at present, somewhere the ancient tradition regarding this is followed and a white bed-sheet is spread upon the bed so that the marks of blood can be seen easily on the next morning of first night. When ladies of the house see that spot, they become delighted as this is an indication that the bride was virgin. In past, if such spots were not seen on the bed-sheet then brides were asked the reason for this and hence the ladies were rarely found keeping illicit sexual relations before marriage because of the fear of the breaking of hymen. The continuous progress done by medical science finished such fear in women as it is said by the scientists that such breaking of hymen may occur because of several other reasons mentioned earlier. Such unauthentic declaration done by the science was rumored on very large scale by sexually corrupt ladies and they frequently started keeping illicit sexual relations before marriage because now they had got a marvelous way, attested by medical science, to hide their sexual debauchment from would-be husbands. All ladies are very familiar with the fact that if they themselves do not speak about the illicit sexual relations they made in past then their husbands will never come to know because by stating the actual indication of a lady's chastity to be her virgin knot as an improper and unauthentic way of judging virginity, medical science and ladies had already betrayed men. Such illusive announcement made by medical science has widely opened the door of prostitution and illicit sexual relations for ladies. In India, it is a certified truth at present environment that less than one percent of the unmarried ladies lose their virginity because of the reasons given by medical science while around more than ninety-six percent ladies lose their virginity because of having illicit sexual relations. A familiar lady, regularly keeping illicit sexual relations before her marriage, was asked by her husband after marriage about the looseness of the vaginal track then she said that in childhood, while playing game, she slipped and a broken piece of glass went inside her vaginal route which was removed through surgery and from then she was having such looseness in her vaginal track. The innocent husband, unaware about the before marriage sexual affairs of his wife, accepted the statement said by her as truth.

Married ladies, when caught red handed by their husbands performing sexual plays with other men, behave in three ways. Most of such ladies immediately blame the concerned men for forceful sexual mating and pretend themselves to be innocent. Whenever during such illicit sexual course, they suddenly find husband or other relatives arrived, they start shouting and weeping so as to pretend that they are being sexually raped and are helpless. It is also found that when first time a husband finds his wife performing adultery, he becomes shocked and furious and hence becomes violent for his wife and for that other-man. In most of such instances, the other man escapes immediately leaving the lady alone.

Husband wants divorce from his wife but he is never able to prove that his wife is an adulteress. Now the wife shrewdly puts false blame on her husband for asking dowry or physical harassment. In such instances, ladies are also found putting false blames of sexual impotency on their husbands. Sometimes they falsely blame their husbands for having illicit sexual relations with other ladies and sometimes for compelling wives to do prostitution. This is the extreme of the disgusting nature of women. In very rare of such instances, a lady accepts her fault but still she persists on saying that it was her first mistake. She now pretends being seduced by that man and starts weeping to emotionally blackmail her husband. She keeps on saying that she was unaware of the malicious intentions of that man. Now the stupid husband thinks that his wife was right and she was seduced by a man. Whenever in future she finds her husband to be normal, she starts performing adultery again but now she takes utmost precautions. Fifty such instances were sorted out through intensive surveys which revealed horrible facts. In two of such instances, shocked husbands did not say anything to their wives and committed suicide. In four such instances, husbands killed their wives and then committed suicide. In five matters, husbands killed their wives and surrendered in the police station. In two matters, husbands killed the lover of their wives and wives helped them in doing so just to pretend to be faithful to them. In seven matters, husbands filed for divorce but in such five matters, they were falsely blamed for asking dowry and physically harassing their wives to compel them to perform harlotry while in rest of two cases, they were blamed for keeping illicit sexual relations with other ladies. In five instances, wives escaped with their respective lovers and in such two matters husbands were blamed by the parents of their wives for asking dowry and killing the wives and they were send to prison while after few years those wives were caught in other cities living happily with their sex-partners with whom they escaped. In rest of the three matters out of above mentioned five, the wives, who were caught red handed performing illicit sexual relations with other men, blamed their husbands for sexual impotency and filed for divorce. Astonishingly, all of such men who were divorced by their wives on the false ground of impotency, remarried later and all of them are having their own children at present. In three matters, husbands scolded their wives and send them to the house of their parents. In seven matters, husbands politely forgave their wives by ignoring their faults. In rest of fifteen matters, wives immediately or in future killed their husbands with the help of their lovers.

The gentlemen residing in India or abroad think that the country is still running on the principles of Lord *Ram* and the ladies residing here are the another form of *Sati Savitri*. People still keep the old assumption in context of the disposition of Indian women but in fact more than three-by-fourth of the ladies have broken all the limits of harlotry and ruined the Indian culture. Again the balance is maintained between the virtuous and awful ladies just because of the ladies of high moral, who are in fact less than twenty percent of the total populace of ladies. It is believed that if ladies are not controlled strictly by the society, judiciary or at the family level then after few decades, India will reach at the extreme of illicit sexual relations and all ladies will perform harlotry or adultery thereby giving birth to crossbreeds.

After the marriage, the bride enters in the house of her husband as a newcomer. In love marriages also, the brides have come like lovers in front of their husbands hence their behavior and performances expressed as fiancées or lovers are quite different than their actual disposition. In all conditions, brides are considered to be beginner in the new family environments. In both of the situations, though almost of them are familiar with the environment of the premises of the husbands but husbands and their family members are quite unfamiliar with them. The bride is taken to the room decorated for the celebration of her first night. There she is made sit among the female relatives of her husband. She is introduced with the female guests and other family members where she is questioned by the ladies regarding herself or her family and she is expected answering by saying yes or no or just giving movements to her forehead. Hence she answers in very brief. An extreme loquacious bride even behaves like this though the brides, familiar to the husbands and their family members from the period of before betrothal are seen little bit joking and conversing at this moment. The bride sitting in the room does the assessment of the decoration by the time her husband enters the room. In the low class and the middleclass families, such decorations or the preparations for the first night of the bride and groom are done very normally because of the busy schedule and the crowd of the guests. The bride remains sitting bowing her head when all the relatives leave the room and husband enters. Somewhere the act of making bride and groom close is performed by the sisters or sisters-in-law of the groom. They spread white colored bed-sheet decorated by flowers and keep some rich edible items including milk for the bride and groom.

It is mostly said that brides are frightened at the first night after their marriage. In fact the virgin girls of less than nineteen years are little bit frightened at their first night. Girls of this age group performing love marriage are less than seven percent. The virgin girls above this age group are little bit uncomfortable or uneasy but not frightened at their first night. Non-virgin girls are not newcomer in sexual mating because of their early experiences and hence are familiar with the psychology as well as the attitude of men while sexual mating. Such ladies neither are frightened not uncomfortable but always pretend to be fearful. Some of such girls are worried with the thought that their husbands might get doubtful regarding their pre-marriage sexual relations though again medical science stands in favor of them so that they may hide their act of harlotry by giving numerous other reasons for broken virgin knot or looseness of the vaginal route.

Lots of men perform kissing, hugging and chatting with their brides at the first night and do not prefer sexual intercourse because they believe that husband and wife should perform intercourse only when both of them become well familiar with each other. They keep the opinion that men should sexually intercourse with their wives only when the friendly environment or relationship is built in between them so that wives unaware about sexual relations might not get embarrassed. Such thoughts of men seem to be ridiculous in present environment because more than ninety-eight percent unmarried ladies know every thing about sexual course. It is found in surveys that out of these ninety-eight percent ladies, more than sixty-eight percent have done complete sexual course multiple times while seventy percent have done oral sex before marriage. More than ninety-four percent brides are practically familiar with hugging, kissing and breast massaging done by guys with them before marriage. Less than six percent brides keep only the verbal knowledge of sexual plays provided to them by indecent literatures or friends. Such brides, who have already been involved in illicit sexual relations before marriage, find ridiculous when their husbands talk to them about their relatives, hobbies, education or jokes etc on first night and they consider such husbands to be dumb. They pretend being very interested in hearing the talks of husbands and present themselves as a virgin thereby scared of the sexual touches done by husbands even after being expertise in the art of making sexual relations. Less than six percent virgin just married brides who are practically ignorant about the sexual relations, should be treated delicately by husbands because they are worthy of respect. Such ladies get embarrassed while making sexual relations hence men should avoid making complete sexual course with them in the first night. Less than eleven percent men have performed complete sexual course before marriage while twenty-six percent keep the experience of kissing and hugging. More than seventy-six percent of the grooms are unaware about the exact location of vaginal route and brides keep the edge of their penis at the opening of vagina on their request. Some interesting figures regarding the situation of men at the time of their first night can be understood by the fact that the seminal fluid of the five percent of the grooms fall just by the glance of the naked breasts of brides. Thirteen percent of men face the discharge of seminal fluid while disrobing their wives. Twenty-one percent men lose their seminal fluid when they see their wives entirely naked. Nine percent of the men experience the discharge of the seminal fluid while kissing or pressing the breasts of wives. Nineteen percent of men get discharged when they touch the vagina by their penis or just try to enter the penis. Twenty-two percent men get discharged when they just make their penis in-out three to four times. Remaining Eleven percent men in actual succeed to perform sexual course properly in the first night of their marriage. The basic reason behind such figures is that at present scenario, most of the unmarried men are novices in sexual course while almost of the unmarried ladies are expertise in such sexual plays. It is found that very decent men also keep desire of lustful behavior to be shown by their wives to them. They prefer their wives showing indecent lustful gestures and producing lustful hissing sounds while performing sexual mating.

As women have nothing to do with masculinity hence they are not anxious because of the fear of being unsuccessful during sexual courses while such fear always troubles newcomer guys performing sexual course first time in their life with their wives. Women just have to present their *Yoni* or vagina either willingly or reluctantly to perform sexual course with their husbands while men positively have to invoke sexual excitement in them because they can not perform sex being reluctant. For sexual courses, penis should be fully excited and should take proper shape but women are free from such compulsions. Women can start performing sexual union even when they are not sexually excited but this is not possible for men. The question for success or failure in context of sexual mating rises with men and women are free from such responsibility because they are always winner in sexual plays. There is a direct or indirect coordination in-between the excitement of penis and the feelings or mental disposition of men hence men can not perform normal sex if they are depressed, anxious or mentally puzzled while again women has nothing to do with this. A man puzzled with the quarrelsome nature and misbehavior of his wife keeps himself busy in the mode of earnings and always afraid from the ladies. Such depression negatively effects the sexual capabilities or the excitement of penis hence he does not perform illicit sexual relations with other ladies while wife to such a man is found to be uneasy till she is with her husband and the moment he goes to office, she becomes perfectly normal, ready to commit adultery. In contrary to all of this, depression, anxiety or mental puzzle invokes sexual craving in women and provoke them to perform sexual courses and this is the reason that wise aged lustful men seek such other's housewives to fulfill their sexual craving. Such men are familiar with the temperament of ladies and hence they know that women are never satisfied by their husbands hence live in depression caused by themselves. As such depression is helpful in stimulating sexual desires in women hence almost all married ladies can be approached for adultery. It is usually asked to groom by his friends after his first night whether every thing happened proper or not. The same question is asked to brides by their mothers-in-law or friends. Though such question is separately asked to both husband and wife but the intention is simply to know whether husband could perform sexual course. All of such questions are related to sexual capabilities of men. The question of sexual impotency also comes with the husbands while women are free from such blames. Again such probability of being successful or failure in sexual course worries to men only.

In context of making sexual relations before marriage, the ratio of girls is very high in comparison to the boys. Less percentage of the men have performed sexual course before marriage while almost of ladies have done it before marriage. The basic cause behind such big difference in the ratio of girls and boys regarding keeping illicit sexual relations is that almost teenage young girls prefer experienced aged men for sex hence unmarried young ladies often allure married men for illicit sexual relations. Again the reason behind the selection criteria of young ladies is that at present, ladies do not want to impose the probable liabilities of sexual relations on themselves hence they keep sexual relations with married men because they know that such men will never emotionally compel them for marriage. Making sexual relations is like a game for ladies but the responsibility of the family or performing marriage is like a burden to them hence almost ladies want to sexually enjoy in their bachelor life and then marry with rich men to make their future safe and to get a legal as well as social clean-chit to commit adultery. If a husband to such a lady asks about her love affairs then she strictly denies to it and innocently says that she has never even touched any man in her unmarried life because she was taught by her parents that such act is the biggest sin. A girl who has gone through multiple abortions also says the same to her husband. In contrary to this, men seldom hide their love affaires of married life with their wives though few of them hide their pre-marriage illicit sexual relations. It is found that men add a lot to embroider such affairs and tell extravagantly to their wives. If a lady confesses her previous love affairs in front of her husband then he always gets embarrassed because it is a fact that no lady can remain sexually untouched while performing love affairs. A husband, who unfortunately got familiar with the past love affair of his wife, could never behave normal and told that he spend half of his life in studying and preparing for higher competitions. He said that after a big struggle in his career, he achieved a good job and then parents arranged marriage for him. He did not even talk to strange ladies and he got the wife who was having illicit sexual relations before marriage. He said that he was in deep distress because when he asked about such relations, his wife denied and blamed him for unnecessary having doubt.

Such situations are very normal and can be easily seen in the families. Though it is considered that husband and wife should forget about each other's past and live happily following the codes of conducts and it seems to be an appropriate way of living married life but it does not provide solutions to two probable problems. Firstly, a lady involved in sexual relations in her unmarried life never feels any kind of guilty conscious after marriage and considers her husband to be foolish and unnecessarily quarrels with him to humiliate and harass him. The second problem that arises is that such a wife easily hides her sexually adulterated past from her husband and hence she achieves a self confidence to perform negative attitude which ultimately induces her to perform adultery in future and makes her daring to perform illicit sexual relations.

The exceptions to this can be seen in the examples of the concept of changing of internal disposition and the theory of changing the stage of the properties. In such examples, sufficiently big gentry of ladies who are of extreme abandoned disposition with quarrelsome nature and are often involved in sexual relations, become generous, trustworthy and devoted wives after the marriage. Such ladies are so generous and husband devotee that no one can even imagine about their adulterated past. This is true that if the husbands to such ladies are simple, innocent and decent then they decorate the life of husbands by their changed praiseworthy attitudes.

Again if the husbands of such ladies are simple and decent then they do not hesitate to sacrifice even their lives for the welfare of their husbands.

The virginity of girls is considered to be their invaluable wealth. The virginity means the chastity and trustworthiness in case of married ladies while for unmarried ladies, it literally means by the unbroken virgin knot or hymen. It is considered that at the time of marriage, girls are given to their husbands with their invaluable wealth of virginity. If virginity is the precious wealth of girls then also almost of them have already sold or gifted it before marriage for the sake of sexual pleasure or money. It is said by some scholars that the current level of the dowry system is just to compensate the demolished virginity of ladies. It was considered to be a big crime when such a licentious and sexually adulterated girls were deceitfully married with decent men. Now the ancient customs and culture in context of women are lost. Unfortunately men can never prove the involvement of their wives in making illicit sexual relations during their unmarried life and even after marriage hence they accept such sexually corrupt ladies as their brides either by-mistake or with full consciousness. Again initially the concept of judging virginity was entirely based on breaking of virgin-layer at the first night and was a certified truth but as the medical science revealed false reasoning behind the breaking of hymen thereby making this eternal truth to be skeptical, unmarried ladies started involving in sexual relations on large scale. Now women are having false reasoning to justify their sexually corrupt performances and unfortunately such logics are certified by the medical science. Though somewhere this concept of blood discharge at the time of first mating is still followed and it is always proved to be true but as the judiciary, laws or the society demands the proof and hence the false logics certified by the science are supposed to be true and therefore men are helpless to take any action against their wives. As mentioned above, this concept of the discharge of blood at the time of first mating is found to be true in around ninety-seven percent matters but benefit of doubt of the three percent is given to all sexually corrupt ladies. As the benefit of such legal doubt is taken by more than three-by-fourth of the women population hence the invaluable vagina or chastity of women has become cheap.

The men and women who follow the second theory of judging the virginity of unmarried girls insert their finger in the vaginal route of ladies and guess about the virginity by feeling the prominence of flashy muscular ring shapes. Loose muscular rings situated at the vaginal route are the indication of ladies being sexually corrupt. Though it is found that the girls, who work for hours in agricultural fields or in some other jobs where such sitting posture is needed, experience decrement in the thinness of their vaginal route. Ladies with broad vaginal mouth are also the exceptional cases of this theory. As per the opinion of the followers of this stream, if a finger is inserted in the vagina of a virgin lady then clear tightness of vaginal route can be seen when finger crosses three different zones.

The persons, who follow the third concept of judging virginity, say that one can get about sexual purity of his wife while inserting penis in her vagina at the first night. They say that such judgment can be done by experiencing the tightness or the looseness of the vaginal route. A virgin man experiences failure number of times while performing sexual course with his virgin wife unless he puts some oily substance on his penis. If anyone of them have already performed sexual course then they do not feel trouble in performing complete course. In fact all of the three theories are almost true but can not be legally accepted because of the lack of scientific evidences and acceptance of the science.

The concept of honeymoon is not limited to higher class families and nowadays it can be seen in almost middleclass families. The grooms go to visit some popular tourist place or hilly area with their brides for the sake of some change and to plan something new in their just started married life. Though the duration of such visits vary from few days to few weeks but this is sufficient for both of just married husband and wife to know each other. The concept behind honeymoon is to keep the newly married couple free from family obligations, provide them sufficient duration to know each other's disposition and let them freely perform sexual union. During the period of honeymoon, husband and wife live together paying complete attention to each other because of the absence of the relatives. All ladies are in favor of honeymoon because they have to enjoy this period living alone with their husbands performing sexual relations and this is the very initial period when they can control over all the probable situations of their future married life by assessing the temperament of husbands so as to mould them as per their typical feminine behavior. For a lady, married to a man living in a joint family, the period of honeymoon is like a qualifying exam in which she has to influence and divert her husband by revealing her body and sexual skills so that husband might follow only the guidance given by her for the rest of his life. She pretends to be innocent, unadulterated and unaware and makes her husband realize that he is having complete right on her because she is just made for him. To keep the thoughts of possessiveness for husband and to dominate over him, she deeply scrutinizes the shortcomings of him. If the husband is of emotional nature then in the views of wife he is emotional fool whom she keeps in control either by emotional blackmailing or by mental harassment. She wisely utilizes the whole period of honeymoon and gets familiar with the fact that her nude body is sufficient to destroy the consciousness and conscience of husband. When she finds her husband to be caring and conscious regarding her, she becomes happy because this is an indication of her victory. She wisely creates some situations to make her husband conscious. For this, she innocently changes the cloths in bathroom without closing the windows or while roaming with husband, pretends to adjust her upper clothing etc. When she finds her husband caring for her by closing the window so that no one may see her naked or staring at other men when she adjusts her cloths in public or making her sit either with him or with ladies while traveling in busses or auto rickshaws, she gets overwhelmed as being successful in invoking possessiveness in her husband. She knows that now her husband will be with her when she will harass or humiliate in-laws.

As per the ostentatious disposition of a lady, honeymoon is a splendid initiation of married life and love making while as per her actual disposition, this is a chance in which she has to perform any act so as to prove other relatives of husbands to be secondary in comparison to her and to build a thought in the conscious or subconscious mind of husband that parents, real brothers, sisters and other relatives have only exploited him financially or morally in past and she will stand with him as his only well-wisher to fight against such relatives. As per the opinions of the husbands, a pre-decided and successful honeymoon provides a way to influence the newly married brides and impress them. The old aged people or the young, who believe in following the customs, consider the concept of honeymoon as an attempt to isolate married men from their joint families. Every mother is against of her son going on honeymoon with his newly wedded wife because she knows that during that period, her son will be out of the range of her jurisdiction hence will easily be influenced by the shrewd women psychology of his wife though she seldom discloses her actual opinion regarding honeymoon. In this situation, mothers consider their daughters-in-law to be other ladies in context of their sons while the fathers are free from the conflicts of thoughts regarding achieving dominancy. A couple, who is a part of joint family, when returns back to home after honeymoon, seems to be separate identity from the joint family. Again as per the views of aged ladies, the concept of honeymoon is a silent but practical consent to avoid other family members and considering them to be disturbing elements. During the period of honeymoon, a bride has been familiar with the nature and behavior of all of the family members including her husband. Though the description of the nature of the family members is done by husband as per his own views but she hears such opinions of her husband carefully and keeps the right to take final decision in context of the temperaments of the family members in her hand. She pays least attention when husband tells her about the nature of the gents of the family while she becomes conscious when he starts telling about the female members of the family. She has to represent and prove the good qualities of her female in-laws, as her mother-in-law and sisters-in-law etc, told to her by the husband, as the awful qualities of them. Actually the facts about the nature of the family members and the honor of the family with whom a bride should get familiar gradually living with husband and in-laws peacefully for years, she becomes familiar with all of that before marriage because of the stupidity of her husband. Hence a prejudice can be seen in her behavior with the in-laws. After coming back from honeymoon, the glory of the eyes of the bride silently reproaches to her mother-in-law by saying, "I have done what I desired to do."

As per the men's psychology, almost of them have informed about their past to their wives. Men consider it as their smartness and tell their wives extravagantly about all incidents happened in their life by keeping themselves as a hero. In contrary to men's behavior, ladies mostly hear the stories told by husbands silently. Almost men think that their brides are impressed by them therefore listening to them very carefully but in fact, wives just patiently tolerate such rubbish stories told by their husbands and seldom react. Sometimes this situation remains for days or for even weeks and ultimately the moment wives have grasped the gist of the talks done by husbands, they start reacting. In this process of assessing the temperament of husbands, the awful and virtuous qualities of women assist them and this tendency of women has nothing to do with their education, financial status and family backgrounds. After marriage, in context of sexual behavior and basic feminine tendencies, a rustic uneducated wife with rural background behaves the same as a highly educated, modern wife belonging to a sophisticated family. The actions or reactions shown by ladies regarding sexual plays and their general behavior are same. Hence it can be said that in context of husband or all the men society, ladies possess same sexual craving and attitude though it does not seem to be true by their visible appearances. The real relatives, society, education, honor of the family and financial level never prove to be successful hurdles at the moment of arousing sexual craving, passion for love making and performing sexual relations, because ladies never care for such factors. Again in the attempts done to sexually seduce men, causing distress to others, suppressing or harassing or humiliating others, showing women's peculiar character, flirting and performing sexual courses, all women behave in similar way. Some husbands are very wise hence they never disclose their secrets and actual behavior to their wives and such wives sometime take months to years to comprehend their husbands' temperaments but again the moment they get familiar with the dispositions of their husbands, they get mentally prepared like a warrior to oppose them by quarrelling with them and humiliating them. All of such ladies make the house as a battlefield. Almost men avoid and forgive their wives on the mistakes and indecent attitude performed by them considering it to be their childish nature but in actual it is an indication of arousal of the rebellion tendency in the wives which should be viciously suppressed by the husbands. Such rebellion tendency aroused in the wives make them presumptuous in performing awful deeds and gradually they go through a perverted enjoyment in expressing their awful tendencies. At this stage, they do not have to live wearing the mask of innocence and virtuousness because now they are free to behave like this and feel pleasant in performing negative activities and in showing negative attitude. They always present themselves against of their virtuous husbands and innocent in-laws because they have the negative reasoning to justify own ill-deeds as virtuous deeds. They never listen the proper advices given by family members and retort aggressively in an indecent way even to their well-wishers. In this situation, the probabilities of improvements in ladies are nil. The extreme of aggressiveness and the tendency to take revenge can be often seen in the instances where ladies kill their children and commit suicide. Such incidents are never seen where men kill their children and then commit suicide. Often men, extremely humiliated by their sexually corrupt wives, commit suicide but they never slay their children. When such instances, where ladies killed their children and did attempt of suicide but fortunately saved by the doctors, are scrutinized then almost ladies confessed that they killed the children and then did the attempt of suicide so that their husbands may not find any objective to live peacefully with children. No lady said that she killed the children with the intentions that husband's new wife in future may not harass the step children.

If a wife behaves indecently with her husband and in-laws then her husband should not get frightened from her instead he should stop her by keeping generous restrictions on her. It is often seen that married men are very conscious regarding the opinion of the family members and society hence they forgive or avoid the misdeeds of their wives while almost married ladies are morally nude in this context and they never care of the family or society. Men should physically punish their wives if they do not show any improvement in their activities. Wise husbands never hit at the face or head of their wives instead they prefer hitting them at their breasts and buttocks because ladies feel same pain on these body parts as they feel when they are slapped on face. If ladies are punished by their husbands by hitting on their faces then they become shameless and obstinate to redo the same misdeeds. Wives should be physically punished by husbands in a close room in the absence of other family members because again if they are punished in front of any other family members then they become unabashed. It is often seen that morally corrupt ladies, when find themselves to be incapable to harass their husbands, start harassing and misbehaving in-laws. In the absence of in-laws or if they are not capable to harass in-laws, they start physically harassing their children. The overall aim of them is to humiliate their husbands and for this they are always ready to perform anything which irritates their husbands.

The husbands familiar with women psychology never disclose their opinion regarding their blood relatives to their wives and never tell their past to them. They let their wives know themselves about the nature of the family members and strictly stop them scolding the family members. Such men are almost succeeded in their family life as they never converse unnecessarily with their wives. They perform love making and sexual talk with the wives within the premises of the bedroom. If a wife attempts to humiliate or harass such a husband on the basis of the requests made by him for making love or the cheap sexual behavior he showed with her in the closed room then he strictly suppresses her behavior. It is often found that when wives do not get any solid point to act against husbands then they try to impose the cheap requests for love making done by husbands on their whole character. The husbands, who are successful in their personal lives, make clear to their wives that the requests for love making done by them are not a part of their personalities and this is their right which should be achieved by them forcefully but they are generous hence request for such needs. Men never discuss about their marital sexual lives with even very close friends but ladies do it in their very close circle. Ladies are also found sharing such moments of their marital sexual lives with their close female relatives. They describe the sexual relations with their husbands in such a vulgar and indecent way that if some one stranger hears it then he gets ashamed. Again the very personal discussions done among very close ladies are around eighty percent more indecent in comparison to the discussions that take place among very close male friends. Ladies in actual come close to each other only when they start conversing on indecent sexual topics with each other. Hence their ideological proximity or closeness with even other ladies takes place only when they start sharing sexual topics. Hence everything or every aspect of ladies is directly or indirectly attached to their sexual attitude and their peculiar interpretation of sex.

It is assumed that all married ladies should live in joint families at least for few years so that they may comprehend the customs and culture of their husbands' families. This duration of living in joint families is helpful for them to maintain closeness with the family members. Ladies are never found willing to live with their husbands in joint families and if they do so, there are solid reasons behind that. Ladies live in the joint families with their husbands when husbands strictly deny to leave their parents and wives are incapable to compel them because they pretend themselves to be least attracted by the sexual charm of the wives or the in-laws are wealthy as well as having valuable assets and wives seek financial benefit in living with them or husbands are financially not sufficient capable to live separately with their wives leaving parents alone. In rare families, it is also seen that wives prefer to live with in-laws because they are physically harassed by the alcoholic husbands and hence they feel safe with the in-laws. Except of above mentioned factors, there are no other reasons behind the ladies living in joint families. The over aged and sick parents living with their married sons seldom get generous treatment and respect from their daughters-in-law.

Most of the ladies complain physical problems or sickness like headache, backbone pain or pain in lower parts of the body after their marriage. Some pregnant ladies suffer from excessive vomiting. If they were already having pre-menstruation pain before marriage then they feel the same after marriage. A renowned lady doctor said that if such physical problems were not there during unmarried life then almost of such problems as headache or body pain about which married ladies complain are in fact psychological. Such pains never exist in women body and these are only false appearances of their mental disorder hence such ladies should be taken to psychologists instead of gynecologists. Almost of such ladies never feel pains and get recovered without taking any medical treatment when they go to their parents' residences. This is perfectly psychological and it has nothing to do with physical pain. It is found in extensive surveys that more than ninety-eight percent of ladies tell lies about such pains of sickness just to draw the attention of their husbands and to show them helpless to perform family responsibilities or house jobs. A popular psychologist told that at present, all ladies consider making sexual relation with husbands as their only duty for the family and it seems that they are obliging to their husbands by allowing them for sexual course. They feel pains or illness when they are given the normal house jobs by the mothers-in-law. At present, almost parents never teach the house jobs to their daughters hence when they have to perform such responsibilities, they feel uneasy and ailing. All ladies complain back ache and waist ache during washing utensils and sweeping floor. According to gynecologists, vomiting is a normal symptom in pregnant ladies and the pre-menstruation pain only occur when it has been in the unmarried life also. Though some ladies experience extreme pre-menstruation pain in the lower part of the body but this sustains not more than four to five hours.

The affection for the parents frequently invokes in the married ladies while they are in depression because of their own attitude or as a usual course. Married ladies of arrogant temperament are usually found to be stubborn to go to their parent's residences just to humiliate and mentally harass husbands and in-laws. Though parents of such corrupt ladies provoke their daughters to quarrel with in-laws by making conflicts and to come back leaving behind husbands and aged in-laws alone but this is also true that such iniquitous parents feel uncomfortable when their daughters live with them for long duration. Such married ladies start creating complication even in their parents' house and make the life of their real brothers' wives like hell. If the parents allow their married daughters to live with them leaving the residence of husbands then they never leave any chance to scold and falsely blame the in-laws of daughters. Now if such married ladies living with their parents have to do house jobs then they do it willingly though they never like to do the same in their husbands' premises. In numerous matters, it is found that wherever the environment of the house of the parents of such ladies is women dominating and the wives of their brother's rule over their men, there such married ladies who live with their parents leaving their husbands alone, have to work a lot. This is the reason that ladies with such parental background seldom live with their parents by leaving their husbands. While if their parents' residences are governed by the petticoat rule of their mother then mothers are involved in humiliating their daughters-in-law and in such conditions, ladies readily leave the house of husbands to live with parents and often found humiliating and harassing their brothers' wives with the help of their mothers. Such morally corrupt married ladies with the assistance of their cruel mothers perform physical as well as mental torture of their brothers' innocent wives to achieve perverted sexual pleasure. It is found that parents of the young unmarried ladies often say that their daughters are expertise in house jobs but unfortunately almost of such ladies are novice in such works and they learn it from their mothers-in-law. The genuine parents, who perform their duty for the daughters in actual sense, never permit their daughters to come back to home after marriage without the consent of their husbands and never interfere in the family matters of their daughters because they know that in almost of such matters, new brides are wrong. Again unfortunately such parents are seldom found.

To avoid some situations, men keep their wives in front. If some unwanted guest comes then often a husband says to his wife to tell lie by saying that he is not available. Few husbands even keep their wives in front to face the family complications. Few husbands end their relations with some friends or relatives on behalf of their wives. Though the husbands get instant remedy by keeping their wives in front to break the relations or to solve some complications or to avoid visitors and relatives by making them tell lies and shockingly wives also get happy in doing so because these are their favorite jobs but in fact such husbands create big problem for themselves for future. Such mistakes done by husbands are like a boon for the wives and when in future wives are caught red handed while telling lies or misbehaving in-laws, say brazenly that they have been taught to act like this by husbands. Somewhere changes can be seen in men after marriage because the opinions of surrounding persons or relatives changes for them. Almost parents believe more on their unmarried children in comparison to their married children. Often parents hide some financial matters or other secret matters with their married sons. Even a married lady keeping good and healthy relations with her brother-in-law starts keeping jealousy and hostility with him when he marries. Somewhere married men starts avoiding the company of their bachelor friends in such an absurd way that it seems their unmarried friends are a kind of danger on the never existing chastity of their wives. Such men are ultimate dumb because they are always busy obeying their morally corrupt wives and wives too comprehend that their husbands are bovine.

A very peculiar behavior is found in married men that whenever someone familiar man asks for financial help to such a married man, he helps him with the instruction that he was helping just without informing his wife hence it should not be disclosed to his wife. A survey is conducted to know the veracity of such happenings. More than ninety percent men say such statements, while helping to their real brothers, close family friends, nephews etc, like "Don't say about this to my wife." This is shocking but true that men say such statements while financially helping to only those who are very close to their families. More than sixty percent men behave like this because they are afraid of their wives and are frightened that if the wives will come to know then they will unnecessary create conflicts. The rest of the near about thirty percent men say this so that the men borrowing money may be compelled to give it back on behalf of the wives. The seventy-eight percent men, who are living separate from their parents, financially help their parents and sixty-seven percent of them provide such financial help to their parents by hiding it from their wives. More than eighty-nine percent ladies put objection to their husbands if they take care of the kids of their younger brothers. More than seventy-eight percent of such ladies falsely blame their husbands for keeping illicit sexual feelings or relations with the wives of their younger or elder brothers so that they may stop helping them financially. It is often found that when a man living in joint family brings candies or some other edible items for the kids of his brothers then his wife scolds him and falsely blames him for keeping illicit sexual relations with the mothers of the kids who are his real sisters-in-law.

A wife carefully assesses the daily routine of her husband. Gradually she gives negative advices regarding the friends of the husband with whom he spends more time. She starts seeking mistakes of such friends or relatives or colleagues of the husband whom she doesn't like. She complains to her husband regarding those male friends of him by falsely blaming them for keeping indecent and lustful behavior to her. If such friends are female then she blames her husband for keeping illicit sexual relations with them. The husband with no discretion or conscience considers his wife to be decent and trustworthy hence gradually breaks his relations with such relatives or friends without investigating about such false blames. In case of female colleagues or friends or relatives like wives of the elder brothers etc, when he is falsely blamed by his wife for having sexual relations, he makes her understand the truth but as usual never gets succeeded in that and hence ends up such pious relations. Usually a wife can be seen saying to her husband that some of his friend or brother looks her with indecent glance. Hence almost ladies destroy the pre-marriage social circle of their husbands and this is the reason that men can be seen taunting to some married friend that he has been changed after marriage. Though it seems that social circle of men begins when they get married but this is not true. In fact all married men are made skeptical by their wives regarding their male circle. For this reason, married men avoid carrying closeness of unmarried friends. Now such blames on the male friends are kept by the wives in the numerous situations. When a friend of husband converses to wife only when it is very essential or avoids talking to her then she feels herself and her beauty to be neglected by him and provokes her husband against him by falsely blaming him. This situation is also seen when friend of husband tries to talk vulgarly or behaves indecently and the virtuous wife dislikes this but such probabilities are found very rare. It is mostly seen when wife desires the friend of her husband to act something indecent to her but he does not react. In future, husband ends up all the relations which his wife dislikes. A wife diminishes the conscience and discretion of her husband in context of herself. Most of the husbands consider the false blames put by their wives to be the ultimate truth.

The over-affection of a married lady for her parents is always harmful for her own family including husband and in-laws. Normally wise husbands send their wives for a sufficient big duration to their parents' premises when they create unnecessary complications in the family and do not keep any kind of verbal communication with them for that period. This method is almost successful in making improvements in the behavior of the wives. This is always found to be true that if a husband reduces his affection and sexual inclination towards his wife and becomes stubborn regarding his morals as well as on the codes of conduct of the family then even a sexually corrupt and immoral wife gets under control. Though it is said that a husband should be polite with his wife and should ignore the misdeeds done by her by-mistake but as all the ladies perform such misbehavior or unpleasant acts being entirely aware of their wrongdoings as well as of the consequences of that hence wise men always keep a close eye and strict restrictions on the behavior and acts of their wives.

There are few desires about which all ladies keep ultimate expectations from their husbands though the husbands, who are having conscience and discretion, never fulfill that. Such desires of ladies affiliated to their husbands are as immediately informing wives for reporting of their arrival from office, taking dinner in the bedroom along with wives only, informing wives about the incidents happened and routine of the whole day, giving whole of the salary to wives, being in touch with the wives through telephone during office hours, informing wives proper reasons if they have to go outside alone or with some other family member, respecting the family members of the wives and dishonoring own parents. If a husband fulfills such desires of his wife then he spends whole of his life with compromises and his position in the family is like a pet dog. If he does not follow such instructions then his wife tries to make his life hell by unnecessarily quarreling. Again a man, blindly following the instructions of his wife, is considered to be born from his wife. A man, following the immoral instructions of the wife patiently and performing as per the sayings of her considering it to be his moral responsibility, in fact treats his wife as his mother. As for a son, mother's behavior can never be immoral or indecent hence it is an obligation to man to follow the instructions of his mother. Men keep sexual relations with their wives and hence if they blindly obey their wives, they give them the respect which should be only given to mothers. Hence such men are considered to be having sexual relations with their mothers. Therefore the mothers of such men are always humiliated and harassed by their sons who are in control of their wives and such mothers face a dreadful end of their lives.

A working lady when goes to the office after marriage, her wearing changes. Before marriage she visits the office in her desired wearing but now as a married lady, she has to follow the codes of wearing of the just married lady. Wise women perform little bit decoration and wear *Sari* as a traditional married lady's wearing. They put vermillion mark at their forehead as an indication of their married status. As most of just married ladies visit their offices after the honeymoon hence they are the center of attraction among the colleagues. The female colleagues welcome them and usually ask the phrases being double entendre like "Was everything all right?" They have to perform house jobs after coming from office and mothers-in-law always keep an eye on them. Such working women have to face double burden of their official duties as well as of house jobs. They are provided leave from the office during their last few months of the pregnancy. The in-laws and the husbands make sure them not performing excessive work during the pregnancy. Doctors advise them not to pull heavy luggage and take rest properly. All such advices depend upon the work style of them in their past unmarried life. As nowadays, the parents of the young daughters never teach them to do house jobs or any kind of physical labor hence after marriage such ladies face problems during their pregnancy though exceptions to this are found in the ladies of lower class families and working ladies. Therefore doctors advise such ladies not to perform any heavy job and take rest because they know that modern ladies are not habitual of performing physical work. The ladies of villages or the one involved in farming and the ladies of low class can be seen working hard till the time of their delivery. The concept of medical science, of taking rest during the pregnancy, has been proved wrong in the context of such laborious ladies. It is found in a survey that the ladies, who perform physical work till their pregnancy time, face no trouble or pain during delivery while the ladies who take rest and avoid any kind of physical work before pregnancy face lots of trouble and pain at the time of delivery.

While living in joint families, married ladies try to behave normally with their sisters-in-law. The younger sisters-in-law give proper respect to them. They do normal joking among each other if the family is governed by gents. As women are very sensitive in grasping negative attitude and awful temperament of each other without applying their own conscience and discretion hence gradually the awful properties of new brides and mothers-in-law or sisters-in-law are adopted by all of the females of the family. It is often seen that a sexually corrupt bride adulterates the chastity of her sisters-in-law though the reverse situations of this are seldom found. Thus on one hand, ladies in joint families live with each other being united and on the other hand quarrel with each other hence men interfering in their matters are considered to be foolish. It is seen that the temperament of ladies is utter flickering hence when they quarrel like enemies and when they become united like good friends, is entirely unpredictable that is why men are advised never getting affected by the conflicts of their wives with other ladies unless the limit is crossed.

The conflict of a married lady with her mother-in-law is a very normal matter. A mother-in-law never gets satisfied with her daughter-in-law doesn't matter how much decent and obedient she is. Similarly a bride always possesses a prejudiced ill-feeling for the mother-in-law doesn't matter if she considers and treats her as her own daughter. A visible-invisible or direct-indirect strained relationship can always be seen among brides and mothers-in-law. Men of the families have big role in controlling over such situations. A man should pretend to be neutral in front of his wife and mother in context of their conflicts while he should assure his wife alone that he is in her favor and the same he should tell his mother. He has to be diplomatic in family conflicts. It is found in surveys that more than three-by-fourth men disrespect and avoid their mothers because they are frightened with the behavior of their wives. Rest of the men either take the favor of their mothers or manage by any means to live with their wives in the joint families or stand against their wives under the guidance of mothers. In between the mother and wife, if wife is right and genuine then less than one percent men harass her by taking the favor of mother.

The beginning of the sexual relations of a husband and wife starts from touching, embracing, kissing, pressing breasts or massaging body parts and reaches to the climax of mating. Normal sexual course is not the final destination of the sexual relationship. A wife, even after being expertise in sexual skills, always behaves like a novice in the initial period of her married life regarding the sexual plays. After marriage, when husband and wife get familiar to each other's sexual disposition because of having regular intercourses, they seek new postures or methods of performing sexual plays and this is the reason that normal sexual course is never the last step of the sexual plays. They perform sort of researches and new inventions are done by them in context of sexual plays. Initially husband performs sexual mating by lying upon his wife and this is the most popular way because of being easiest for the husbands and wives, who are novice in the field of sexual plays. Few husbands, practically unaware about the copulation, put the legs of their wives on their shoulders and try to insert penis into their vagina during first mating. As mating with such posture is only possible by the experienced men or the experienced ladies having loose vaginal route hence newcomer husband and wife are not able to perform mating in this posture. This is the reason that if the husbands are inexperienced in mating then they take many days to perform complete sexual mating and experienced wives seldom help them performing sex because they know that their assistance done may invoke a doubt about their previous sexual performances in the thoughts of husbands. Sometimes the narrowness of the vaginal route of a virgin lady also creates hindrance in performing intercourse.

When husband and the wife have become expertise in sexual plays, they prefer copulation in the posture of animals and in this husband inserts his penis inside her vagina from the back side. Sometimes husband keeps the legs of his wife on his shoulders and then performs mating. Experienced men change their postures during sexual mating without making penis out of the vagina. Men prefer their wives lying upon them and performing the sexual pushups as they do when they lie upon their wives during mating. It is often said by men that their wives don't permit them for oral sex and anal sex. This is not true because it is found in surveys that the ladies involved in pre-marriage sexual relations avoid anal sex and oral sex while ladies who are virgin till their marriage, give consent for such sexual plays. This seems to be very contradictory but is true. If a husband pretend to be novice about anal sex and oral sex and asks for such plays to his wife then often she becomes ready. It is said by few experienced men that if a man asks for such plays in the initial period of married life then wife gives her consent while in later years, she seldom gives permission for that. It is often said that anal sex is hatred, painful and complicate sexual play. Experienced men keep oily substance on their penis as well as at the mouth of anus of their wives before performing anal sex so that it may easily get inserted. Mostly men perform anal sex with their wives when they are menstruating. Oily substance protects from the particles of shit sticking on the penis.

It is found in an extensive survey that more than eighty-two percent ladies prefer making oral sex but they seldom accept this. More than seventy-eight percent ladies love oral sex to be done with them while from remaining around twenty-two percent of the ladies, nineteen percent do not like this but never put objection. More than eighty-five percent ladies desire for rapid and robust sex to be done with them. Sixty-eight percent ladies desire to be beaten by husbands. Such ladies told that they behave in awful and indecent manner with the husbands and in-laws so that they may get physical punishments from the husbands. Forty-nine percent ladies prefer to be beaten during sexual plays. Ninety percent unmarried girls desire their lovers to make harsh sexual intercourse with them. Twenty-nine percent lustful ladies up to the age group of twenty-three desire to be sexually raped. Sixty-one percent lustful ladies lying in the age group of twenty-nine to fifty-one desire to be sexually raped. Ninety-seven percent lustful ladies of the age group lying in between fifty-one to sixty five keep such perversion of being raped.

Doctors advise to take precaution while performing intercourses during last three months of the pregnancy. Men are advised to perform mating with medium pace and not apply weight upon the abdominal area of wives. Hence wives sexually excite their husbands before penetration, who take time in ejaculation of semen. Men also experience early discharge of semen when they are verbally abused by their wives with indecent sexual phrases during sexual plays. Men also prefer anal sex in this duration. Some ladies experience regular itching or shivering at their vaginal route hence they need regular copulations to be done with them during pregnancy. Peculiar habits of chewing some edible or non-edible item can be seen in ladies while their pregnancies. Some of the ladies prefer chewing betel nut, betel leaf and clove while some like chewing inedible items like white clay or chalk, slaked lime and pieces of lime stone etc.

The information about the first pregnancy achieved by a lady is delighting for her husband and other family members. She is expected giving birth to a male child in her first delivery. A pregnant lady belonging to lower middleclass or lower class orthodox family trapped by the snares of illiteracy always undergoes the fear of giving birth to a female child. She will become a true mother in true sense when she gives birth to a male child because giving birth to a female child will make her incomplete mother. The men of the family seldom differentiate among a male child and a female child but the mother herself and her mother-in-law puts restrictions on the birth of a female child. It seems that the ladies are like an eclipse occurring to diminish the glory of the birth of their own daughters. Though it seems in the families that only mother-in-law and other aged female in-laws of a married lady feel distressed when she gives birth to a daughter but this is not true because the mothers themselves get upset while giving birth to daughters. They pray to God so that they may give birth to a male child and the same they desire from their daughters-in-law in future. It is found in surveys that Ninety-nine percent of ladies and twenty-one percent of men desire for a boy as their first child. The figures in context of desire of a male child in women were drawn by the surveys conducted on aged ladies having pregnant daughters-in-law and shocking results were exposed. Seventy-one percent ladies, who said that they desired for a daughter but they could not express such feelings because of the in-laws, lied because they are found expecting the male child from their daughters-in-law. The percentage of men desiring for a male child increases when they have daughters only. It is often seen that when a married lady gives birth to daughters only then in her further pregnancy if she comes to know through ultrasound that the child in her womb is female then she goes for abortion and pretends as she was bounded by the mother-in-law though she herself is willing to abort. If the probability of experiencing physical harm during abortion becomes nil then all the mothers, who always proclaim ostentatiously about motherhood, will prefer abortion instead of giving birth to female child. Normally married ladies justify their act of going through an abortion by saying that they were compelled to know the gender of the child in womb by the mothers-in-law and husbands and the moment they hear that the child is female, they force them for abortion. To know the truth of the statements of the married ladies, a survey was conducted among aged wet-nurses who were in this profession of doing abortions of married ladies since more than twenty-five years. Few of such were affiliated to government hospitals and were involved in performing such abortions secretly at their residences. All of them told that in the very initial period of their profession they did such abortions at their own residences or at the residences of the pregnant ladies. Though at that time, there were no facilities to get the gender of the child in womb but still the ladies having number of daughters preferred to perform abortions so that they may not give birth to female child anymore. Most of such ladies were those who gave birth to number of daughters for the desire of a male child. Even number of ladies used to come to slay their female children. They all say that they were compelled for this by their mothers-in-law. As the science developed, it became easy to know the gender of child in womb through ultrasound. Those nurses being reliable or being family wet-nurses of such ladies did the abortions of their daughters-in-law in future. They said that before performing the abortions they always ask to the pregnant ladies whether they are doing it by their own will or they are compelled. All the pregnant ladies answer that they are forced by in-laws which is entirely false. If this is true then why they compel their daughters-in-law for aborting female-child or for giving birth to male child. They said that in all such instances, more than sixty-seven percent matters of performing such abortions are not in the knowledge of the fathers of the unborn babies. They again said that seldom any lady speaks truth regarding this because whenever she feels that she is going to be blamed she puts the culpability on others. This is the reason that for such social crimes, a bride blames to her mother-in-law and the mother-in-law blames to her.

After giving birth to a child, ladies achieve the most praiseworthy rank of mother from a bride. Women are considered to be at highest level bestowed upon them by God when they achieve the deferential status of mother. They put their head up with arrogance when they give birth to male child. By giving birth to new generations they have provided successors to their husbands' pedigree. As the responsibility of upbringing and nurturing of the infants are upon them hence they find themselves in an entirely new role. Breastfeeding to the infants provide them a peculiar sensation and the feeling of motherhood. They are not helpless in the society because the male child in their arms provides them protection from the lustful glances of sexually corrupt men. Men give them respect and offer them their own seats while traveling. Such respect is also provided to pregnant ladies but this is the honor of a mother not of a lady. Though young and middle-aged ladies seldom give their seats to other aged or pregnant or sick ladies and shockingly when some guy offers his seat to such a young healthy lady then she asks about her probable malicious intentions by blaming on his character.

Birds make their kids learn flying so that they may go and live their own life. If birds have to seek their own interest then perhaps they would have not taught kids the art of flying even when they are fledged, thereby making them sort of handicapped. Similarly wise parents give proper education to their sons and daughters so that they may become capable to live their lives and become independent. Hence it is a social obligation of parents to educate their children but if the same act of providing education is done by a husband to his wife then it becomes painful for him. It is seen that if men educate their wives or invoke awareness in them or make them social then it ultimately causes distress to men. To educate a wife is a right step only when she has to spend her life separate from her husband after being independent. It is found in a survey done on hundred families that the men who provided education to their wives considering them as close friends, always faced antagonism of their wives because in all such matters, wives stood against of their husbands saying, "Why did you provide more education to us when ultimately we have to follow you?" In ninety-eight of such matters, wives said that it was the duty of their parents to teach them not of their husbands and when the husband allowed them to take further education and live freely to show themselves broadminded then why they are putting their objection now when we desire to live unrestrained life. One of such lady revealed the facts by saying that higher education and lack of restraint in context of ladies start from making illicit sexual relations and ends on adultery. The husband, who educates his wife, is foolish because he is unaware of the women psychology. Another lady said that when parents educate their daughters and send them outside for higher education then they become abandoned and started making illicit sexual relations. Girls keep sexual relations with their teachers and when they go to take shelter of some religious priests or spiritual orators, they perform sexual course with them. When husbands provide higher education to them then they consider such husbands to be illiterate and fool. Hence knowledge of women has always been a curse for their family members including their parents and husbands. This is a bare truth that to provide the opportunities for the education is the duty of parents not of husbands and wherever the husbands broke this law by making their wives more educated, there the bifurcation of families occurred because of such knowledgeable ladies.

Middle Age

There are no specific standards to define the exact age group for the middle age because for women, it mostly depends on the age at which they marry. Some girls marry at the age of even twelve to fourteen years while somewhere this figure goes beyond forty. If we consider the start of middle age by the physical symptoms like looseness in the body figure and sluggishness in the physical beauty then it can be said that at the age of thirty-eight, the middle age of women starts. It is often said that starting of downfall of natural physical beauty indicates starting of the middle age. Somewhere the women are said to be of middle age when their children achieve the age of fourteen or fifteen years. Such laxity in the built of body figure and in the natural beauty makes a lady realize that she has stepped in the middle age group. A lady who reaches at this stage suddenly one day realizes while looking at mirror about the degradation of her beauty. Initial symptoms like visibility of wrinkles on the face or appearance of white hair perturbs her. At this situation, she increases the level of cosmetics and almost succeeds in hiding the physical changes of starting of middle age. If some young boy addresses her as aunt, she gets utterly offended but cleverly hides her gestures. If her children or husband makes her realized about such physical symptoms of being aged appearing on her body then she hides her helplessness and changes the subject by smiling. When some youth addresses her as aunt, she gets offended and thinks of sexual union with that youth to make him realize that she is as young as he is. As she is attached with the family and society hence she feels inconvenient and unsafe to express her sexual desires publicly. In contrary to this, she finds her children quite mature at this stage hence she feels sufficiently free from the responsibilities of the children and diverts herself towards satisfying her uncontrollable sexual craving from other men.

A lady at this stage of her age finds her family complete. This is the stage of her life where she becomes stagnant and faces emptiness. Sometimes while arranging a wardrobe, she finds some object or album which reminiscence her about her past then she emerges in the deep valley of thoughts of old memories. Even at the night, she recalls the whole day routine and her past like a movie before sleeping. Ladies need not have to do any effort for this because this is a natural process happening with them. Sometimes they feel that God betrayed them and for this the responsible persons are their husbands. A lady with her husband and children considers them to be two sides or faces of a milestone in which her desires are crushed. At one side she finds her responsibilities for the family and society and on the other side resides her unsatisfied sexual requirements. Such ladies take active participation in kitty parties etc to get rid from normal and monotonous routine of their life. Though newly married ladies are taken to such parties by their mothers-in-law but they can not behave freely because of the presence and strictness of the mothers-in-law. Ladies willingly join kitty parties when their children grow up to the age of seven to eight years. Again during middle age, they almost get free from the responsibilities of their children. The fear of husbands and the opinion of the society, about which ladies care little bit in the initial period of their married life, have been diminished entirely. By the increase of age of children, the sexual craving increases in ladies unless they get physically restricted by the nature. Ladies consume their internal energy in such outdoor programs or get-togethers. In such types of activities, even if a single lady is involved into making illicit sexual relations then she diverts the whole group of ladies towards it. The ladies, who are the permanent guests of such parties, criticize women who are not the active members of such gatherings or are absent. The female members involved in speaking ill about the personal life of other ladies or reproaching them are always found rumoring and making indecent fake stories about them and seldom found discussing about the recipes of some peculiar dish. They also discuss with each other about their sexual lives or extra marital sexual affairs and often seen performing extreme vulgar and indecent discussions. Thus such functions of ladies includes of low-level gambling, menacing or scolding or rumoring about other ladies, small scale demonstrations of cuisine and achieving verbal sexual pleasure, nothing else.

Ladies of middle age apply heavy make up in the functions. The level of such make-ups increases as the age of ladies grow and this is always found in the ladies of middle age because with growing age, deterioration in their natural beauty takes place. To hide the growing age symptoms, they visit beauty parlors. Due to increasing of age, such deterioration in beauty is seen in the ladies more rapidly in comparison to men. Hence between the same aged ladies and gents, the ladies look more aged. Ladies quickly adjust their frequency at the gatherings of the parties. They watch young guys lustfully with a side glance conversing to young girls. Though they feel sexual excitement when they see their daughters or the same aged girls talking to guys but still they seek faults in the natural behavior of young boys and girls expressed for each other. Socially they pretend to be against of smoking, taking alcohol and adultery but all of them are eager to inherit these activities in alone or in their very personal friend circle. The ground of all such very close friend circle of ladies is entirely based on sex, doesn't matter whether such circle includes of their male friends or female friends.

A middle aged lady, who keeps the craving for sexual satisfaction, always finds her husband to be repulsive for her sexual desires. At this stage she finds her husband gradually being unresponsive towards her sexual appearance. She becomes more possessive for her own body rather than her husband's body. Her physical dullness and looseness in breasts as well as in vaginal route prevents invoking sexual feelings in husband. To make sexual plays with such a wife becomes a boring obligation for husband. A lady distressed due to her unsatisfied sexual cravings, is attracted towards young men of the age group of her children. When the children become well matured then such licentious lady finds it difficult to perform adultery in the house even when husband is outside for work but meantime she is free from her liabilities for the children hence visits outside for achieving sexual pleasure with other men. The ladies faithful to their husbands involve themselves in house jobs instead of wandering and gossiping with other ladies when their husbands are outside for the official work. The more a lady involves herself in house jobs or other work thereby making her busy, the more she is protected from her own perverted sexual craving. Ladies, who involve themselves into unnecessary and useless conversations or arguments and do not fulfill their family responsibilities, their sexual feelings become uncontrollable and superimpose over their other qualities.

In middle age, a wife is quite assured about her husband. She knows that her husband can not pressurize her to do anything against her desire and not even can compel her to act as per his opinion. She has been familiar with the fact that which type of attitude shown by her upsets her husband the most. She has been expertise in emotional blackmailing to her husband on behalf of herself or her children. She often utilizes the weaknesses of the behavior of her husband to harass and humiliate him. Such nature is often seen in the ladies who possess excessive sexual longing. Rich men and high-profiled businessmen are unaffected by the peculiar irritating nature of their wives because they are very busy and come to their homes for taking meals and rest only, still the wives and young daughters of them are often involved in making illicit sexual relations because availability of plenty of wealth and utter busy schedules of the men of the family provide them carelessness and abandoned behavior. It can be easily seen in the normal middleclass families, where men are busy in earning money by any means, that the ladies of the family including sisters, daughters and wives are involved in making illicit sexual plays. Almost men showing cruel or inhuman behavior in their profession or in daily routine are either frustrated because of the behavior of their ladies or are afraid of the nudity of the ladies of their family or are crossbreeds. Sufficiently big crowd of ladies, at this stage, involve themselves in sexual relations with the men in relation hence most of such ladies are incest. Most of them can be seen keeping sexual relations with the servants, guards or watchmen, washer men and milk men etc. It is found that the ladies of low class are enjoyed sexually by middleclass and high class men whereas high class ladies satisfy their excessive sexual need by performing adultery with middleclass and low class men. Though it seems that rich ladies are under control in context of performing adultery due to strong financial status and dignity of family while middle or lower class ladies prohibit themselves not performing adultery because of the fear of their husbands but this is all senseless and false because ladies belonging to all of aforementioned three categories openly performs adultery on a very large scale.

A lady reached to the middle age has her complete family. In this situation, she finds herself to be entirely safe because she had spent the prime years of her married life and now she is the mother of young children. As she lives in the family of herself hence she willingly participates in the activities of her children. She advises her growing daughter about menses and comprehends her own gradually decaying beauty when she looks at the growing beauty and youth of the daughter. She experiences the mixed feeling of hatred and jealousy when she finds her daughter menstruating but never reveals her internal feelings. She advises her daughter to wear bra when she finds her breasts growing and being visible from outside. She desires to bathe her growing sons and daughters by herself but again she is unable to perform this because of the family environment. She wants to see her children nude because she gave birth to them. She always keeps an eye on the lower undergarments of her son and daughter and if she washes the cloths of her children herself then she smells the undergarments worn by her son and licks it with the tongue to feel the taste. Though such affection of a mother for her son is peculiar yet not indecent because it can never be even assumed to be affiliated with sexual pleasure still this is the extreme perversion or sexual insanity that can be seen in almost ladies. Almost ladies, who wash the cloths of their husbands, feel peculiar sexual pleasure in washing the undergarments of them and often smell it and lick it before washing. The reason behind this is that a lady possesses the feelings of hatred for such activities until she has performed mating. As by the time she reaches middle age, she has been expertise in sexual plays hence she does not feel any hatred feeling towards any kind of sexually perverted activity.

In middle age, a lady finds negative changes in her physical appearance and degradation in her attractiveness. She realizes sluggishness in her activities and decrease in physical stiffness. Her breasts remain no more in proper shape because of looseness and waist becomes fatty. Ladies always become anxious and depressed when they find the physical symptoms in them like double chin, fatty thighs and decrement in the sensitivity as well as in the narrowness of the vaginal route. A husband who always roamed around her and proposed her for love making in the initial period of married life now even avoids looking at her unattractive body. A lady, who has experienced pleasure of sexual union with her husband frequently and even more than twice in a day, now finds it difficult to achieve such pleasure regularly and gets such opportunity once in days or weeks or months. In this age, the ladies who desire for sexual union but never express it verbally to their husbands usually keep their hand on the penis of the husbands while sleeping and try to sexually excite them by rubbing their penis by thighs. After such efforts, if husbands are not ready then they express their desire verbally. Because of the increment of loose fattiness of the vaginal route and the decrement in the sensitivity of the vagina due to decrease in sensitivity of the clitoris, they prefer violent sex to be done with them. They take unnatural deep breaths and produce hissing sound while performing sex and to make their husband sadistic during sexual play, they often abuse them or provoke them by stating indecent phrases. They are readily agreed for oral sex and desire the same from their husbands. Again as they have been expertise in sexual plays hence they seek different ways to perform sexual courses to calm down their sexual perversion. They lick in between the anus hole and penis of their sex partners by their tongue so as to excite them and put testis of them in the mouth to produce sexual excitement in them by marvelous coordination of tongue and saliva. Again they desire men to perform oral sex with them but often men lick by their tongue up to the clitoris of them and at the vaginal route or anus hole, they feel disgusting and hence seldom lick their. A lady is not able to completely wash out the area surrounding their anus hole because of fleshy buttocks and hence the smell of shit and even small particles are always left behind which can be sensed by men while licking the anus hole of ladies. This is the reason that ladies do not feel hatred while taking penis inside their mouth and sucking the semen and even licking anus hole of men while the same act of licking vagina and anus hole of ladies, done be men, is seldom seen. This is often seen in middle aged ladies and they even say that semen tastes to be little salty gum like substance. They never put objection when anal sex is performed with them and the anus hole of ladies, regularly involved in anal sex, can be seen wide and always open up to the width of thumb. Because of the expansion of the vaginal route, the rapid sexual pushups produce sound. The growing children, when hear the artificial hissings and natural sequential sound of sexual pushups produced by their mothers, they come to know that the parents are performing sexual plays in their bedroom.

Ladies at this age group always desire to perform sexual courses with young guys. It is quite unproblematic for such ladies to allure the young novice guys and seduce them sexually as the young guys never consider or feel the sluggishness of the breasts and broadness of the vaginal route of middle aged women because they are unfamiliar with the pleasure of making sexual plays with virgin girls. Young guys living in hostels or as paying guests, far from their hometown, in order to achieve higher education of engineering or medical, are the center of attraction for such ladies. Such students become the main source of fulfilling the perverted sexual craving of middle aged ladies. Most of the guys, studying in the private colleges of higher education situated at different states of the country, who are from other states and live either in hostels or at rent, are trapped by the licentious and sexually corrupt ladies of local areas and hence ruin their career as well as virginity. Almost of such students take six to eight years to complete their three to four year courses because of getting strayed from the path in the proximity of such sexually corrupt middle aged ladies. It is found in an extreme wide survey that almost of such students are trapped by married ladies. It is also seen in many instances that a middle aged lady and her daughter satisfy their sexual need by keeping illicit sexual relations with the same guy. For making illicit relations, such ladies remove all the hindrances of the route and when their children and husbands leave the house, they invite such students. They often financially help students by giving them money for their fees or other expenses. Though such guys studying in private donation colleges belong from sufficiently rich family backgrounds but still they are trapped by these adulteresses. Such instances can easily be seen in the private Engineering colleges of South India. Most of such ladies invite the students to teach their daughters or sons and appoint them as tutor so that they may come to their home and husbands may not put objection on their presence. Ladies pretend being worried about their children's education and make sexual relations with such students whom they appoint as personal tutors. Almost of such students achieve the first knowledge of sexual course or lose their virginity through such ladies. When such students were surveyed then they disclosed the truth on behalf of not exposing their names that such ladies, while giving the first lesson of sexual course to them, remove their cloths to perform oral sex and even insert their tongue inside their anus hole. Few of such instances where the husbands caught their wives red handed, ladies staying in the age group of thirty-five to forty-five, blamed on the underage guys by pretending themselves being sexually harassed. Almost of the parents, who send their sons to the higher engineering colleges by spending a lot of money, are not aware of the facts that before the professional education is provided to their children from the institutes, the education of performing sexual courses are taught to them by married ladies residing in local areas. Many students are unable to complete their education within the prescribed duration because of their involvement in such sexual plays and again this situation is mostly seen in the colleges of South. Such students pass by the help of their teachers on providing additional amount or by giving bribe to some clerk or some lower level employee of the examination cells who changes the copies by taking money. Ultimately when such students pass out from the institutes, new students come to take position of them to act like callboys satisfying the sexual needs of sexually corrupt middle aged married ladies.

Rich middle aged ladies often take the services of callboys to attain sexual pleasure. It is frequently seen in metro cities where rich ladies stop their cars near young guys and ask their charges. A popular high ranked lady officer posted in *Uttar Pradesh* was regularly involved in illicit sexual relations with young healthy home-guards. For this she did appointment of new home-guards for the security of her residence. One of such home-guard told that all of the young guards including himself have to fulfill the sexual desire of that popular lady. She always did oral sex with the guards and compelled them to do the same with her. She used such indecent conversation during sexual course that no one could even imagine her being a high-class government officer. In metro cities, aged lustful ladies often arrange orgies where a young guy is compelled to dance being entirely nude on the table while the ladies sit around it. They all perform sexual plays with such callboys and even bite at their different organs. In some instances such guys die but the matters are never disclosed. There are some instances where guards or lower male staff appointed at girls' hostels were lost and were never seen again. Such matters are always hidden because of the involvement of some girls of renowned and rich families.

At this stage of life, women working in government offices are improper for the job because of the laziness, unwillingness and sluggishness of their body. This situation can be seen in women at the age of forty-two. They are found weaving sweaters and reproaching others in office hours. Though such indolence in them is also because of sluggishness of the environment of government offices but in fact they adopt idleness in their behavior from starting as they find it to be a suitable way of working in government service without actually working. Presence of such ladies itself make the environment of offices lethargic. They can often be seen unaware about all such facts and busy in their own life style. Male officers and colleagues communicate with them with utmost precaution and only on urgency. Male officers avoid communicating with them and even are frightened with them because they usually perform ill attitude and indecency while conversing. Almost aged ladies take the advantage of this and possess indecent behavior because they know that they can not be compelled by a male officer to perform any job as they are female. They know that men are afraid of the nudity shown by women publicly. If they are posted at the divisions where there are chances to gain black money or bribes then they ask for it more brazenly in comparison to their male colleagues. Every working lady considers her female colleague as her prime opponent.

Working women living far from their offices, reach their through bus, trains or other transport services. Most of them pay for monthly seasonal tickets so that they do not have to purchase tickets everyday.

Such ladies performing regular up-down for their offices are found to be more ill-mannered and shameless. Though it is assumed that the ill experiences faced by them make them shameless and indecent in behavior but they often express such brazenness and indecency as an inseparable part of their temperament. During the journey, if an old man sits near to them then they pretend to be very decent and well mannered. If some young man sits beside them then they squeeze themselves pretending that their chastity might get adulterated. Again in such situations, the woman inside them awakes and they consider the presence of a man near to them as suppression of whole women society hence they expend their thighs and arms brazenly to make a heavy touch with that man and experience pleasure of sexual thoughts. They even do not hesitate touching a boy of the age group of their sons to achieve such kind of sexual pleasure and their entire concentration and thoughts are towards young guys sitting next to them. They fold their arms in such a way that their breasts become visible to others from the sides and may get touched by the elbows of the guys sitting near to them. They pretend to adjust the edge of their *Sari* on the *blouse* which is already at proper place, so as to attract men towards their visible breasts from inside the blouse. In this process, they come to know without raising the eyes that who is looking at the valley in-between their breasts. While sitting with the men of same age group, they keep touch of their body parts with such man showing carelessness and unawareness. If another lady approaches them for sitting space then they seldom give place to her but if they have to give space because of the pressure of other passengers then they keep staring that lady with abhorrence while smile when have an eye contact with her. Such female middle aged daily passengers are expertise in using indecent phrases or abusive terminology while conversing. Such ladies, who wear *Sari*, pass urine in public toilets in standing posture like men. They are found to be most responsible for sexual molestation of young novice guys. Such tendencies of making indecent touching to opposite sex, can frequently be seen in men. Men often pretend feeling drowsy or sleepy so that they may not be blamed while they touch girls indecently.

The middle aged ladies, who are involved in their business or husbands' business, are sufficiently aware and active and hence they keep control of the house as well as financial matters in their own hands. Such one-sided control of wives in financial matters as well as family matters restricts the freedom of husbands. Somewhere it seems to be genuine because of extravagant husbands. Though the reasons behind wives working in offices or business are effortlessness of husbands, incapability of husbands to perform the family responsibilities, poor financial position, wives possessing government job, attractive salary achieved by wives, uncontrollable desires of wives for living luxurious life and incapability of financially strong husbands to forbid their wives for working outside. Businessmen and men working in some traveling jobs especially in the field of medicines as medical representatives can often be seen keeping illicit sexual relations. The children of businessmen also want to involve themselves in business but often avoid joining the family business especially when the family business is not running with a good pace. The children always give preference to the sayings of their working mothers instead of working fathers.

In the families where both of the parents are working and grandparents are absent, the young daughters experience the pleasure of sexual plays with servants or other relatives. Girls with unrestrained behavior prefer to invite their boyfriends to their own houses in the absence of parents to perform sexual plays because they feel their own residences to be safe most places for such illicit activities. The daughters of working women also take sexual education from their distant relatives and cousin brothers. Seldom real brothers elder to them touch them with sexual intentions while they are sleeping or awakening but again this is because of lack of sexual knowledge or lack of sexual discretion in them.

The middle aged men and women involved in business never let the customer bargain regarding the prices. Purchasing done with a young shopkeeper is always beneficial for the customers as there are always multiple ways to bargain while middle aged shopkeepers seldom give discount to customers rather charge more for a particular item. Ladies at this age group are more money minded and often cheat while selling their items. Again wherever both of the husbands and wives are involved in business there wives take the responsibility of taking charge of money matters and expenditures and give limited pocket money to their husbands.

A middle aged lady finds her family complete when her children have become youth. If she has been living in joint family from the beginning of her married life then she still prefers to live in joint family. She has been familiar with the fact that in a joint family, if the rules and disciplines are maintained by an elder male member while other family members follow the codes of the family and seek the welfare of others instead of gratifying own desires then such families never bifurcate and ladies are very rarely diverted from the virtuous track of morality. If the married lady has lived in the joint family for few years of the initial period or her married life and after that she is living separately from the in-laws living with her husbands and kids then she finds an affection in her for her own parents and brothers while hatred for in-laws at this stage of life. She whispers into the conscious mind of her husband against her in-laws and tells him indecent imaginary incidents regarding them. She falsely blames and scolds her in-laws, who have supported her a lot in past during the initial period of her married life and in her pregnancies, to achieve perverted delight. She always keeps visible or invisible sexual feelings for her brothers-in-law, younger to her husband. During the initial period of her married life, she always remains sexually thirsty if her brothers-in-law are morally strong and do not pay attention to her with sexual intentions. In this situations, she always blames and scolds her brothers-in-law when she lives separate in her own family including her husband and kids only while if brothers-in-law are morally loose and perform sexual course with her then she never blames them even when she starts living separate with her family from the joint family.

Normally a man can live with a lady bearing her awful attributes and despotism for longtime only when he is by any means directly affiliated to her *Yoni* or vagina. In this, only two kinds of ladies are considered. One who gave birth to him as his mother hence he is born from her vagina and the other one is his wife as he is desirous to insert himself in her vagina through his penis or his lover because he keeps such desire of copulation with her. As he comes out through the vaginal route of his mother and is desirous to go through the vaginal route of his wife by the help of his penis hence he often can be seen confused and helpless when these two women overlaps his personality thereby making him morally and physically impotent. When these two aforementioned relations are superimposed upon his temperament then he is always in dilemma as what to do and what not to do. Now if he has to choose one of them then often he favors his wife because his objective from mother's vagina is achieved while the purpose of the vagina of his wife is still to be achieved in future. He knows that his mother will survive at most ten to twenty years more while he has to live whole of his life with his wife. Now a husband is bound to obey his wife by bearing her immoral activities because he performs sexual course with her but as male relatives like brothers-in-law etc, of high moral, do not perform sexual course with her hence they put their objections when they find her to be iniquitous and indecent for other members as for her mother-in-law. Married ladies are often frustrated if their brothers-in-law pay no attention towards their sexual appeal. In middle age, such ladies often say to their husbands that they were sexually molested or abused by brothers-in-law and the stupid husbands blindly believe on such fake statements of their wives hence break the relations with real brothers. Such false indecent blames put upon the male relatives of husband by a lady are in fact the visible reflection of her sexually perverted thoughts. Again if such ladies had illicit sexual relations with their brothers-in-law in past then in this situation they never blame or criticize their brothers-in-law instead they reproach their wives. A lady, who has kept illicit relations with her brother-in-law, wants to humiliate and debase his wife by saying that he has slept with the one whom with she sleeps now being his wife but controls over her such perverted desire because of the fear of the opinion of the family and the society. In a joint family, if any man is having weak financial position in comparison to his real brothers then his wife is treated like servants and is bound to perform house jobs alone by the wives of other brothers. A middle aged married lady besieged by disgusting charm of performing adultery and the fear of the society reproaches all the men of husband's family with whom she always desired for sexual course but could not achieve because of strong character and high moral of them.

If a middle aged lady has always lived in a nuclear family after her marriage then she never behaves normally if she has to live in a joint family. She is never able to keep close affinity and affection with aged in-laws. As she has never lived with in-laws hence such distance always keeps her relations to be smooth with her in-laws but still she never keeps aged and sick in-laws with her when they need assistance of their son and daughter-in-law.

The resemblance of eunuchs can be seen in the behavior and attitude of middle aged ladies which disappear when they become of old age. Middle aged ladies with arrogant and despotic temperament can often be seen working in women welfare organizations. Young sexually corrupt married ladies, who are of indecent behavior, or the virtuous brides of the decent families diverted from the right path by other ladies, when visit to such organizations, are often misguided by such middle aged ladies instead of being advised the difference of virtuous and awful behavior. Again as such freedom seekers women welfare organizations are less in favor of ladies but more against men hence they seldom help ladies who are really in trouble and even never guide the culpable ladies approaching their for asking help by saying them that they are wrong and hence responsible for their so called problems. They never advise to a young corrupt married lady that she is the only cause behind her problems and in fact she has no problems because she herself is a big problem for a decent family. It is seen that innocent married ladies, who are actually in trouble because of their husbands or in-laws, get benefit of such organizations but again unfortunately such decent ladies are less than two percent of the total ladies who say that they are in trouble. Some of the middle aged ladies working in women welfare organizations have been psychologically reinvigorated up to such an extent that they feel the need of men only to perform moral or immoral harlotry. They are often involved in adultery which is immoral and they never consider their husbands to be more than an animal hence performing moral sexual courses with the husbands is also a kind of harlotry for them. A friend working in a multinational company had a conflict with his wife. The wife was of quarrelsome nature and she left for her home after the hot argument. After few days the husband was called by a women organization. He was happy to imagine that perhaps the experienced and well qualified ladies belonging to organization have given his wife some proper guidance. The situations were just opposite of what he assumed. The ladies made his wife more aggressive and stubborn by making her realized that she was right and hence wife was more against of him. The lady of the organization said to him, "Wives do not know what their husband do in the offices hence it is the right of wives to live their life by their own lifestyles. A lady has the right to perform all the activities which are done by men but if a man is impeccable and innocent then also he has no right to even think of his wife to be immaculate because women have their own identity entirely separate from men." It is a usual tendency of ladies to imagine for a perfect, wealthy, strong character and professionally successful husband but they themselves put the morality aside from considerations and want to be ever merged in the chasm of illicit sexual relations. A female aged social worker who has worked in the women welfare organization said, "The crimes related to women will never end unless women get severe punishments for their involvements. The only way to keep a curb on the continuous increasing sexual debauchment performed by ladies and their indecent behavior is that the names of the married ladies or unmarried girls found performing harlotry should be made public. There should be registration of prostitutes and if any lady is caught making illicit sexual relations then she should get punishment and her name should be kept in that list. As per the rules specially made for the safety of ladies, if a man is found to be guilty then he should be punished at any cost but if it is found that a lady blamed falsely and spoke untruth just to take the advantage of such rules then she and her parents should be severely punished equally."

The sensual lust and the passion for love of ladies increase when they reach to middle age but they are distraught and depressed with the busy schedule and repulsive attitude of their husbands. Almost men are busy in earning more money or fame or both at this age group. Ladies, sexually neglected by husbands, start visiting *Satsangs* or prayer assemblies and for this they join some group. In such religious assemblies, the religious priests or priestesses impose their thoughts on the audiences and teach them the various ways of achieving *Moksha* by neglecting the family responsibilities. The female spectators are most influenced by such virtuous gurus as they are taught to be indolent by not performing house jobs. A sufficiently big gentry of middle aged Indian ladies ruin their family life by neglecting family duties and adversely affect the life of their husbands and children because they get influenced by such religious priests. Though the biggest contribution in diverting women from right track and making their husbands' and in-laws' life like hell is of the women based television serials, mostly produced by female directors, based on the disgusting and shrewd attitude of the ladies in joint families. In such serials, they represent the awful and disgusting nature of women quarreling with each other and busy in intrigues to make others down by any means. It is found in a big survey conducted in India that more than sixty-five percent of the total ladies are sexually and morally ill-influenced just because of these serials. More than ninety percent of men are against of these serials and around fifty-two percent of them find their personal lives being ruined by their ladies who are regularly watching these serials since more than a decade. A renowned lady, who regularly watches such serials, said that allowing such serials to be shown in televisions was a big conspiracy against Indian family culture, customs and all men. She said that she was wondering that such serials, which are mostly responsible for making women sexually and morally perverted and are responsible for the devastation of the joint families, are running smoothly and no one dares to raise his voice against such serials. She said that in India, men never raise their voice against women and women are not going to raise their voice against such serials because they are negatively inspired by these episodes and hence they are stimulated to invoke negative attitude in them very rapidly. More than ninety-eight percent housewives, having time to watch television, prefer to watch such serials regularly. It is also found that such ladies leave their meals but never forget to watch such episodes. The difference among both the aforementioned matters is that a lady regularly joining *Satsang* quits from her responsibility of performing house jobs and obeying her husband and considers such reluctance or laziness to be spirituality while the ladies influenced by such women dominating serials, full of family conspiracies, ruin the family life of their husbands and other female members. Such serials performed a major role in introducing dirty politics and conspiracies in the families because it is an eternal truth that women are more influenced towards awful deeds and are most sensitive for such disgusting performances. In previous case, a lady who had illicit sexual relations throughout her previous life pretends to be religious and hence quits from the remaining family obligations of her while in later case, the female based episodes make the ladies of all the age groups, to be quarrelsome, sexually corrupt, sadist, perverted and violent.

Ladies become anxious by seeking the physical changes occurring in their bodies. The stage of Menopause or sudden end of menstruation cycle provides them a feeling of sexual impotency. Menopause is in fact permanent cessation of ovarian function typically happening in ladies during the age group of around forty-five to fifty. Again to make understand themselves that they are still sexually attractive and capable, they are oriented towards young guys. Ladies of this age group have to do least efforts for making illicit sexual relations because young guys are easily available to them. The perceptible or imperceptible sexual craving in the ladies is at the peak during this stage.

Such middle aged ladies, regularly visiting to some religious orator or priest, who proclaims his own theory regarding human existence and God, give a part of the grasped incomplete and senseless knowledge to their husbands and children and always pretend to be erudite and different from others. Ladies visiting to such religious orators regularly or in weeks or in months consider their husbands to be worthless and exhibit as if they are impressed by those orators and hence are obedient to them instead of their husbands. They extract and adopt only such episodes of the so-called religious expositions by which they can humiliate others and distress to family members by showing reluctance in performing family obligations. Again they define such reluctance or laziness in performing duties as the prime step to confront God. The religious orator describes his self drawn connotations of religious sayings and one-by-hundredth part of that is actually grasped by ladies. Then such ladies interpret the incomplete grasped religious lectures and utilize it to fulfill the objectives decided by their perverted psychology. In this way, such religious orators are never able to give the proper guidance to ladies instead create complications and distresses for the husbands and children of them. If the orator is male then the female audiences keep a peculiar affection for him. All the middle aged lustful ladies, joining such religious assemblies, keep sexual feelings for the religiously established male priest, doesn't matter whether he is a young man or a middle aged man or an old aged one. As all ladies are willing to see every more knowledgeable or efficient men to be bowed in front of them hence they keep desire for sexual course with them because this is the only way by which they find men to be helpless and submissive in front of them. If the orator is female then also the count of female audiences approaching to her is large. The lustful ladies hearing to female orator either keep the lesbian feelings or are free from sexual desire because of their overage. Somewhere aged ladies, who are sexually unsatisfied in their past and are in dilemma in context of their future, join such religious assemblies. Ladies unwilling to perform family duties also bent towards such priests. A kind of ignorance, laziness, effortlessness and reluctance produced in middle aged ladies because of such religious assemblies create obstructions in the daily routine of their husbands and children but as usual, ladies never care about the grief of other family members and continue visiting to such prayers to experience the pleasure of spiritual sexual union.

The middle aged parents desire to select brides themselves for their marriageable young sons. Somewhere young children are engaged in affairs and ultimately willingly or unwillingly, parents allow them to marry with their chosen life partners. As much a middle aged mother cries at the time of *Widai* of her daughter or at the last step of marriage ceremony when her daughter leaves her premises with her husband, the more she is full of the peculiar mixed feelings of pleasure and sorrow when her son gets married and a new lady enters in her premises as her daughter-in-law. She is happy because the male infant whom she nourished in her womb for nine months, gave birth through vaginal route and nurtured by breastfeeding has been a complete man. She is the creator of men, the most powerful entity of the universe. Her creation has been matured and is ready to give birth to generations. When her son spends his time with his girlfriends, she never becomes distressed because she feels sexual pleasure when she finds her son sexually molesting virgin girls. She desires her son to sexually rape the ladies in front of her whom she does not like but she can not express such perverted desires of her. She, even after being a woman, wants to take revenge from all the women through her son but again such desires are never expressed by ladies. Her son can not perform sex or keep attraction with her vagina, the vagina she gave birth and the vagina related by blood relation to her own vagina but he is allowed to enjoy sexually with rest of the females. She is depressed and frightened to see her daughter-in-law because as per her opinion, the influence of a mother on her son is over once he gets married and produces his own children. Though she never keeps sexual attachments with her son but she feels sexual pleasure when she imagines her son performing sexual course with his wife. She used to guide her son in the way she wants but now another lady has come in the premises of her son in the form of his wife to guide him and rule him. She always considers the presence of her daughter-in-law as a dire misfortune and danger over her possessiveness and rights for her son. She thinks that her daughter-in-law should take her permission and benediction before entering in the room in the first night as well as in further nights but she can not compel her for this. She keeps a sharp eye on the gestures and the face expressions of her daughter-in-law entering in the bedroom at night and coming out in the morning. She is the future of her bride hence she is well familiar with all the techniques performed by young ladies. She desires that all the household jobs should be done by daughter-in-law after taking permission of her but meantime she wants to arrange the general necessities of her son by her own. She considers it as her absolute right to guide her daughter-in-law even if she is perfect because this gives her feelings that everything is under her control. Again she thinks of her daughter-in-law asking permission before performing any work. She desires to see her daughter-in-law as her son's servant cum keep who is expected to perform house jobs as well as to provide sexual services to her son. Though she is very conscious but still she finds gradual decrements in her rights. She knows that if she will not behave strictly with her daughters-in-law then they will spread adultery and create complications as well as conflicts in the family on behalf of their husbands or her sons.

Her son going outside for office work or for some other reason informs to his wife instead of telling her. Now the information of the income and investments done by her son is limited to his wife. From this moment, the foundation of the well known visible or invisible conflicts, which take place between mothers-in-law and daughters-in-law, is built. This is true that they both are bound to live with each other and if the motiveless affection is seen in-between them in any family then this is mere ostentation which they have to perform either because of the fear of the opinion of the society and family or because of the financial need of one side that can be fulfilled only by other side. As a lady never behaves honestly with even her mother, real sisters and daughters hence imagining her to be keeping flawless affection with her mother-in-law or daughters-in-law is senseless.

Parents of the young girls select bridegrooms for their daughters. All mothers desire to marry their daughters as soon as possible. The presence of the daughters is like an obstacle for them in performing the activities of their liking. A middle aged lady never accepts the pious affection of her husband for his young daughter in a normal way but still she wants to put daughter in the form of an alluring sexual object in front of him. The love or affection which a son gets from his mother, if the same is obtained by a daughter from her father then mother gets suspicious about it. The presence of a lady in the role of a daughter bifurcates the affection of a man that he keeps with his wife when he was having no daughters. A mother wants her monopoly back as soon as possible by marrying her daughters and sending them to their husbands' premises because she never accepts her daughters to be a part of her family. She always becomes happy when she finds her young daughters keeping jealousy with each other or quarrelling with each other but she pretends to be guiding them to be united. Middle aged ladies, who keep active enmity with their husbands and daughters and often humiliate them, never desire their daughters to get married early because they never want their daughters to get rid from the hell made by them. In contrary to this, if the daughters are seen standing against of such mothers by favoring their decent fathers then mothers are in support of marrying them as soon as possible so that no one may interfere while they humiliate their husbands. If the house is run by a disciplined man, who never let his wife performing ill-deeds, then middle aged ladies of such husbands are bound to live peacefully with their daughters without humiliating them. In such families, fathers prefer their daughters marrying late so as to give them higher education or because of the over affection of them with daughters. An immoral middle aged lady never gives proper guidance to her daughter and tries to mould her daughter as per her iniquitous temperament. She teaches her daughter peculiar attitude of feminine nature so that she may be able to ruin the life of her husband and in-laws. She knows that ladies are by nature eager to adopt awful properties and habits hence she behaves with her husband in a disgusting way in front of her daughter so that she may learn all of such immoral behavior and in future may apply in her own family. This is the knowledge which she provides her daughter very deceitfully. Again she knows that young girls are most affected by seeing relations of a husband and wife where wife dominates over husband and they inherit awful properties of such a wife in their life so as to apply all of that in their own married life. A middle aged characterless lady gradually dissolves slow working poison of awful habits and ill-nature in the temperament of her daughter which ultimately in future ruins daughter's family life specially causing humiliation and harassment of the would-be husband and children. Rare mothers keep themselves free from such visible or invisible ill-feelings and jealousy towards their daughters.

Almost ladies on the one side hate prostitutes and prostitution while on the other side they are eager to adopt the sexual life of prostitutes. In this age group, a lady who is characterless and hence is involved in adultery always desires her daughter to perform the same but never expresses her desires openly to her. Few of such ladies even perform sexual mating in their own house in separate rooms with the clients or lovers in the form of visitors, in such a way so that their young daughters may watch this. They know that young daughters get sexually excited if they see their mothers performing sexual plays. Some professional morally corrupt ladies of this age group allow their customers or sex-partners to have a look at the beauty of their daughters with the intention that perhaps they may continue their visit to perform sexual course with them with the desire of having sexual course with their daughters. Gradually such ladies are successful in diverting their daughters to perform harlotry. If the middle aged lustful ladies are financially strong then somewhere they keep their daughters in hostels. The conflict of a middle aged lady increases with her daughter if she is her only child. In this case, as both of them possess feminine properties and women psychology hence they are very familiar with the wickedness and shrewdness of each other. If daughters get the support of a worthy father or brother or lover then they start opposing their mothers involved in immoral activities. At the occasion of the marriage of a daughter, her father wants to give her gifts in the form of dowry as per his capabilities but her mother always provoke him not to do so. Again each lady wants to give minimum dowry at the marriage of her daughter but her desires for asking dowry while marrying her son are unlimited. As per the opinion of a normal man in the role of a father, the wealth is earned for wives and kids hence it is genuine to give dowry to daughters because this is the right of a daughter on the parental property while as per a normal lady in the role of mother, her daughters have no rights in the parental property. This has been already mentioned based on the figures drawn by various surveys.

A middle aged lady expects for all kind of support from her children. When she goes outside with her young children, she considers herself to be their elder sister. If someone thinks her and her young daughter to be real sisters because of the resemblance in faces, she becomes very happy. If some boy does eve-teasing with her daughter then she comes forward to oppose him. Ladies at this age group, who consider social norms as mere pretence, are capable to solve any conflict by taking active participation. If she gets the complaint against her son about harassing a girl then she is ever ready to argue in the favor of her son even when she knows that her son is wrongdoer. Some of them are extremely uncivilized even after being educated and they are often found saying, "Men can do nothing against of us because we can bear numerous men at a time in context of sexual plays while a man can not handle completely even only one of us." When they get complaint against their sons for distressing young faultless girls, their attitude of always supporting feminism now ignores the humiliation of innocent girls and they take the favor of their sons by falsely blaming on the characters of the offended girls. The penis as a symbol of a man birthed from their vagina is having the right of molesting other vaginas. In case of the love affairs of their daughters, they expect them to elaborate their romantic moments spend with lovers. Such coordination with the daughters provides them homosexual feelings. She desires to watch her children naked. Sometimes, when the children feel some problem related to genital organs, she herself inspects their organs before taking the advice of some doctor. Again vulgarity and indecency can never be assumed in the relations of a mother with her children. She knows that the physical relations of herself with her son are limited to giving birth to him and breastfeeding to him. Very rare mothers keep sexual relations with their sons and in fact they are neither mothers nor human beings. Such relations of a mother with her male progenies can be seen only in animals still few mothers achieve sexual pleasure from their sons in imaginations without actually performing sexual course with them.

Men spending their life happily with their families are fortunate because the count of such men is less than twelve percent. Though it appears that around sixty-eight percent men are happy with their families and this much men even confessed that they are happy with their family life but when deep survey is conducted about their actual life then it is revealed that eleven percent men out of them are beaten by their wives. Total count of men who are physically harassed or beaten by their wives is sixty-three percent but unfortunately men never disclose this to maintain their pseudo mannishness. Now out of those sixty-eight percent men, who say that they are happy with their families, thirty-one percent were usually scolded by their wives and their parents were in deep trouble because of the humiliation done by the wives of their sons. Out of remaining thirty-seven percent men, twenty-four were living their family life just like a pet animal tamed by the wives. Hence in fact only thirteen percent men were happy but one percent of them were having a verbal contract with their wives that both of them will not interfere in each other's life style. It is a rumor especially spread about India that the society and families are men governed. In fact it is seen in surveys that the rise of the family depends on men and the degradation or devastation of the family entirely depends on women. If a family is renowned and decent then a man is responsible for that while if a family is baseless and indecent with no ethics then a woman is responsible for that. We can understand this as women are always responsible for breaking of joint families and they are the only cause behind the violence, quarrel, adultery, intrigues, humiliation and harassment in the family while men are responsible for wealth, peace, dignity and fame of the family. The exceptions to this are only found in the families where gents are very alcoholic or expend their whole income in gambling. A man has to struggle a lot to make his family ideal and renowned while a woman just has to protect herself from her awful properties including sexual debauchment. In the present scenario, almost families are guided by ladies and they appoint men in earning wealth. This is the reason that financial crime or corruption and rate of taking bribes or black money have been highly increased in India. Men are happy because they are earning black money thereby fulfilling the desires of their corrupt wives but meantime they never admit that they are governed by their wives. More than seventy-six percent men are depressed and frustrated by the behavior of their wives hence they release their frustration by harassing the people in destitute of the society. Men keep busy themselves in earning money by any means so as to compensate their eloped family happiness and to make them unaltered by the family conflicts. Again most of the men speak lie to their wives because they are frightened from them. Men know that wives are happy to see the black money earned by them and it provides men little comfort and safety from their wives. In a survey it is found that less than five percent ladies desire to live a simple life with simple husbands while more than ninety-five percent wives desire from their husbands to earn money by any cost. Money is the first desire of ladies because sexual relations they can perform anywhere meantime they know that if they will compel their husbands to earn more money then they will be almost free to perform illicit sexual relations because husbands will not get time to watch them. Again a survey revealed the fact that all big mafias, contractors, builders, transporters and all men involved in the business or offices where they earn black money through their physical or administrative power are in fact coward and afraid of their wives. More than ninety percent of the wives of such persons are involved in illicit sexual relations because such men are over confident about their power. More than ninety-seven percent men, who keep ill tendencies and pretend to be strong, brave, practical and cunning in their professional life, act like a pet dog in front of their wives.

Middle aged ladies with such family environment often can be seen morally humiliating and harassing their husbands. Such ladies make their grownup daughters quarrelsome and lethargic like themselves and with the help of them they emotionally blackmail to husbands. Girls affected by their corrupt mothers hence disrespecting virtuous fathers tends towards making illicit sexual relations and ruin the lives of their husbands and in-laws after marriage. Such affection of mothers for their daughters is always proved to be disastrous for their married life in future because they provide unrestrained and unethical temperament to daughters. If a corrupt mother does not possess such affection with her daughter then she stands against of her husband as well as of her daughter but now daughter stands in opposition to her mother to help her father and presents herself as a woman to oppose an unethical woman in the form of her mother because she knows that the only solution to stop the behavioral nudity of a lady is the nudity shown by another lady. She knows that a woman can neglect and control over the depraved behavior shown by other woman. Now in this situation, such a middle aged lady even blames her husband and daughter for keeping sort of immoral relations because she knows that this is the only false blame which if she puts on her husband and daughter then they will not be united to oppose her anymore. This is often seen in Bengali families. Such middle aged ladies take bath being entirely nude and without locking the door or change the garments in front of husband and daughters so as to sexually harass them and to produce shameless situations in the family. They are sexually and morally perverted and try to generate lustful environment by such activities so as to invoke sexual feelings among their daughters and husbands. They often provoke and sexually excite their daughters to keep proximity with young guys and if this is done by their daughters then they blame on their character in front of husbands. Such middle aged ladies are extreme indecent and lusty. They are very hygienic and sometimes seen to be insane because of their over consciousness for physical purity. They wash the house and the cloths many times in a day and they feel hatred when husbands touch them with sexual intentions while they are always sexually attracted towards other men. Some ladies of this age group keep dogs and perform unnatural sex with them considering them to be the men of their liking.

Middle aged ladies, who are very active, often keep the salary earned by their husbands and give the limited pocket money for their expenses. Such tendency in married ladies grows during the early years of their married life, when they get prominent in their roles towards their husbands, and sustains for lifelong. They keep the full information about the salary earned by their husbands and their investments as well as bonus amount or salary increment they get from their offices. Hence husbands in jobs hardly manage to hide some money for own expenses from their wives. Men in business have this facility because they do not have a fixed salary. Such kind of ladies take the salary earned by husbands and do not care for the future activities done by husbands. They often say to their husbands, "Give us the whole salary then do whatever you want." Such behavior is usually shown by ladies if they find their husbands to be alcoholic. Again they often found saying to their husbands, "We want money to feel security and you can do anything in your life if you assure us getting the whole amount earned by you." They let their husbands taking alcohol when they get whole of their salary. Such husbands seem to be normal but live their life in depression. As they get a very limited amount of the salary they draw hence to manage for their other expenses, they perform taking bribes in the offices. They often hide their other sources of earnings from their wives and sometimes do not inform their wives about the increments in their salary. These men sometimes steal their own earned money from their residences in the absence of wives. Such ladies often say to their husbands, "Take bribe or do anything to earn if you want to fulfill your desires." More than eighty percent lower class employees in government services take bribe because of their wives. Husbands keep the plenty of illegally earned money in the house for their wives and children and seldom utilize this for own pleasure but wives and children take full advantage of this and spend luxurious life. There is not even a single wife who stops her husband from taking bribes or for earning money by illegal ways. No wife discloses the black money earned by her husband to public or government's taxation department instead they all enjoy it. Ladies, who often forcefully impose their desires, women stubbornness and awful qualities to their husbands, never stop their husband when they earn black money and never accept that their husbands are involved in illicit earning activities because they have a perfect coordination with the illegally earned money of husbands. If their husbands are caught red handed by the crime bureaus then they say that they advised their husbands numerous times not to earn black money but they did not pay attention. Again they pretend to be helpless and unaware about their husbands' habit of earning black money on behalf of which they are spending luxurious life. Another situation where ladies keep the salaries of their husbands can mostly be seen where husbands financially help their blood relatives. Almost wives become angry if their husbands financially help to their relatives and hence almost wives keep the salaries of such husbands with the thought that by this they will stop their husbands helping to their aged and physically sick parents or younger brothers and sisters.

The lives of the husbands become hell if they are not able to take bribes or earn black money for their greedy wives. Such men avoid taking vacations from the office and are not willing to go back to their residences even after office hours. They prefer sitting alone in solitude, watching movies or spending time with close friends instead of going back to the house. Their wives do not let them live a peaceful life and often scolds them to earn more money. Their self made home is made hell by their licentious and quarrelsome natured wives. More than thirty-two percent men openly accept the awful nature and disgusting attitude of their wives by considering that as an inseparable part of their destiny. These men say that after coming home from the office, the kind of peace a man imagine in his life is not found at all. When ladies unnecessarily quarrel on baseless topics then men either sit quietly or go out of the house. Seventy percent of such wives when interviewed very personally then they said clearly that they can not sit quietly without making complications and can not see their husbands sitting peacefully. One of such lady told very personally that as there are no definite and strict codes of conducts for married ladies hence almost of them humiliate and harass their husbands and in-laws. A renowned middle aged lady said that if the existence of the joint families is still maintained somewhere in the country then the reason behind this is the compromises done by men in almost of the families. Married ladies with arrogant nature start seeking the shortcomings and weak points of their husbands from the very initial period of their married life. Sometimes they argue on husbands' drinking habit and sometimes they make a baseless doubt regarding husbands' probable sexual relations with a lady whom husbands even don't know and hence make their life hell by quarrelling. A husband falsely blamed and humiliated by his wife on such numerous topics has no explanations. The most interesting fact is that if a man is of arrogant nature and physically harasses his wife after taking alcohol or has been involved in illicit sexual relations in past and even at present, then wife of him never says anything to him. Such a man rarely seeks any conflict or complication in his family. In contrary to this if a husband intakes alcohol occasionally in very limited quantity and behaves very decently in such a manner that no one can even imagine that he is drunk or had no sexual relations before marriage and is trustworthy to his wife then he is always blamed and humiliated by his wife for having aforementioned bad habits which in fact he does not possess. Again if a man had emotional affection with some lady in his bachelor life while never had sexual relations before marriage but unfortunately he has told about his fair love to his wife then he is always blamed by the wife for having sexual relations with that lady whom he even never touched. Ladies often quarrel with the husbands if they give some kind of gift to their mothers or sisters. Such wives often complain that their husbands never give some gifts like jewelries or garments to them. They take away all the money earned by husbands and give them just sufficient amount for their expenditures and even after that they expect for the gifts. They often reproach and argue with their husbands saying that they are not having luxurious items like air-conditioners, luxurious cars etc. When a husband is distressed by the arguments done by his wife regularly, he takes some loan from financial institutions or banks and purchases such items for his wife. When the installments of loan are deducted from his salary then wife says that there was no need to purchase such luxurious things. Now he is humiliated by his wife for the unpardonable offense of taking loan for fulfilling her desires. Hence if a man acts as per the directions given by his wife then also he is humiliated by her. The humiliation, harassment, responsibility, anxiety, conflicts and complications enters in a man's life the moment he marries with a licentious lady of awful nature.

Mostly the salaries of fourth class government employees, who are excessively involved in drinking alcohol or gambling, are directly given to their wives instead of them. For this, their middle aged wives give their request in written to government departments where their husbands work. It is very essential because workers of such lower ranks, working in government organizations, are harassed by their wives as well as by their own habits and seek the peace in wine and gambling hence they spend almost of their earned money in that. The consequences of this are faced by their children and wives as they live in financial crisis.

In middle age, the appetite of ladies increases and they feel more hungry for food. They often complain that their stomach is burning because of hunger. They get more attracted towards different and delicious dishes. Ladies, who are not conscious for health and figure, live their life for the charm of eating delicious foods. They enjoy almost dishes in dinner parties and are unable to control over their excessive eating habit. The ladies, even suffering from diabetes, do not stop eating dishes which are harmful and prohibited for them instead they prefer regularly taking medicines or diabetes-injections with the delicious food. Some abnormal tendencies can be seen arising in ladies during their middle age. They usually show few peculiar habits as drinking the water while gargling, belching with sound, yawning with sound and passing the air or farting with sound. In fact they become very eager to achieve freedom for everything and they think that by such activities they may come out from their feminine obligations and become free as men are. They don't understand that men performing above mentioned activities in public are considered to be uncivilized. Their psychology and opinions become baseless and they consider performing adultery is also an essential symptom of women's freedom. Some more abnormal activities or habits that they inherit are; they pass urine while standing, pass gas while keeping the palm near anus-hole and then smell their palm, they smell and lick the undergarments of their husbands and children before washing, smell their sweat behind the arms and smell and lick their own seminal discharge. They stop their husbands washing the penis before oral sex because washed penis is seems to be a piece of raw tasteless flesh in mouth. During sexual intercourse, they prefer more than one man and are often interested for orgies. They are always eager to rape some boy of the age group of their sons and desire to get rapped by men. They insert some object resembling penis inside their anus-hole so as to narrow the expansion of their vagina. Ladies, who like to lick their own vaginal fluid, often perform oral sex with their sex partners after mating.

As the ladies of this age group have solved their sexual curiosities hence they desire to go beyond normal sexual relations. They do not hesitate to break the standard and universally accepted codes of sexual mating. Some of them are eager to breastfeed their grownup sons. They often pretend to love the friends of their sons like mothers but in fact they betray the pious love of a mother because they are having sexual intentions in doing so. They never hesitate to make illicit sexual relations. Financially capable mothers provide different soaps for taking bath to their daughters while they desire their sons using the same soaps that they use. A lustful housewife of this age group has sufficient time for all of such nuisance. They seek perverted sexual pleasure in very small things or activities and shockingly they always succeed in that.

Middle aged married ladies are always skeptical regarding the character of their daughters-in-law. They want their sons to perform sex with their wives cruelly and roughly. They spread white bed-sheet on the bed of their sons during their first night after marriage and investigate the presence of blood spot in the next morning. When they find blood spot because of the breaking of virgin knot in the first night, they become happy by imagining the momentary pain of breaking of virgin knot faced by their daughters-in-law. Some mothers assist their sons if they behave cruelly with their wives. Most of the middle aged ladies keep one sided homosexual feelings with their daughters-in-law. They desire that their daughters-in-law should elaborate the sexual plays done by their sons with them in the first night. Some of the married ladies share such feelings of their first night of marriage with their real mothers but they never share this with their mothers-in-law. Again such verbal sexual debauchment is somewhere done by married ladies with their mothers because they keep lesbian feelings with their mothers but as the mothers-in-law are unfamiliar to them hence they do not keep homosexual feelings or emotions for them and hence do not disclose their first night happenings to them.

Middle aged ladies often get sexually excited imagining about the first night of their own daughters. They are filled with sexual feelings during the first night of their daughters. When a lady gets married and goes away with her husband then her mother desires that the son-in-law should perform all such sexual plays with her daughter which she desired to be done with herself in the first night. She desires to defeat a man in the form of her son-in-law by the help of *Yoni* or vagina of her daughter. She wants to perform sexual course with her husband at the same time when her daughter intercourses with her husband first time. Hence often middle aged ladies keep indirect sexual attachments with their sons-in-law. If a lady is married at the early stage of her life and hence at the time of her daughter's marriage, she is not very aged then somewhere she is found keeping illicit sexual relations with her son-in-law. This situation is also seen in the matters where the son-in-law is quite aged than her daughter. As the son-in-law sexually intercourses a *Yoni*, as a symbol of her daughter, taken birth from her *Yoni* hence if a son-in-law asks for sexual plays to her then she seldom denies because directly or indirectly she desire the same.

Old Age And Death

The sexual feelings and sensations do not exist at old age hence a lady of such age group finds herself with no existence. As all attractive ladies want to represent themselves as a source of lust in the form of their body even when they are equally capable as men are hence they consider their existence only till they can sexually entice men by representing themselves in a body-form. If at this stage of the life, a lady can gain perverted pleasure of making complications or conflicts among the people of her family or can rule her family or society then also she finds her existence because the pleasure that ladies achieve in this is very similar to the pleasure they get while making sexual courses. A lady lives her whole life freely with abandoned behavior and performs awful activities including adultery under the shade of pretending to be helpless, harassed, humiliated, constrained, embarrassed and incapable. If a lady faces the illness and physical incapability in her old age, she becomes hopeless and distressed. The hatred feelings for their bodies in men make them highly depressed and to protect themselves from this, they take the shelter of religion. In this age, a little bit consciousness and positive thinking rise in them for the worth of their existence when they visit such so-called highly spiritual sermons. A lady, who has lived whole of her life for the prime aim of achieving sexual pleasure and causing distress to others, now becomes ascetic. Even some of the ladies, who were very despotic in their previous life, become renunciant because of the incapability to further rule the family or the presence of other female autocratic family members like daughters-in-law etc. Such a lady makes coordination with the spiritual orator and tries to engross herself in the religious sayings. As she has always been pretentious in her life hence even now she pretends to hear the orator sincerely. She lies from herself by betraying her own soul. She makes herself understand that she is the most devoted listener but in fact she has nothing to do with the religious sayings. Again she visits such religious ceremony just to pass her time and pretend herself to be spiritual. She has lived whole of her life depending on lies and betrays and these have become an essential part of her identity in such a way that she can not quit from such temperament. She believes that the spiritual sayings of the orator are in fact coming from the inner feelings of her own heart. This feeling provides her the pleasure of virtual and spiritual sexual union. As she has spent entire of her life for the sake of sexual pleasure and falsehood hence every aspect of her life till her death is based on these two propensities of her. She becomes affectionate and emotional for the orator. This is the only affection of her life which has nothing to do with physical sexual feelings. Some ladies accept consecration by some religious priest to achieve a life of ascetic. The sacred verses, by which one can achieve *Moksha*, are told by such gurus to them with the instruction of not disclosing that. They tell that spiritual verse told by guru to all of their close relatives and friends and say that they are warned by the guru not to tell this to anyone but they are just telling this to only them. Thus as usual they can never hide secret things because disclosing of the secret matters provides them perverted pleasure and satisfaction.

A lady often seeks her married sons being in full control of their wives. Her children, whom she gave birth and nourished, assuming them to be a part of her own body, consider her to be an unwanted member in the family. She did numerous prays and wishes to conceive a male child and gave birth him but now that child has been young and feels disgrace to declare in front of his friends that she is his mother. It is found in an extensive survey that the children born after numerous wishes and prays almost found to be black sheep of the families and never proved to be any kind of helpful for aged parents.

If such a lady has kept the control of the family in her hand from the beginning and is financially capable then she prefers to keep her son and his family with her. If her children are posted at distant places and hence are living with their family separate from her then she lives with her husband alone and in the absence of husband, prefers to live in solitude. Again if such aged ladies are widow and financially capable then they prefer living alone so as to live a life with no compulsions. She never accepts her son's or daughter-in-law's restrictions on her life style. Almost aged ladies and gents keep negative attitude for youngsters. They prefer menacing and scolding youngsters. They become happy when some family matters are put in front of them for their advice as they always assume themselves extraordinary experienced and practical and hence seek themselves in the role of a judge.

As the remaining affection of sons for their parents reduces when they too become parents hence an aged lady feels a kind of rivalry or competition with her grandchildren. She pretends to embrace her grandchildren and always keeps a jealousy feeling for them. She feels that the affection or care, she should get by her sons and their wives, is completely taken by her grandchildren. She sometimes behaves like a child to draw the attraction of her sons. In fact she is highly depressed because she knows that her grownup children are not willing to keep her with them. If she is fortunate then she gets food and medicines at proper time otherwise mostly she is thrown in a secluded room and is entirely neglected by young family members.

An aged but active lady, with the tendency to rule on others, living with her children's family, keeps a perfect control over the female and male family members. In fact such ladies just keep strict control over their sons and hence never let their wives dominate over them. Such kind of aged ladies are seen in lesser families. They behave with their grandchildren as a principle of school. If aged ladies are served by their daughters-in-law then this is mostly because they are having plenty of money and properties personally on their name. An aged lady can keep her rule maintained in the family only when she possesses such property on her name or her wealthy husband is alive. If aged parents transfer their property or distribute the assets to their children in their life time then in ninety-seven percent of such matters, they face misfortune and distress after that, which is provided to them by their own sons and daughters-in-law. If a simple and innocent aged lady is widow with no financial stability then she is bound to live with her children's family. Almost such ladies experience grief and distress in their remaining life. All of such ladies are morally and physically harassed by their daughters-in-law for which their sons either give silent permission or just ignore this. When the aged ladies were interviewed and surveyed then horrible facts were revealed. Daughters-in-law of such aged ladies treat them like servants. Young ladies compel their mothers-in-law of the age group of around above seventy years, to perform all the house jobs and give them very little and rotten food. Such financially helpless aged ladies have to work like hell and the house jobs which they are bound to do are sweeping the house, cleaning utensils used by all the members, washing cloths of whole the family and sweeping toilets etc. They are given remaining food and somewhere they are compelled to eat stinking food. They are not given medical treatment when they are sick. When some of their organ becomes rotten due to some disease, even then they are not given medical treatment and are kept isolated from other family members to die painfully. They spend their last time painfully and being entirely neglected and hence always desire for death. They are not allowed to meet with the guests and if some friends or guests of the daughters-in-law ask about their identity then they are introduced as a family servant. All of ladies are found to be scolding and menacing their aged and incapable financially poor mothers-in-law. The facts that were disclosed by surveys indicate that ninety-eight percent aged and financially incapable ladies are harassed and humiliated by their daughters-in-law. As mentioned above, almost of the aged parents who transfer or distribute their all property to their sons spend their remaining life in distress and being entirely neglected by the children. Only around twelve percent of man physically regard and take care of their aged parents while fifty-nine percent of ladies take care of their parents even after being married. Out of such fifty-nine percent married ladies, only two percent were found taking care of their in-laws. Out of eighty-eight percent married men, who never physically care for their aged parents, seventy-six percent are compelled by their wives for discarding the aged parents while twelve percent men are very money-minded and are not willing to even see the faces of their parents. Hence ladies are quite faithful for their parents but extremely disloyal for in-laws. Out of the total count of the financially helpless aged ladies living with their children's families, ninety-eight percent face misbehavior and ignorance from their daughters-in-law out of which eighty-six percent are treated just like servant. Sixty-eight percent are given remaining food while forty-two percent are given stinking food. Twenty-one percent are physically tortured. Fifty-seven percent are compelled to live in separate room. Thirty-two percent are not allowed to meet with the guests. Thirty-nine percent are not allowed to mix-up with their grandchildren. Sixty-two percent are abused by daughters-in-law. Seventy-two percent of aged ladies, who can not move and hence perform excretion on the bed, are made bathed once in a week and their excretion is washed by daughters-in-law incase of twenty-one percent matters while by husbands in forty-eight percent matters and in rest of the matters this is done by female nurses or servants. Twenty-one percent very aged ladies are humiliated and tortured by pinching with fingers or nails or needles and are touched by some very hot metallic object like tongs or burning wood on their feet by their daughters-in-law or by the granddaughters on the direction of their mothers. Seventy-two percent aged ladies are not given food at proper time. Sixty-one percent aged ladies are not given sufficient food. Forty-one percent of them often sleep empty stomach. Seven percent daughters-in-law spit on the food given to their aged and sick in-laws. Seventeen percent aged ladies are bound to eat inedible items including non-vegetarian meal. This all seems to be utterly shocking but this is the exact situation of overage sick ladies living under the shelter of their daughters-in-law. This is a naked and utmost disgusting form of Indian ladies who are considered to be a live symbol of mercy and kindness and always pretend to stand in favor of the rights of ladies but actually behave to aged female in-laws in such aforementioned hatred way.

During aged life, the sensitivity for urine secretion decreases in women and they are unable to control over passing urine hence they are found passing urine even while sleeping. When they feel little pressure for urine excretion, they excrete it at the nearest possible place and even pass urine while standing. Very aged ladies need proper assistance to accomplish their daily routine. It is seen that their sons make them pass urine or shit and help them in taking the bath before going to office and when they come back; they change their bed-sheets on which they have passed urine while their daughters-in-law almost neglect them. Again if they are somewhere served by their daughters-in-law then this in only because the strictness of their sons done over their wives.

Very aged or sick ladies are helped by their daughters-in-law in two situations. In the first case where a young or middle aged lady helps and serves her aged or sick mother-in-law can be seen when the lady was living with her mother-in-law from beginning and she has seen her in healthy situation and the second condition occurs when the lady has never seen her mother-in-law in healthy position. In both of the cases, ladies serve their mothers-in-law only when they are bound to do this by their husbands or they seek some financial benefit from the aged mothers-in-law. An unmarried son takes care of her sick and aged parents easily but the situation changes if he marries. Some men send their aged and sick parents to the asylums made for aged people because of the pressure of their wives. When few of such men were interviewed then they told that their parents were not given proper food by their wives. Neighbors told them that their wives physically harass and scold their parents when they go to office. They requested to their wives not to do so but no improvement occurred. Ultimately they send their parents to the house of old aged people. Many of the men left their wives for misbehaving with the parents but the parents of the wives put false blames on them and ultimately they have to accept their wives. A man very puzzled with the misbehavior of his wife for the parents told that he left his corrupt wife so that he may be alone to take care of the aged helpless parents but the parents of the wife lodged a fake complaint against him and he was arrested. Now nobody was there to take care of the parents. Ultimately he accepted his wife to get rid of the troubles and left his parents. Very wealthy men admit their aged and sick parents in the nursing homes so that they may get proper services and treatment and hence they become free from taking care or looking the faces of their lean parents. They give a lot of money to such nursing homes or private hospitals. Most of the sons feel uncomfortable to keep their aged mothers with them but they seldom feel inconvenient with aged fathers because their wives never tolerate the presence of mothers-in-law while they have least problems with fathers-in-law. If there are number of sons of an aged lady then almost of them are slaves of their wives hence no one of them agrees to keep parents with him. If because of the fear of the opinion of society or relatives they have to keep their parents with them then they distribute the responsibility of the parents among them and one of them keeps father with him and other one to mother. This sequence rotates among all the sons but unfortunately none of them dares to keep both parents together because of the fear of the wives. When such morally corrupt wives were interviewed very personally then they brazenly told that if the in-laws are kept together then they become united to oppose the harassment of them done by daughters-in-law. All ladies think that their mothers-in-law and fathers-in-law should be kept separate otherwise they become united to make conspiracies against daughters-in-law. This is shocking fact that pairs are made in heaven but they are converted in to hell by ladies in the form of wives. Similarly the pairs of husbands and wives are destined by the God but when they become old, they are bound to live separate by ladies in the form of their daughters-in-law. If fortunately any of the sons is devoted to parents and keeps parents with him by any cost by never caring the opinion of his wife then he is publicly menaced and scolded by his rest of the brothers and their wives and they try to harm him. Such aged parents are fortunate who can visit or live with any of their children but again such situations exist only when they have plenty of the wealth which allures their daughters-in-law.

Aged women are seen becoming mentally retarded when they undergo longtime sickness. In this situation, they often scold and abuse their husbands, sons and daughters-in-law. Some of them become violent and beat the other family members. Mostly the feeling of the insecurity and the very conscious attitude of them becomes the ground of their unnatural behavior in their aged life. In the aged period of the life, ladies feel the irrationality of the life and they find themselves being betrayed by everyone including themselves too. Almost ladies, who utilize whole of their life making illicit sexual relations and doing ill of others, fall in a kind of delusion in their aged life that they had been harassed in whole of their life. They do not get rid of the habit of deceiving themselves by making them believe that they were right and the others were wrong. Most of such ladies break all the laws and idealism they made in their early period of the life. Somewhere they ask for non-vegetarian meal even after being pure vegetarian throughout their life. They desire to intake the foods which they never liked in their lifetime. It is seen that if the sexual sensitivity does not become nil then a lady, who has followed the codes of chastity in her lifetime, would become a harlot. They are eager to break the laws of prohibition that they pretended to impose on themselves in whole of the life but they are physically unable to express their desires for illicit sexual courses that were forbidden for them in young age. They want to quit from their pseudo disposition and habit to feign. A literate aged lady, who is fond of reading literature, finds it easy to pass her time if she is financially capable. If such ladies are having married daughters then they often get financial as well as other kind of services from their daughters. If aged parents have only daughters then they are more cared and hence are more secure. Most of the ladies with no sons live with their married daughters. Very rare young or middle aged ladies respect and care their in-laws considering them as their own parents but this is also true that such honest and generous ladies are found in the same society where no lady wants to take care of in-laws. Such ladies, who take care of their in-laws without any self-interest, are extremely virtuous and seen rarely. One of such lady said, "My mother-in-law is ill since past eight years and she is not able to stand up or walk herself. She had a paralysis attack hence she is unable to perform her daily routine. She takes meal and excretes urine and shit on the bed. I help her performing daily routine with the assistance of my husband. I always consider my mother-in-law as my real mother and never ever bother her. I know that I am not doing any favor on my husband or mother-in-law because this is my duty and is the only way by which I can justify myself to be true. If I make some delay or laziness in providing service to my mother-in-law then my husband strictly warns me. In fact a wife serves and behaves properly or not to her in-laws entirely depends on the husband of her. Masculinity of a man has nothing to do with his capability of performing sexual courses to satisfy the sexual need of his wife because women are never satisfied sexually. Hence as per the sexual perspective, all men are impotent. The exact meaning of masculinity of a man is to make sure that all the family members of his family get the rights, facilities and the respects they deserve for. A man has to make sure that no one is harassed of humiliated in his family by other family members. The codes of mannish nature never allow interfering in-between matter of ladies and prohibit for roaming around ladies but it instructs men to keep a proper strict control over the ladies of the house. If a lady does not perform house jobs even after being physically fit and compels her mother-in-law to do it then the husband to that lady is impotent. If a lady unnecessarily harasses and humiliates to her daughter-in-law then the son of that lady is impotent. If anyone of the family members asks for more dowry from a married lady and obliges her to bring money from her father then husband to that lady is impotent, if such verbal consent for giving money is not done by the parents of the bride before marriage. Mostly it is found that the normal house works of an unmarried man are done by his mother or unmarried sisters now if this situation sustains even after his marriage then it would-be more better to take the services of a prostitute for sexual pleasure instead of getting married. Young ladies should comprehend that they are going to the house of their husbands not only for achieving sexual pleasure or the happiness of married life instead they are entering in the married life by leaving their abandoned and flickering nature behind to sincerely perform family duties. They have to prove themselves by performing family duties perfectly because this is the justice they do for their existence. Almost mothers want to marry their daughters so as to get rid from them. Even a lady, who is said to be performing the whole household job in her unmarried life, becomes tired and sick when she has to do even a part of that in her married life. In the society, a man marries with the intentions that he will have his own wife who will assist her in living a smooth life and give birth to his children. If even after marrying a homely lady, a man has to perform official job as well as house jobs and his family members are humiliated by his wife then what was the intention of marriage? If a man remains quiet even after seeing all this happening in his family then he is an impotent. No lady is willing to serve and respect in-laws and a man has full right to punish his wife if she does not follow the codes of the family. Most of the married ladies humiliate and misbehave with in-laws to harass their husbands and they are often succeeded in this. Somewhere the same technique, that ladies apply to harass their husbands, is adopted by the husbands to improve their wicked wives then it is seen to be effective. Such husbands say nothing to their quarrelsome nature wicked wives and they just go to their parents' house and publicly menace or socially harass them." Another lady said, "Almost ladies pretend performing childish nature. As a child is punished by his parents if he commits something immoral similarly a lady should be punished if she is iniquitous or performs mischievous activities. In India, if a mother beats her child for his mistakes and the underage child goes to police station then no one hears him and this has happened in some matters in the country. Then why the judiciary is eager to hear or take favor of married ladies against their husbands and in-laws. My neighbor's wife, who did love marriage, is a good lady but very aggressive by nature and when she becomes aggressive, she does not see anything. Once she had a quarrel with her aged mother-in-law then she went to nearest police station and complained against her mother-in-law. Her husband got a call in his office from his in-laws house that wife's father is serious so he went immediately to other city where the parents of the wife live with the intention that wife will be unnecessary bothered if she will come to know about her father's ill health. When the wife came back from office, she was told by me that there was a telephonic call from her parent's house that her father is serious. Lady moved to her father's place immediately with the intention that husband will manage the things when he will come back. Now both of them went from the city and when police came to their residence for investigating about the complaint filed by the wife, they got a doubt that wife has been killed by husband and in-laws and husband has abscond. They arrested the aged parents. Unfortunately the father of the lady died hence they both took three days to come back. As the couple did the love marriage hence aged parents were not having any information about the parents of their daughter-in-law. Both of the aged parents spend three days in the lock-up where the local police made their life hell. When the couple came back then they were released."

One incident of city *Lucknow* is of very importance to mention here. A man told that he was living in his house since past twenty years. His neighbor was a lean widow lady having a son. The lady was of very peaceful temperament and he never saw her speaking loudly or abusing anyone.

Her son was also of very decent nature. She married her son and after few months of that, she was heard abusing and shouting on her daughter-in-law. The daughter-in-law was also seemed to be very polite. Man was shocked that why that old lady abuses her daughter-in-law while the daughter-in-law's voice was never heard. As he was familiar with the old lady since a long time hence he was wondering why she has abruptly been arrogant. There was a big wall in between his house and the neighbor's house. He brought a ladder and once when old lady was loudly abusing her daughter-in-law, he took the help of ladder to find what exactly is happening there. He was shocked to watch that the aged widow was sitting in a corner and abusing to her daughter-in-law while the daughter-in-law was standing in the shade of tree making the lower part entirely nude and pretending as masturbating through a brinjal and was irritating the old lady by making indecent gestures. As the boundary of the neighbor's house was sufficiently high hence no one from the outside could view the actual situation.

A lady, knitting the warp and woof of intrigues, jealousy, aversion, strife and vengeance throughout her life, finds herself incapable at the old age. She has lived her life as a creator. Because of possessing the quality of giving birth to human, she considers herself equivalent to God. She becomes shocked when she is forcefully made away by nature from the whirlpool of her self-made hallucination, at the old age. The lord of death is eager to embrace her but she is not prepared for death. She wants her adolescence back so that she may again get a chance to fulfill her ever unsatisfied cravings. When she desires for death while her extreme physical incapability or sickness, she does not die. God has to make her realized forcefully about the sins, she committed in her lifetime because she never confesses and hence is never ready for repent. It is seen that the last phase of the age is more painful in the case of ladies in comparison to gents and hence they die after bearing pain or longtime sickness. After death, their body is kept on the earth. Their body, giving birth to human from *Yoni*, gets intermingled in the soil to achieve another *Yoni* through a *Yoni*.

Stages of Women's Life

Unmarried Lady

The continuous changes taking place in the body of a girl make her suitable for marriage till she approaches age group of eighteen years. If we consider the opinion of the society then the proper age of a girl to get married is eighteen to twenty-four. After this age group, physical decay starts taking place in her though such symptoms are not easily seen up to age group of twenty-eight to thirty in unmarried ladies. If ladies are health and beauty conscious and devote a sufficient time in physical exercise or stretching then their physical decay is not visible up to the age group of thirty-six. Unmarried ladies find the mannish qualities arousing in them after the age group of twenty-six years. The unmarried ladies who seldom perform sexual relations find their physical beauty maintained and even enhanced but they face gradual internal physical decay. If an unmarried young lady is continuously involved in illicit sexual relations then the decay in her physical beauty can be seen after few years but again this all depends on her life style. A girl of the age group of thirteen to twenty-two possesses rapid increment in the size of breasts when her breasts are regularly pressed by a man. Similarly, deformation of the shape of breasts or increasing the size of breasts unsymmetrical indicates that the lady is allowing such breast massaging to be done to her by men. Again if in a girl of eighteen to twenty-six, with completely developed breasts, the looseness or shapelessness or improper increment in the size of breasts is seen then it indicates that lady is performing sexual plays including pressing of her breasts regularly. The unmarried ladies, performing abortions, lose the tightness of their breasts from the base while the upper tips remain as tight as they were earlier. It is seen that unmarried ladies with lean and figureless body achieve attractive appearance when they perform sexual courses and such changes are so drastic that it becomes difficult to identify them. Again it can be seen that an unattractive unmarried lady, who does not keep sexual relations, when marries, becomes more beautiful and attractive. The decay of the women's internal energy through the sexual plays brings beauty and attractiveness in them for the initial years only. At present, mostly ladies marry at the age group of twenty-two to thirty though somewhere this crosses the limit of thirty-four to thirty-five years. Ladies involved in some business or jobs often marry late. The exceptions to this are seen in the ladies who perform love marriage. The ladies involved in the professions like acting, modeling, bar dancing or air hostesses etc, where the beauty and figure of them are the essential and qualifying qualities, marry late because of the fear that they may lose their beauty if they marry and have regular copulations. Very ugly or handicapped ladies, who are without virtues, are not able to get married unless their parents are having sufficient money to purchase grooms. In western countries, almost women prefer late marriage and enjoy sexually before marriage.

The ladies, who willingly do not marry in whole of their life, live an unrestrained sexual life like married ladies of flickering nature. The difference between their spontaneity is that married ladies live freely but hide their capriciousness so as to avoid the work load on them and blame to their in-laws for keeping restrictions on their freedom while unmarried ladies do not have such option to speak lies. Unmarried ladies deny the existence of men's society because they are not bound to live with a man as their husband but unfortunately married ladies living with their husbands also never let the rule of their men to be imposed upon them. Unmarried ladies do not need men for the assistance of any kind because whenever they feel sexual craving, they fulfill it by keeping illicit sexual relations secretly. Whenever they perform sexual courses with men, they never lie below men and always perform sexual plays sitting or laying upon men. They prefer their sex partners to suck their breasts like an infant and this desire is also seen in the married ladies elder to their husbands. The unmarried ladies of the age group of above thirty-five years seldom disrobe themselves entirely while performing sexual plays. They often look and consider married ladies with hatred views and merciful glance because as per them married ladies have everything of their husbands and nothing their own. Almost of them regularly perform illicit sexual plays and consider married ladies to be concubines of their husbands.

It is found in the survey that the count of ladies who are willingly not performing marriage is very less in comparison to those ladies who are unmarried because of their ugly or unattractive appearance, physical inability, suffering from incurable disease and financial incapability. It is very unfortunate that almost good looking or rich girls perform no special effort in their life till their marriage and involve themselves in illicit sexual relations then suddenly one day, princes of their dreams come to marry them or such princes are purchased for them by their rich parents while the girls who are unattractive and penniless, remain unmarried or could marry after a long struggle done by their parents even when they are worthy and morally high. Some parents make delay in marrying their daughters and hence such ladies never get a man equivalent of their age group while somewhere parents deny or ignore the marriage proposals coming for their daughters to seek better groom and hence gradually the girls become overage. Almost unmarried ladies, after the age group of thirty-eight, only give their consent for marriage when they are unemployed or are a burden on their aged parents or are unable to fulfill their sexual craving. Again such working unmarried ladies involved in illicit sexual relations, consider marriage to be useless and baseless. As mentioned above, the ratio of ladies, who could not marry because of ugly features or some physical disorders, is very high in comparison to the girls who willingly do not marry. Wherever the girls could not marry because of some problem or lack of worthy groom, a kind of arrogance or roughness starts appearing in their behavior. This happens only with the unmarried girls who maintain their virginity. They often compare themselves with the wives of their elder and younger brothers, who are younger to them and hence get depressed. This situation rarely happens with the guys who are unmarried till the age group of thirty-six years while after that; a kind of frustration can be seen in their behavior. When a boy reaches the age of marriage, his parents seeking him roaming here and there in the evening hours, say that he should get married then only he will become stable while for a girl in the same situations, they say that she should get married because she has reached the age of marriage. That is why almost parents can be seen saying to their marriageable daughters," Whatever are your desires or ambitions, fulfill that in your husband's premises." Or "If you are desirous to study more then do it after marriage."

Unmarried homely ladies, who are financially capable, involve themselves in the social activities by joining some organizations. They prefer to join social or self service organizations, women organizations or some kind of teaching career. Teaching and nursing are considered to be best options for them which provide them money as well as make them busy hence almost of aged unmarried ladies are found in teaching profession or nursing profession. Wherever they work, they always follow the strict discipline and never let others to break social or official laws. Such ladies, who are in actual virgin, are very strict and indecency in their behavior is never seen. In contrary to this, the unmarried ladies, who are involved in sexual relations, are very practical and an indecency can always be seen in their behavior. Virgin unmarried ladies are very aware for the cleanness and they sometimes appear to be mentally disturbed like widows showing the excessive consciousness for the physical neatness. Such unmarried ladies pretend to be very idealistic and are of extreme despotic nature.

Unmarried chaste ladies working in schools or educational institutes are often found financially helping poor girls. If a teacher is absent then they come to teach the students of that batch for that period. Whenever they find students sitting idle, they start teaching them so as to utilize their precious time. They seldom found making amusements among students and colleagues. Students fear from such teachers or principles and follow the codes of discipline in their presence. Such unmarried lady teachers of the girls' colleges tell their students the ill attitude and thoughts of men and often warn them to be aloof of even with the shade of young guys. They become offensive when someone interrupts them while speaking or opposes their opinions. They give importance only to unmarried ladies elder to them, senior ranked ladies and widows. Again such despotic natured unmarried female teachers never tolerate interference of the parents of their students in their way of teaching. They are often very punctual of the time and are desirous to give a proper shape and schedule to their life.

The almost unmarried ladies affiliated to medical services as nurses are very lustful and licentious by nature. Such unmarried nurses perform illicit sexual relations or harlotry on a very large scale. A big range of such nurses perform sexual debauchment just for the sake of fulfilling their sexual cravings thereby not taking money while the rest earn from illicit sexual relations. They are deprived of the dignity of motherhood and social possessions as well as of the rights of a wife even after keeping sexual unions. Hence they are neither a wife nor a socially accepted prostitute.

They are nun or nurse in the opinion of the society which in fact they aren't because of their regular involvement in illicit sexual relations. They have to prove and justify themselves to be a nurse or nun while the codes and morals of such dignified status are not followed by them since a long period by performing harlotry. To pretend to be normal with such uncertainty in thoughts, can be done by a lady only. Such behavioral contradiction brings cruelty, mercilessness and insensitivity in them for their profession and this is very essential for them for their so called performance of social service. This is the reason that the nursing profession is meant for ladies. They are ever ready to perform any kind of disloyalty to their profession by taking bribes or because of the greed of achieving sexual pleasure. They are fully involved in the illegal activities performed in nursing homes, maternity homes, private hospitals or government hospitals. It is found in a survey that nursing is the profession where more than ninety-nine percent ladies are sexually corrupt. When three hundred young and physically capable middle aged nurses were approached in a survey for their sexual services then all of them gave their consent for such relations. Two hundred and twenty-one of them became easily ready for sexual courses just by proposals while twenty-six of them became ready when they are provided some gift or dinner and rest of the fifty-three became readily managed when they are provided money.

Some of unmarried middle aged ladies like childless widows give shelter to many dogs in their residences. They nourish them as if they are human beings. Sometimes the count of dogs tamed by them becomes very high and it becomes problematic for the neighbors. Some of them perform all kind of sexual experiments on these animals. They perform unnatural sex with dogs and make male and female dog to perform copulation so as to enjoy looking this. They wrap the nails and mouth of a bitch by a cloth and perform her masturbation by an object of the size of penis. They perform oral sex with dogs and make several dogs to have sex with a single bitch continuously by binding that bitch by a rope. They feel extreme pleasure when they see blood coming out from the vagina of bitch. They put chilly powder and sprit in the vaginal route of bitches. They are not inhuman for dogs but they are cruel to bitches. They tie the mouth and nails of a dog before performing unnatural sex with him so that he may not bite or scratch them. They often pick the penis of small boys, coming to their home for candies offered by them, and suck their penis meantime they put their hands on their vagina. Aged men with homosexual feelings can be seen doing the same act with children. Lustful unmarried ladies can not make sexual relations because they are socially not permitted hence whatever they do to satisfy their sexual desire, is either immoral or very hatred, disgusting and inhuman. Publicly they pretend to be very neutral and unaffected towards the sexual attraction for men because this is an obligation imposed on them by the society hence gradually such harshness becomes a part of their behavior. They consider the worth of men only up to the sexual satisfaction and hence they never give importance to them more than pet dogs.

Widow Lady

A lady is said to be a widow when her husband dies. Widowhood is a kind of curse for the life of a lady. The sad demise of a man breaks the ambitions of his wife into pieces. For the ladies residing in village areas, backward areas or remote areas, the widowhood diminishes all the possibilities in the life. When a married lady becomes widow, her all desires and expectations for the future get ruined. It is seen that a widow lady becomes mentally strong and almost any kind of grief does not make her easily bothered. The rest of the life of widows depends upon the background of the families they belong to and the duration after marriage when they become widow. On the basis of the circumstances and situations in which a lady becomes widow, we can classify the widows in the following categories:-

If the parents of a girl and a guy have done the betrothal and the would-be husband dies after engagement but before marriage then such kind of a girl is considered to be a widow of the first kind. Though as per the laws and judiciary, such a girl is not considered to be a widow but still as per the religion, she is considered to be a widow. Again the Hindu society never considers her as a widow but in fact in all the religions she is supposed to be unfortunate or ill-fated for her spouse. As only the betrothal has taken place hence the girl is said to be virgin. Somewhere the broad minded and generous parents of the demised boy marry their younger son with the same girl but such instances are seldom found. Somewhere backward society scolds such lady by calling her as "a witch eager to slay the husband" and orthodox families avoid marrying their son with such a lady. Lady becomes uncertain of what to do, when she comes to know about the death of her would-be husband. She becomes distressed when the would-be husband dies, with whom she imagined a lot about future married life. Her parents become sad but are thankful to God that this happened before marriage. As some time pasts, she is married somewhere else. Very rare of such widows do not marry in future. Virgin child widows, who do not remarry, are also considered in this category. Such examples are seldom seen where the child widows do not remarry and obviously are virgin till the death of their husbands.

Ladies whose husbands die after marriage and before three years span from the marriage, are considered to be the widows of the second category. Such widows, who are childless, often remarry with some widower or aged unmarried men or with divorced men. They give preference to childless widowers or divorcees. If such widows have their own children then they experience problems in remarrying but again for remarriage they give preference to childless men. Very few widows of this age group do not remarry and spend whole of their life with their children. Almost of widows of this category, who do not remarry for the sake of the welfare of their children, experience negligence and humiliation by their children when they are married or grownup.

We can keep those widows in the third category whose husbands die after three years and before eighteen years of the marriage. Some of such widows remarry with some widower and some prefer to live alone with their children. The percentage of involvement in illicit sexual relations is found to be highest in such widows and more than ninety-eight percent of them, who do not remarry, are involved in illicit sexual relations. Their daughters are also found to be involved in such relations and are presumptuous and abrasive in nature while sons are decent and matriarchal. If the sons have achieved the age of understanding right or wrong and are of arrogant nature during the life time of their fathers then they become problematic and cause distress to mothers when father dies.

Ladies, who become widow after the eighteen years and before fifty years of the marriage, are found remarrying only when they are intellectual or are very innocent. They spend rest of their life with their children and we can count them in the fourth category of widows. If they were dominating over their husbands in their life time then they seldom get depressed after the death of husbands and provide courage to their children for not being distressed. They are internally powerful and hence never get easily diverted when they face troubles. If they have lived their married life immorally by performing adultery and are of arrogant nature then the demise of their husbands hardly affect them.

Ladies, who become widow after the fifty years from their marriage, are considered in the fifth category. Such widows seldom remarry. They become very normal on the sad demise of their husbands and if they have ruled their family in past then they prefer to live alone instead of living with children. The widows, who are of simple and decent nature, spend their rest of the life with their children but unfortunately their last phase of life is full of distress and pain given to them by their own children.

The widows belonging to first category are often child widows. Such widows are seldom seen in the society because the concept of child marriage is limited to very interior villages only and has been almost finished. Yet few aged widows can be seen who were married when they were child. Almost of such ladies not marrying again are affiliated to some society or live under the shelter of some male relatives and provide them their sexual services hence live a life of concubine of them. Though the ambitions of such widows are limited because of being widow at the very initial period of the life still they are found to be very shrewd and always spreading dirty politics in the family matters. If the widows belonging to the second and third categories do not remarry even after being childless then the basic cause behind this is their desire for living an obligations free life or the unavailability of suitable men. If they are having children then they are seen marrying with widowers or divorced or aged unmarried men. Ladies, whose husbands are in government job, almost get the job at some lower rank in the same department on the demise of their husbands. Such widows seldom remarry and all of them, who do not remarry, can be seen involved in harlotry for the sake of sexual pleasure or earning more money. Again such widows remarry if they have no other way to earn living but still most of them prefer prostitution instead of remarrying. If they have daughters then they too get involved in making illicit sexual relations. Some of such widows motivate and compel their young daughters to perform prostitution. Again even after having the possibilities of earning by making efforts, they prefer the shortest route of harlotry to earn money. The widows of fourth and fifth categories are found involved in illicit sexual relations when they are excessively lustful. They often keep sexual relations with their nearby relatives. They are found keeping young girls in their house as paying guests and providing customers for them for sexual plays. This is the safe most way of earning and they take their commission from such young girls for providing a permanent and safe place for prostitution. They work in such an efficient way that no body can even guess that they are running a kind of brothel in their residences.

There is no meaning of being widow for a wife to a rich man because she never experiences financial problems and becomes free to live her life without any hindrances. It is seen in financially very high and renowned families that marriage is a kind of ostentation for ladies and the intention of marriage for them is limited to experience pleasure and to pretend themselves as a faithful married lady in the society hence such ladies are never affected by the death of their husbands. In very low class and low class families, almost women are involved in harlotry to earn money or sexual pleasure even when their husbands are alive hence the demise of the husbands never bothers them. The opinion kept by them on the demise of their husbands is that a family member died whom they were authorized to humiliate and harass. All of such widows, who do not remarry, perform harlotry irrespective of their financial status.

In some very orthodox families of interior rural areas, widows are prohibited to go outside. Non-vegetarian edible items, brinjal, jack fruit and other spicy items are banned for them. Somewhere a widow is not allowed to eat rice, pulses and beans. She has to wear white *Sari* and make her appearance to be unattractive if she is living with her highly orthodox in-laws. Jewelries and other make-up items are restricted for her to use. She has to break or remove the symbols of a married lady like bangles, vermillion, necklace and reddish wearing. Her presence in the traditional religious prayers or in the rituals, where deities are summoned by chanting spiritual verses, is considered to be strictly prohibited because she is considered being cursed and misfortunate. Just married ladies are kept away from even her shade because it is assumed that she will bring distress in the life of brides by making their husbands cursed to die. Somewhere she is prohibited to visit marriage ceremonies and her presence in the group is only limited to mourn or cry on the demise of some relative. Married ladies performing the fast and obligations of the festival *KarvaChauth* to enhance the age of their husbands, consider her presence on the festival day as a danger on their chastity as well as on the lives of their husbands and avoid to have a look even of her face. She is not allowed to sit together with other members of the family. Her rights of living the life are finished with the death of husband and she can not make amusements or smile. Almost ladies of the family and neighbor consider her as a witch bringing misfortune to kill the husband. She has to perform her daily routine by rising early in the morning so that she may not become hindrance in the daily routine of other members. It is said to be an awful omen for the day to see her face early in the morning. Her real married female relatives do not allow their husbands to take any edible item given by her. She has a lot of restrictions on entering in kitchen and prayer room. Somewhere young widows are bound to live like a corpse with no desires and feelings. Such forty widows were surveyed to get the truth then during very secret conversations; they told that the restrictions are kept upon them by ladies not by men of the family. One of such young widow said that she is considered to be hatred by married ladies because they are frightened with her. She said that the ladies keep the view that widows are sexually ever unsatisfied and are eager to sexually corrupt men hence married ladies are frightened from widows thinking that their husbands or young sons might get sexually allured by them. She said that her mother-in-law fears that she will sexually molest young brothers-in-law or aged father-in-law. Real sisters fear that widow sister might sexually divert their husbands. Such opinion for a widow can be seen everywhere. A widow, who was quite literate, said that women belonging to women societies often say that they will not let a widow get harassed by men. Those practically unaware and illiterate ladies don't know that widows are harassed in very few cases, basically belonging to interior villages, and at present, such cases rarely happen in the society. Now wherever widows are humiliated or harassed and are bound to live in hell like situations is in fact because of other ladies not by gents. Widows either get sexual pleasure, financial support, mercy and moral support or negligence from men. Men never harass widows and in fact they support widows either socially or financially or sexually. When a familiar lady affiliated to a women organization was asked about this then she said that they have to pretend to be in favor of widows showing them to be humiliated by men. She said that Indian culture is quite different from other countries and here actually the system runs on the myths and rumors. Hence they have to highlight such fake instances to draw the attention of the society towards their organization. She said that she found her young son number of times conversing with a widow residing in the adjacent colony. She warned her son not to be in touch of that widow but when she again saw her son doing the same, she went to the house of that widow. The widow was living alone there and was popular among lustful men for providing sexual services. She said that she warned that widow that if she will find her next time conversing with her son, she will bind her to leave the colony by blaming her for prostitution. She confessed that at present almost all of the widows, who are physically attractive or are physically able to perform sexual courses, are involved in illicit sexual relations.

A widow seems to be very conscious in the society, protecting herself from the indecent glances and touches of men. The lustful men, aware with her widowhood, look her with peculiar intention. If she is beautiful with attractive figure then such men desire to get her sexual services. Licentious men want to approach her for sexual plays because they know that widows are easy to lay for sexual pleasure and are safe. To perform sexual course with a widow is safe because her husband is not an obstacle in this and she can not pretend of losing her virginity. Sexual experiences of married life protect her being pregnant as she knows about the several precautions taken for not carrying undesired child in her womb. When lustful and sexually corrupt men perform sexual union with prostitutes, they use condoms to ensure a kind of safety from sexually transmitted disease. Such precaution of using condoms brings a decrement in the extreme of sexual pleasure but it is not necessary to use while performing sexual course with a widow because a man assumes that a widow had sexual relations with her husband only and hence he is the only one except her demised husband who is having the opportunity to intercourse with her. Again every man keeping sexual relations with a widow keeps the opinion that he is the only one performing sexual plays with that widow.

She wears a veil of sincerity and strictness on her face while visiting some place where majority of men reside. If such face expressions and gestures are shown by an unmarried or married lady then men become frightened from her to perform something indecent but such expressions are obvious in case of widows hence familiar men never afraid of them. Lustful men give their consolations and assure them for not being worried, just for the sake of achieving proximity of their nude body in future. If a widow is living alone with her children in the city then such men, which mostly includes of her demised husband's colleagues, regularly visit her and help her financially. Men of morals and ethics avoid visiting to widows personally because of the fear of the opinion of the society but help them if they ask. A widow lady is quite aware with the intentions of the men coming to visit her personally. She is also eager to trap, like a parasite creeping plant, to the nearest powerful man to get the support of him. She crookedly applies her discretion to find the best one and hence offers her emotions and sexual services to all of them personally. She seeks a man who can fulfill her all financial desires because she knows that she can get the sexual pleasure anytime from number of men. Unfortunately such financially strong men eager to get her proximity are married hence either she lives like a concubine of one of such rich man and ruins the family life of his wife or keeps sexual relations with number of such men and live a luxurious life by financially exploiting every such man by making each of them believe that she is only available to him.

Some of widows possess stubbornness in performing responsibilities and hence a kind of harshness can be seen in their behavior. Such widows are entirely dedicated for their duties and become introvert after the demise of their husbands. Their some properties abruptly change when they face the shocking incident of their husband's death. They hate of the company of men and also dislike married ladies or mothers even when they too are having their own children. Such widows normally do not perform harlotry and if they keep illicit sexual relations then they do it very secretly with renowned men of the society only. They can be seen working as the principle of some schools or colleges. As working at the post of principle of some school, they often can be seen being of very autocratic nature making their own rules and strictly compelling students and teachers to follow those rules. They even treat the parents of the students roughly and straightforwardly and are unkind for female students in comparison to male students. Again such widows can be seen working as principles of schools or colleges based on so called convent culture. Some of them willing for sexual pleasure when find themselves restricted by the society, get helpless and depressed and ultimately the consequences of their frustration is faced by the girls of the schools. When such principles were interviewed then they said that if they do not keep strict restrictions specially on the girls then the environment or atmosphere of the schools will get entirely demolished because as per their long experience of working as head teacher, the girls are more arrogant, shameless, wicked and are directly or indirectly responsible for all the ill activities happening in the schools. Lustful widow teachers can be seen making small boys nude as a punishment in front of their whole classmates. A widow lady in the form of a teacher relinquishes her sexual frustration by making a man in the form of a small boy nude publicly on his mistakes. They touch penis of small guys and perform other disgusting ways to calm down their sexual anguish. The same act done with a small girl by her widow teacher is rarely seen because least widows possess homosexual tendencies. It is noticeable that such act of making a boy child or a girl child disrobed in the classroom is never performed by a male teacher. It is found in a survey that in almost schools, widow or unmarried teachers perform such act of making a male child nude. Up to which extent, gender biasing is there in the society can be understood by this that as per surveys, more than five thousand small guys are made nude in the schools in front of their male and female colleagues every day while hardly any female child faces the same situations. Again such acts are always done by female teachers and never seen done by some male teacher. When a small girl is made nude by her female teacher in a school then the parents of that girl, society and media raise their voice against this but never any objection is raised when thousands of small boys are made entirely naked by female teachers in front of the whole class. Again lots of incidents can be seen where a male teacher punishes his students on some wrongdoing. In almost of such matters, boys are punished while if a girl is punished by teacher then her parents make a scene by blaming that teacher. Somewhere such stupid and senseless parents visit to school with some media-people to threaten the concerned teacher. It is found that in all of such matters, girls are either very egoistic or are keeping one-sided sexual infatuation with such male teachers. Almost of such girls falsely blame their male teachers when they seek themselves unable to draw their attention towards them. Sincere girls immediately inform their parents if they are indecently behaved or touched by male teachers but they never complain when they are punished on their mistakes like other students.

Widows belonging to all communities or categories perform some job to earn when their husbands die. If the late husband was in government job then often she is also provided a job in the same department. If her husband was a businessman then she takes the responsibilities to run the business in her hands. If the husband was in some private job then she feels more trouble and manages some other way to earn as per her qualification. If she is already working in some department or taking active participation in husband's business then she does not have to worry about earnings after the death of husband. It is assumed that widows adopt harlotry for earning money if they are having problem to earn by some job, not financially assisted by other members of the family and are not having property left by husbands especially on their names. In fact, it is found in surveys that more than seventy-eight percent widows, who perform illicit sexual courses, do this even when they are financially capable and are having other legal ways of earning the livings. Hence most of the widows are indulged in illicit sexual relations willingly without having any kind of pressure including financial crisis. If a widow remarries then she is seldom found performing adultery perhaps because now she has her own man to fulfill her sexual desires. It is also found in surveys that ladies performing adultery in their married life when experience widowhood and remarry then more than seventy-two percent of them quit from such adultery though such ladies remarry in very rare instances. Widows are mostly failures in giving proper guidance to their children if they have only daughters. If they do not marry their daughters in the early stage then they too get involved in illicit sexual plays. Again all widows, having beautiful looking and attractive physical standards, seen involved in making sexual relations. The ladies visiting to gynecologists or maternity homes for going through an abortion are widows or unmarried and very less percent of them is of married ladies. The ladies who insist or motivate or provoke their daughters for harlotry are widows or prostitutes or extremely corrupt married ladies and their percentage is highest in widow ladies. It is also seen that some wealthy client of such a lady, whom with she keeps illicit sexual relations, in future keeps sexual relations with her daughters too. Again ninety-eight percent of the widows of the age group of twenty-one to forty-five are found involved in illicit sexual relations. The habits of conversing indecently and abusing while sexual plays are more found in widows in comparison to prostitutes. In a survey, almost widows expressed their interest in living the life by performing harlotry instead of remarrying.

The mothers of young guys strictly prohibit their sons making any kind of conversation or affinity with widows. Men almost behave normally with a widow but ladies always keep a hatred view for her. Widows are considered to be very expertise in sexual plays hence no lady gives her permission to her young unmarried son for marrying with a widow. These kinds of views of mothers in context of widows have nothing to do with the welfare of their sons because in fact they just seek their own benefit. A mother knows that if she brings an unmarried or a so called virgin girl as her daughter-in-law then that newly wedded bride, being a novice, will take time to be expertise in standing against of her while as a widow lady is already expert in sexual affairs and indecent ways usually performed by married ladies hence such bride will take no time in being prepared against her. She knows that if her son is willing to marry with a widow then he has been captured by the net of sexual delusion of that widow and as he is not listening to his mother's advice when he is unmarried then certainly after marriage, he will openly stand against her with that widow as his wife. When a father prohibits his son marrying with a widow then his intentions are quite different from the opinion of a mother and he in fact seeks only the benefit of his son. A father knows that his son is felt in infatuation and the social norms should be followed while taking a major decision like marriage. He is not against of the marriage of a widow but in fact he is against of the mismatch because he considers the codes of morality and immorality while mothers have nothing to do with morality or immorality. A father knows that in the society, almost widows are sexually corrupt hence he is frightened that might be his son has been trapped in the infatuation. A mother always considers the marriage of his unmarried young son with a widow to be an instant jeopardy on her regime in the residence.

Some widows prefer living alone in the house made by their husbands after performing the marriages of children. Mostly such situations appear with them when the children are working elsewhere. Such ladies are aware of the society and are conscious towards their responsibilities. They visit to their children occasionally or when they become sick and after spending some weeks or months they come back. In this situation, their attitude and behavior become mannish because of living alone in the society and gradually it superimposes on their personality and this can be seen while they converse or walk. They become very skeptical and always keep a view of doubt for others. They spend most of their time in reading literature, watching specially ladies based serials or episodes, movies and visiting religious assemblies. They often advise married ladies residing in their environment and menace the attitude of young girls and boys by scolding them.

The ladies, who have always ruled over their husbands, when become widow, prefer living in solitude. They never bow down or accept their errors or repent when they commit some mistakes or when they are proved to be wrong. Hence because of the fear of the probable conflicts, they prefer living in solitude. They prefer eating sweet dishes as chocolates or candies like minor children. If they live with the families of their sons then they never follow other's instructions. Their sons never retort them in an indecent manner and always respect them but they always keep an antagonism with their daughters-in-law. Such financially capable widows live with their daughter's family even after having sons only when they are blindly obeyed by the daughters and for this they often make conflicts among daughters and their in-laws.

Divorced Lady

Perhaps to maintain the harmony between male and female by letting them to follow few codes, the concept of marriage was invented. It was assumed that men and women will live together being a single entity after marriage by performing their responsibilities for each other and for their progenies.

The concept of divorce was introduced so as to allow the husband and wife in a couple to live separately from each other when some peculiar adverse circumstances arise in-between them. Divorce is a process which breaks the concepts and ideology that exist behind marriage. When a husband and wife seek it impossible to live with each other because of any reason and there are no possibilities of any kind of coordination or compromise then they are allowed to live separately by taking divorce from each other. As in the present era, neither the concepts behind marriage could be maintained nor could the ladies maintain devotion for a virtuous moral life hence the divorce came into existence in a natural visible form. Though the legal process for achieving divorce is made complicate so that a couple may think several times before performing this but in actual judiciary could not maintain the basics of marriage even by keeping complexity in the divorce process. The judiciary gave the consent for some rules and opinions considering it to be healthy for a married life but unfortunately all of such rules are now misused. Again unfortunately such right to misuse the laws and codes of conduct was limited to ladies and whenever a lady found herself incapable to motivate her husband's virtuous opinion or to suppress her in-laws, because of the strict attitude of husband, even after applying all of the distorted form of the laws, she took the shelter of divorce.

Lots of cases are disclosed in surveys where the ladies took divorce just after marriage or after some time on the ground of sexual impotency of husbands. It is a general assumption done by society regarding a childless married man divorced by his wife that he is an impotent. Some matters were sorted out where ladies lived with their husbands after marriage for one day or one week and came back to their parents' house blaming their husbands to be impotent. In fourteen of such matters where husbands were blamed by wives for impotency, wives married somewhere else and in future the so called impotent ex-husbands also got married. It is found that all of such impotent men are having children from their second wives and are living happily. When such a lady, who blamed her husband for being impotent and left him on the third day after marriage, was interviewed, said that on the first night, she came to know that her husband was impotent and this was the reason she left her husband. When she was told that her so called impotent husband was having two kids from her next marriage then she denied accepting this. When her past was scrutinized then it came to know that she was having illicit sexual relations with her aged neighbor hence she left her husband. Then why she was blaming to her ex-husband and why she did marriage when she had already decided to leave the husband. She was pressurized by the parents to marry, who were familiar with her illicit sexual relations; hence she gave her consent for marriage and left husband immediately by blaming him to be impotent because there was no way by which her parents could get the truth. One of such lady came back from the house of her husband on the second day of her marriage and blamed her husband to be impotent. As she got the blemish of divorcee hence her parents married her with a guy of low caste with the opinion that a normal guy of same caste will not be easily ready to marry with a divorcee. Meantime her ex-husband also got married with a widow lady and had children from her. When the lady blaming husband for impotency was asked the truth she denied accepting anything. Then it came to know from her neighbors that she was having sexual relations with a guy of lower community. Her parents denied marrying her with that guy then she married with the guy selected by parents and blamed him for being impotent on the very next day of the marriage. She came back to her parental home and remarried to that guy of the low cast because now parents did not make any objection as their daughter was divorcee. When she left her husband blaming him to be an impotent, his life was made hell by the society and relatives because everyone though that he was eunuch. Later he married with a widow lady because no one was agreeing to marry his daughter with a divorcee man blamed by the ex-wife for impotency. Just for the sake of illicit sexual craving and relations with some guy, the lady ruined the family life and status of a man by marrying him and then false blaming him for being impotent. When such ladies were asked that how they came to know in few days about the sexual impotency of their husbands then all of them told that their husbands were not having penis hence they come to know about this in the very first night. Perhaps they were not familiar with the exact definition and differentiation between a sexually impotent man and eunuch otherwise they would have told some other lie.

Somewhere husbands are wrong hence wives apply for divorce. In almost of such matters, wives are very short tempered and are unable to adjust in the joint families therefore they apply for divorce. Wherever the husbands are in actual wrong up to such an extent that no lady can live with them as their wife, divorces are taken in less than one percent of such matters. In almost matters of married life, the compromises are done by the husbands and rarely the voice is raised by them for divorce. Men seldom take such step even when they are assured of the involvement of their wives in adultery and are extremely distressed by the immoral behavior of their wives. The exceptions to this are only seen in Muslim community where men take divorce from their wives on very normal disputes by saying "*Talak*" multiple times but it is useless to describe this here because the divine procedure of marriage itself has no ethics or morals in Muslim community. They allow polygamy and power play of *Talak* in the real life so as to get sexual pleasure though now they are compelled by the judiciary to follow ethical conduct of their religion properly without misinterpreting. There are few instances where wives took divorce from their sadist husbands who usually burn them by cigarettes at breasts and vaginal area or perform other kind of cruelty while performing sexual plays.

A man willing to marry with a divorcee should know about the ground or reason of her taking divorce and similar precaution should be taken by a lady willing to marry with a divorced man. Grounds behind the matters of divorce happening at very high class renowned families become irrelevant because in most of such instances the ego problem makes the ground. More than eighty percent of the total divorce matters happen only because of the quick temper, immoral attitude, extramarital sexual affairs and indecent behavior of ladies.

Woman, As a Lover

The definitions as well as the meanings of the love affairs in context of the opinions of a male and a female are different. The sprouting of the love affairs happens as a peculiar feeling. If the love affairs of the ancient period, medieval period or the present are scrutinized thoroughly then it is seen that the definitions as well as the cause of such affairs have been changed. Ancient love affairs were in fact the motiveless or selfless adoration and the religious devotion was the base behind the feelings of the love. Love of the medieval period was mere sacrifice and dedications. Gradually the meaning of the love changed because of different motives becoming the inspirations behind the love. Elope of the devotion tendency and the increment of the sexual lust as well as other different malicious motives, ruined the sense of actual love. Though the actual love is considered to be free from the compulsions of the castes or religions and even now such examples of true love are seen where social boundaries become irrelevant but this happens seldom. This is assumed that there is no cause or aim or objective behind a true love and love can not be performed because it happens naturally but at the present time, the difference between naturally falling in love and performing love, made the ground of the objectives of love affairs and categorized it into different types. To illustrate different kinds of love affairs, we can classify it into different types as follows:-

The first kind of affair is in fact mutual sharing of feelings among a male and female. In this, a guy makes his feelings disclosed in front of a girl and the seed of love sprouts. They rarely perform physical touching even after regular get-togethers. They meet with each other and sit for hours without making conversations. They look at each others eyes and then bow their heads. No one bounds other and never keeps any kind of expectations because they understand each other's views without any conversations. They get emerged in thoughts while talking and it seems that they have nothing to do with the society or the materialistic world. When such lovers face any kind of restrictions by the society or their families, they commit suicide with the intention that perhaps no one will be able to restrict them in the other world. Sometimes a boy and girl living in the proximity never express their soft love feelings for each other and marry in different families in future. Though in such matters they have never kept their feelings in the knowledge of each other still this can be considered in this category of love affairs. This kind of love affair is very peculiar and as both of the male and female keep utmost emotional attraction for each other hence sometimes they seems to be mentally abnormal. In such affairs, if any of the male or female is attached with the desire of sexual attachment then he quits when seeks the over emotional attachment of the love partner. Such love-affairs are of very high grade hence are found seldom in present scenario and very rarely achieve the goal of always living together by performing marriage.

In the second category of love affairs, almost pairs are in love with the desire of marrying with each other. The male and female attached with each other are often of the same age group. They keep physical touching through kissing and embracing each other. As a girl assumes the outcome of such affairs to be marriage hence her attitude for her lover is always affected by the financial status or career of him and she desires security for herself. A sober and simple guy is always wholeheartedly devoted towards his lover but she is always attentive and practical while keeping such affairs. Guys involved in such affairs are of the opinion that sexual plays are illicit if made before marriage even with a lady with whom they are going to marry in future. Almost of such guys ruin their academic career and social life when they fall in affairs. Guys, who have completed their education or are earning, are found eager to marry with their lovers even if to accomplish this, they have to oppose or disobey their parents. It is found in a survey that thirteen percent of such affairs are reached to marriage while in the eighty percent instances, girls deny marrying. In such matters where a girl quits from the betrothal done by her, she seems to be pressurized by her parents. In actual she has never fallen in love instead she was on a deal done by her with herself that if she will find her lover capable to give her proper future security then only she will perform marriage. Very few girls, fallen in love affairs, oppose their parents to marry with their lovers struggling for career because almost of them seeks security and proper assurance. It is also seen that whenever a girl seeks her boyfriend to be an obstacle in her career or high ambitions, she kicks him. In seven percent matters, such affairs ends up when a girl insists her lover to change the religion or informs him that he has to live in her house after marriage because she is the only child of her parents or when her lover informs her that she has to live like a housewife after marriage. In contrary to this, the instances, where a girl escapes with her financially unstable lover, are either the examples of mere infatuation or are true love affairs.

When the girl and boy belong to different castes then also girl opposes her parents when they bound her to live under the restrictions of their caste because a lady has nothing to do with the religion or caste of the love partner. If she finds her parents ready for her marriage with her lover then she cleverly compels him to send his parents to her house to beseech for marriage. Again as a female, she never desires her parents to go to the residence of her lover to implore for marriage because she considers it as a dishonor of her parents. This is an indication of the false ego of her and the actuality of her so-called emotional attachment with her lover. The guy, who is in deep emotional love with her, bounds his parents to go to her residence to request for marriage. In this situation, the parents of the lady pretend to be unaware of the facts and give their consent unwillingly so that they may not have to give dowry. Somewhere the parents of the lady meet with the guy and give their consent when they find him suitable for their daughter. They know that the guy, trapped in the love feelings of their daughter, will accept any demand of them without putting any objections. They often just inform the parents of the guy that they have chosen him for their daughter hence decided to let them marry. They put their peculiar demands in front of the guy and pretend themselves to be helpless. Some of them say to him that he would have to live with them after marrying their daughter or would have to leave his parents thereby living with their daughter alone. If a guy denies accepting such demands then they emotionally pressurize him through their daughter. The daughter, as a lover, compels her fiancé to accept the conditions mentioned by her parents and if he denies accepting such senseless instructions then she quits from the affair. Parents present their daughter as an alluring sexual object to entice the guy felt in love with their daughter. If he accepts such absurd demands then the parents of the lady get a bridegroom without doing any efforts. Such a bridegroom always acts as per their instructions like a pet dog. The guy in love considers his rustic behavior as his utmost dedication to his lover and just informs his parents that he is going to marry with a girl. Shocked parents of him know that now they just have to perform the formalities of his marriage because almost things he has already arranged with her lover and would-be in-laws. Almost such distressed parents of young guys performing love marriages realize that they actually gave birth to a daughter in the form of their sons and hence they are just performing the *Kanyadaan* of him because after the marriage their sons are not going to care for them.

If a girl and a boy, felt in love, belong to different religions then it materializes depending upon the financial and social status of the couple. Such marriages happening in the society can be seen in the very high class families as they are least affected by the objections put by religious authorities. Such marriages among a Hindu and a Christian can be seen even in the below status families but seldom seen among the lower class or middleclass families of Muslims and Hindus. Most of the guys or girls belonging to normal Muslim families are killed by the men of their own community if they marry with a Hindu. Even a Hindu girl or boy faces lots of hurdles in marrying with a Muslim and hence almost all of such lovers move secretly to different cities to perform marriage and never come back because they know that they will be killed if caught by their community. Though inter-religion marriages are religiously forbidden but it is found in a wide survey that the true love done by a boy and girl as a lover is only seen in inter-religion love affairs.

If the parents of the lady do not give their consent for marriage then if she finds her lover financially capable to provide safe future to her, she opposes her parents and marries with him. As ladies are desirous to get everything readymade hence they never prefer choosing a struggling guy as their husband if he belongs to normal or below normal financial background. It is found in a survey that nineteen percent girls, who seek their lovers to be financially strong, go for marriage even when their parents are against of this. One percent ladies dare to marry with their lovers even when they are struggling or belong to poor financial background. Eighty percent ladies, felt in love, deny marrying because of several reasons. Somewhere parents scare their daughters that they will kill them or themselves or their lovers if they insist on marrying with their lovers and hence ladies quit from their affairs. Some parents physically punish their daughters when they come to know about the decision of love marriage taken by the daughters. In fact most of the girls quit from the affair when they seek future insecurity with their lovers. Such situations happened with the guys are horrible. Somewhere guys, when assured and insisted verbally for marriage by their lovers, apply for marriage in the court to become legally accepted husband and wife. The information is send to the parents of both sides through legal channel and a period is given to them to come to put any objections. This duration is sufficient for the parents of the lady to pressurize or convene her for not performing love marriage and hence at the day pre-decided by the judiciary, she either disappears or says in front of the legal authority that she was compelled by the lover to perform marriage. The legal authority warns the guy not to create such problems for that girl in future. As the parents to that guy have already declared in their relatives that their son is going to marry with some girl hence after getting betrayed by the girl, in future while marrying the son elsewhere, they have to assure the parents of the bride that their son is unmarried. Such difficulties never occur with the parents of the girl. Somewhere a girl puts false blames of sexual harassment or of keeping illicit sexual relations elsewhere, on her lover to break the relationship and when shocked lover tries to meet her to get the reason of such false blames put on him then the girl is made unavailable by her parents. In all of such instances where the relationship is broken by the girls, guys get shocked and take a big duration to overcome from such situations.

In the third category of love affairs, both of the male and female keep light emotional and strong physical attraction for each other. Such lovers usually perform kissing, and oral sex. Though the attitude of the ladies belonging to this category for the marriage is same as of the ladies of previous category but the guys of this category are well familiar with the technique of reaching to the goal of marriage. As per this peculiar technique, it is said that once a guy performs complete sexual course with his lover then seldom she quits from marriage. Such guys are of the opinion that one should perform copulation with his lover so that if she betrays then he will not get depressed that he could not achieve anything. Again in such affairs, if guy avoids mating then in almost of such instances, the situations become similar to the previous case. Almost mothers ask their daughters, who are in love, that whether they have kept physical relations or not. If they say no then they are motivated to marry somewhere else as per the desire of parents. If they say yes then normal parents bound them to marry with the same guy and even help them in doing so. The exceptions to this are found in renowned and rich families where some parents say to their daughters that they should forget the previous sexual relations or may continue it but should marry in a family of equivalent dignity. It is seen that a girl denies for marriage even after keeping sexual relations with the lover only when she has kept sexual relations with number of guys and is assured to get some another more eligible guy in future as her husband. Almost ladies, who have kept sexual relations in past, pretend themselves to be virgin and carry love affairs with their new lovers with the intention of marrying with them. There are uncountable examples or incidents in the society where a guy is betrayed by his lover and hence a wise guy never communicate with his lover in written and always keeps the letters of her safe with him as evidences. Such attitude of them sometimes look like they are not in love instead they are making sexual conspiracies for each other. It is found in a survey that ninety-three percent girls never write their names on the written communication done by them with their lovers for the sake of their security. They often write on the greeting cards as "It's me" or "Guess!" instead of writing their names. In contrary to this, only four percent boys take such precautions and never write their names and do the same as mentioned above.

The fourth category of love affairs is entirely based on sexual attraction or financial benefits. A lady as a lover proposes to confess her feelings to desired guy or makes an alluring environment so that the specified guy himself proposes her. The intentions of her behind such efforts done for starting love affair is either sexual attraction with the guy or strong financial status of the guy or weak financial status of her. A guy in the role of a lover also keeps either the desire of sexual course with his girl-mate or is attracted by the strong financial position of her. In these love affairs entirely based on the calculations, if some boy is affiliated with a girl because of sexual charm or infatuation then he performs sexual course with her. Somewhere girl insists him to marry when they have kept sexual relations numerous times while the lover quits as his infatuation has been faded because of keeping regular sexual relations with her but this happens only when the concerned guy is of utterly flirtatious nature. If the girl belongs to a rich family and possesses attractive features then marriage is materialized in very rare matters while in almost of such instances, the guy is kicked by her or by her parents. Again if the lady belongs to poor family in comparison to the family of her lover then such affair is almost successful and accomplishes the goal of marriage. If she is financially stronger in comparison to her lover then their marriage materializes only when she is of normal or unattractive features and the lover is attached with her with the intention of achieving financial assistance of her parents. If the girl is financially poor then she pressurizes her lover for marriage when she becomes pregnant. In almost of such instances, girls are often found telling lies about their pregnancies to threaten their lovers in order to make a psychological pressure on them. All of such marriages are like an invisible contract or a whole-life compromise. If any of them is attracted because of the strong financial status of the other one then after marriage the one belonging to poor financial status is always seen involved in making illicit sexual extra-marital relations.

The selection criteria of the rich and renowned ladies and gents regarding their life partners can be easily visualized by some facts. Almost of the ladies, who are financially established and are of beautiful looking, never marry with guys belonging to financially low class status. No heroines of the film industry or no world famed female player or no lady with fame can be seen marrying with a financially poor man. All of such ladies either marry with very high class businessmen or some other renowned men. In contrary to this, almost renowned players or heroes of the film industry or other high class popular men belonging to any field prefer marrying with the simple low profiled girls belonging to financially normal families. They all know the truth about the pre-marriage sexual lives of the ladies belonging to glamorous high profile society. Almost all of the ladies of the high society are involved in social, moral and physical harlotry. Wherever such renowned men are found marrying with their equivalent high profiled ladies then this is because those men are already merged in the marsh of immorality or they are under family pressure or they belong to filthy rich and renowned families and hence they have to maintain the dignity of the family or they desire for the ladies affiliated in the same fields in which they themselves are or they are least bothered about the activities and personal lives of their would-be wives because of their utter busy schedule. Again men desiring for working ladies as their wives are either morally impotent or are financially not sufficiently strong or belong to very high society. Exceptions to this are only seen in men who are familiar with the temperament of ladies and know that to prohibit the release of internal energy of ladies in family conflicts, the only way is sending them outside for office work.

A lady involved in the love affairs of first or second category normally seeks the image of her father in her lover. If as a daughter she is impressed by her father then she gets overwhelmed when she finds the good as well as the bad qualities of her father in her lover. If she finds the rule of her mother in the residence and her father is of indolent nature and possesses indecent attitude then she hates with the guys of the temperament of her father. She never wants to keep any emotional relations with such guys but she always keeps a desire to sexually humiliate them. If she is positively influenced by her father and her father lives in strict discipline then also she gets impressed with the men of the nature of her father. In this situation if she finds her father smoking cigarettes or taking alcohol then she considers such bad habits in her lover as his qualities. She is always desirous to reside with her father in the proximity of her lover hence she seeks dual identities in her lover. She asks for small demands from her lover considering him as her father and thus behaves like a child while seeks moral as well as sexual satisfaction, mental peace, assurance and security from him considering him as a lover.

In other categories of love affairs, a lady performs deep scrutiny of the guy who proposes her by confessing about his soft feelings for her. Almost ladies have ability to make accurate assessments of the guys living in their surroundings and they know that which of them may confess in front of them and in fact they have already decided that with whom they will carry the love affair. The opinion or the way of thinking of a male and a female regarding the opposite sex is entirely different. If in the mob of guys and girls of an institute or college or society or office, a guy is emotionally attracted towards a girl then he can never behave normally in front of her while he behaves very normally with other girls. Such uneasiness or hesitation of him for a specific girl gives birth to love feelings in him for her. A lady chooses many guys and always pretends in front of them instead of showing actual behavior. Again such pseudo behavior for the opposite sex becomes the cause of love for them in her. Now if any of the guys selected by the lady confesses in front of her then she keenly observes the probable profit and loss happening in the future and gives her silent consent if seeks herself to be safe and secure with him. Again it is seen that if a lady likes some guy then she never confesses herself instead she makes an alluring snare in such a way that the guy trapped in that himself comes to propose her. She gets affronted if she has to propose someone while she is overwhelmed when proposed by some guy because it satisfies her ego. Every lady desires her beloved guy sitting on knees and asking for her consent for love affair. She always wants to reserve the rights of giving her consent or refusal with her so as to be in safe mode. She considers the love affairs as a game where she is the organizer as well as umpire even when she is also a contestant in the game. When the love affair starts and she becomes happy with it then it goes smoothly while the moment she feels inconvenient or bore or insecure, she quits making herself comfortable with some other guy. When numerous breaking of the affairs were scrutinized, it is found that almost the grounds for separation are prepared by the girls and the step of quitting from affairs is taken by them. Such a lady, when performs the sorrowful ending of the love affair, makes her lover distressed while she remains very normal and shrewdly blames the lover by telling him the numerous shortcomings of him being the ground of the separation. Hence she makes him realized that he was only responsible for such breaking and she was just tolerating him since such long duration. The very next day, she starts searching other boyfriend as a replacement of the previous one. Almost ladies make breakups in the love affairs only when they have already searched the new would-be lovers in their conscious or subconscious mind. Smart guys usually tell stories about their never happened previous affairs in front of desired girls and pretend to be emotional. They say that they were betrayed by their ex-lovers whom with they were in deep love and even still love them. This technique is almost successful for emotionally trapping girls in love affairs. In fact, girls become jealous with the so called ex-lovers of such guys and hence become eager to prove themselves to be more worthy and faithful lover for them.

Actually for a love affair to be successful, it is essential that it should not sustain for very long period. The duration of a love affair should be maximum one to three years and within that period, the girl and the boy should marry with each other. When an affair runs for long period then the relation gets rotted and stinking. Often girls get saturated from longstanding love affairs and try to quit but they control over their flickering tendency because of the dedication of concerned lovers. Still after certain period, depending on their endurance, they quit. Sometimes it seems that they are just bearing the relation unwillingly. The same situations appear with the men, who are married with ill natured ladies, few years after the marriage but they have no option of quitting hence they live their married lives with lots of compromises.

Girls belonging to lower middleclass or lower class families often sexually entice the guys for the sake of earning money to accomplish a luxurious life. They often ask for precious garments, edible items, jewelries, gifts and money from their boyfriends. Their cellular phone bills and other expenses are managed by their lovers. All of such girls prefer making complete sexual course with their lovers because they pretend being in emotional love hence they provide their sexual services to achieve maximum financial benefits from their boyfriends. Keeping sexual relations with the boyfriends is very normal for such girls because they keep the opinion that maintaining the virginity is useless while losing the virginity is profitable. Any man can get the close proximity and so called love of such ladies by just providing some gifts to them and by praising them extravagantly. If a guy becomes emotional and insists his lover for marriage then she quits. Again she becomes busy in managing some other guy to let him fall in love with her. This sequence of changing boyfriends sustains for long. Few of such girls do not make complete sexual course with the lovers while all of them perform other sexual plays like oral sex to allure them to earn money and pleasure from them. When such a lady gets fed-up with her love affairs, she finally chooses a guy and marries with him. Such girls feel proud on their capability of changing the lovers like the wearing. They think that young guys are like a puppet and they can compel them to move as per their instructions. Again if a lover is determined to marry with such a girl then she never accepts his proposal or keeps love affair with him for a sufficient duration to fetch money and other facility from him and then kicks him by falsely blaming or by letting the parents intervene in the matter. They are known as easily available girls in their society. Some of the depressed ex-lovers of such ladies throw acid on their face when they found them roaming with other lovers, with the intention that they may not ruin the life or other guys by sexually enticing them through their beautiful faces. Such act of brutality is done by extremely depressed guys betrayed by their lovers. This is a clear indication of the extreme senselessness and brutality in the guys aroused because of the betrayal done by their lovers. In such fourteen instances where the brutality was shown by a guy on his lover, a survey is done and it is found that in seven matters, the offended girls were responsible because they have betrayed their lovers and had fetched a lot of money from them. In four matters out of the remaining seven, the guys caught red handed their lovers making love with other guys. In one matter, such brutality was done by a guy because he was in love with the girl but she denied and publicly scolded him. In two matters, the guys were extremely possessive for the offended girls and were eager to get their consent forcefully. When the girls refused their proposal then they threw acid on their faces with the intention that they may not be physically worthy to be loved by other guys. Such kind of tendency of taking revenge can be seen in ladies in the worst form. The revenge taken by ladies is more disgusting and hatred because ninety-nine percent of them take the help of their sex organs or sexual skills in that. In India, more than ninety-eight percent of the young guys, who are killed in different matters, are in fact either directly killed by their lovers or wives or are killed in the rivalry caused because of illicit sexual relations. The ratio of the incidences of death of men caused by ladies as their beloved lovers or wives is thirty-one times more to the ratio of death of ladies caused by men as their lovers or husbands. An engineer of a renowned software company was killed on the direction of his fiancée or would-be wife because the date of marriage was very near and the lady felt in love with some other guy. She found it difficult to tell her would-be husband about her latest affair hence she arranged his murder. The very surprising fact was that the lady was in love with her would-be husband since past many years and both of them decided to marry. Such incidents happen on very large scale in India but unfortunately at most three percent are actually solved and in rest of the matters, the culprit fiancées or lovers or wives are never caught while some other men are caught by the police and are punished by the judiciary. There are uncountable cases where guys are killed by their lovers or wives through some professional killers or by the men with whom they were having illicit sexual relations and the culprit men are imprisoned while the brain-behind ladies are roaming freely in the society.

If a guy is emotionally attached with his lover then he seeks the feelings of affection, soft emotions and coyness in her. The guys immersed in pure emotional love with their lovers seek the qualities in them which have already eloped in women long time back. Appearing of such high qualities in the behavior of a lady is like a mirage which seems to be true from distance while in actual exists nowhere if seen by a close view. Such guys, who are emotionally attached with their lovers, bear the lack of prudence and conscience and hence lose their precious time, wealth, education, career and close relations with the family members as well as with the well wishers. In contrary to this if a guy is attached with his lover because of infatuation or sexual attraction then ultimately such relationship ends when carried for long duration because both of them have been fed-up with each other. To make a love affair successful by reaching to final goal of marriage, it is essential that the guy should be attached with his lover emotionally as well as sexually in proper ratio because as a lover, how much affection a lady keeps for the boyfriend and what is her actual opinion regarding her love affair, she doesn't know herself. Again a survey disclosed the facts that ninety-three percent men are emotionally attached with the ladies with whom they keep sexual relations and even fifty-nine percent of them seek such emotions in them even for the prostitutes with whom they perform copulations while twenty-one percent women seek such emotional attachment in them with the men with whom they keep sexual relations while the rest of seventy-nine percent ladies keep a sort of rivalry and hate in them for such men. This is the reason that almost ladies are attached with their lovers or sex partners for the sake of achieving financial benefits and they have nothing to do with their emotions.

Girls never perform their peculiar pretensions and flirtatious airs with their parents as they do with their lovers and husbands. If a guy hides his sexual inclination towards his lover or pretends himself to be least attracted towards her sexual charm then she rarely expresses her whimsical behavior in front of him. The moment ladies find that their lovers are fascinated by their sexual appeal, they start exploiting them. Almost of the girls confessed that they wear properly so that a curiosity may sustain in their lovers for their hidden sexual organs. They reveal their body parts up to such an extent which is essential to seduce lovers. If a boyfriend still remains unresponsive then he is shown more body parts. Almost girls said that if boyfriends behave entirely unaffected by the body charm of them then they will come in birth suit or completely nude in front of them.

In a couple of lovers determined to marry, the good and bad habits of the guy are visible while the bad habits of the girl are almost invisible. As discussed earlier, some habits in the man are considered to be normal while those habits, if seen in a girl, are considered to be her bad habits. Belching with producing sound after taking meal, farting with producing an audible sound, snoring while sleeping, shouting during amusements or in normal conversations and spitting here and there by producing sound are considered to be mannish properties and are counted in awful habits if done by girls. Again scratching publicly on itching at some body parts like buttocks, genital organs, thighs, stomach or at breasts, producing sound while chewing the meal, taking meal impatiently and whistling are the habits which when seen in a girl then her lover becomes embarrassed. As a girl and boy perform their best while their love dating hence it becomes very difficult to get the veracity of their temperament. Again it becomes very difficult to judge about the nature of the girl because she pretends all the time by hiding her actual disposition. The behavior of a boyfriend is not very different from his actual performances because almost the only fact that he hides is regarding his financial status but this is only found in the guys belonging to normal or lower financial status.

A middleclass boy pretends to be financially strong in front of his lover and bears the expenses of her roaming, amusements, parties and gifts. It is believed that the payment of all the expenses should be borne by the man if he is with a lady. Though this is not a difficult job for the guys belonging to financially rich families but when such financial burden are faced by a financially lower or middleclass guy then he has to pretend himself from a rich family. Normally this is the only false ostentation done by boys while in rest of the performances; they act as they are in actuality.

The boy is found almost busy in persuading his sulking lover. Such a series of love making and quarrelling goes on because a boy never seeks any fault in his girlfriend. After marriage, gradually the actual temperament and drawbacks of his lover disclose because a lady can never pretend or perform pseudo attitude till very long doesn't matter how much she is expertise in women psychology. Now a man as a husband seeks entirely different properties and habits in his ex-lover, who has become his wife. If aforementioned mannish habits are shown by a girl in front of her lover during her love affair then perhaps lover would have got embraced and would have quit from the love affair because no guy can accept such very normal tendencies easily if are shown by his fiancée. A man, who has done love marriage, gets depressed when hears rude speech of his wife or seeks rustic behavior of her who has always spoken pleasantly and behaved politely as a lover. The changed behavior shown by a girl as a wife is beyond the expectations of the husband. A man is always eager to give his affection and love to his lover but as a wife, she wants to get love forcefully. Marriage changes the definition of the true love and confines men in boundaries while it liberates ladies and provides them freedom regarding performing illicit sexual relations and ill behavior. The respect and honor of a girl increases in the views of her lover when she marries to him while a guy always loses his dignity in the views of his lover when he marries with her. The practical examples of the consequences of love marriages can be taken from Bengali or Punjabi families. Because of the genetic disorder, almost Bengali ladies are either very faithful to their husbands or are extremely sexually corrupt. On average thirteen percent of such ladies are morally very high while rest of the percentage of them are ultimate disloyal to their husbands. Ninety-seven percent of the Bengali ladies, performing inter-caste love marriage, make their husbands' lives like a pet dog. Though the Punjabi and Sindhi girls performing inter-caste marriages are found in less percentage still they rule their husbands. If the ladies of aforementioned three communities perform love marriages in their own communities then situation remains almost under control. The situation of being disloyal towards husbands is often seen in Bengali ladies because almost men of their community are blind in the beauty and sexual appeal of their wives and always beseech them for their love.

A husband, who did love marriage, said that a boy and a girl in a love couple are like batch-mates or class-fellows studying in the same class. If they do not marry then they get separated after few years like the class mates. If they marry then the progress as well as the overall development of the guy is obstructed while his lover becomes teacher of the same class. Now she starts instructing his husband considering him as her student. As a lady teacher, while educating her underage students, bounds them to go on the track mentioned by her, similarly, a girl who has become a wife, teaches and compels her lover in the role of her husband. This is the reason that around eight percent love marriages are succeeded in the point of views of both the husbands and wives while in sixty-nine percent, men compromises to live a peaceful life. In rest of the twenty-three percent love marriages, the relationship ends with divorce.

Wife-Concubine-Prostitute

Perhaps the term concubine is the distorted form of the other wives of the ancient kings. The concubines of the very renowned persons were respected as their wives. The secondary queens or other wives of the kings were somewhere more renowned and respectable than the wives and this can be seen in the various illustrations of ancient *Dwapar Yug*. Such other wives were considered to be secondary wives but in fact were more brilliant and worthy than principal wives. Almost of them had a proper control over the regime and they were more popular in the public for their administrative power. Some other wives of lord *Krishna* were living deity of the time and are still remembered more than his first wife *Rukmini*. The third wife *Ayesha*, also known as "Mother of the Believers", of great saint Prophet *Muhammad* was a very brilliant scholar by birth and remembered more than his first wife *Khadijah*. Unfortunately the distorted form of other wives termed to be concubines aroused in the period of Muslim emperors. Rich Islamic authorities or monarchs started accepting the beautiful ladies of other religions by forcefully converting their religion and compelling them to live as their concubines. This was the time when the system of *Parda* was developed in Hindu society so as to protect the beauty from the lustful sexually corrupt Islamic tyrants. Initially Hindu ladies tried to hide their beauty by smearing dirty substances like ash of coal or mud over their faces and visible body parts so as to prevent themselves from such forceful change of religion and from being concubines of morally impotent sovereigns. Gradually they started using a veil to hide their faces and termed it as *Ghunghat*. This was the same like *Parda* and both of the systems were to hide the beauty of ladies but actually there was a big difference between the concepts of these two. The concept of *Ghunghat* aroused in Hindu families because the beautiful ladies were abducted by Islamic autocrats and were bound to live the life of harlots while the concept of *Parda* or *Burka* was accepted by Islamic ladies so as to protect them from the members of their own community. Some powerful Islamic autocrats compelled the men of their own community to go through *Talaak* or divorcing their beautiful wives so that they may marry with them. For this, somewhere the Islamic men were given plenty of money by such lustful authorities of their own religion to divorce their beautiful wives. The concept of *Burka* betrayed the innocent Islamic women but was very helpful for sexually corrupt women in performing harlotry or adultery with the close family members under the shade of it. Islamic men were happy to have more than one wives and the supreme right of *Talaak* but they were proved to be physically impotent hence the concept was kept so that anyone of their close family member may satisfy the sexual desire of their wives behind the shade of *Parda*. Indeed *Burka* system made the ground of harlotry and crossbreeds in Islamic community. Some beautiful ladies of Islamic and non-Islamic communities performed harlotry with British authorities during their rule over India and hence even now the breeds of them can be seen in some parts of India.

When a rich man keeps sexual relations with other lady for a long period and provides her all the facilities as he is giving to his wife then that lady is said to be his concubine. Such ladies are not accepted traditionally through marriage still they live like a married one. When a married man, capable to take responsibility of some other lady, keeps sexual relations with her by providing her shelter like a residence and all other necessary items then such protected and cared lady accepts herself to be his keep or other wife. As the term concubine is very personal in context of a man hence there is no difference between a concubine and personal concubine. It is seen that a lady chooses a man of her desire for being his concubine. It is also seen somewhere that a keep is more emotionally attached with a man than his wife. A concubine herself takes responsibility of proving existence or identity to her while in case of a wife such responsibility is taken by her husband. A wife and a concubine both are not a prostitute still the sexual relations of a concubine are said to be immoral or illicit while that of a wife are moral and legal. Wherever the concubines are provided social acceptance there starts the legal polygamy or the custom of having more than one wife. A wife isolates her husband from the other family members and well-wishers because of her possessiveness and jealousy while a concubine always acts as an inspiration for concerned man in performing his duties for his parents and well-wishers. Almost wives make the house like hell for their husbands while such a man, when lives for some hours in the proximity of a concubine, does not feel embarrassing in living in such hell. In almost perspectives considering present scenario, a concubine is better than a wife but her only fault, that her relations are socially as well as legally not accepted, disgraces her life. Men are frightened from the opinion of the society and family and hence always try to hide their relations with their concubines. A man can not produce children from his concubine because those children will not be accepted by the society and will be considered as illegitimate progenies. He can never give his surname or *Gotra* to his children from his concubine. The children from his wife are considered to be legal and he is bound to give them his name even when they are produced because of adultery done by the wife. In present scenario, it can be seen that a wife provides lack of conscience, lack of discretion and moral impotency to her husband while if he is involved with a concubine then he achieves maturity of attitude and mental peace from her, though somewhere this concept regarding concubines is seemed to be broken because of excessive greediness of nowadays ladies for wealth. A concubine provides the significance of living and the realization of the existence to a man. Though a wife and a concubine both are ladies but the one who marries is said to be wife or morally accepted even after keeping illicit sexual relations or performing adultery while the other one, who does not marry but keeps affection and sexual relation with a single man during her life is said to be concubine or characterless even when she actually performs the obligations of an actual wife. This is the reason that in present scenario, marriages on contract are proved more successful than the traditional marriages. If a man has to select one out of his wife and concubine then he gives preference to his wife because of the fear of society and his affection for his children. If society permits such relations with a concubine and the children from concubines are considered to be legal then no one will give preference to marriage because marriage binds men while makes unrestrained to ladies in context of brazenness and adultery. It is seen in a survey that eighty-four percent of the men, who are living in the proximity of concubines or are involved in prostitution, are highly depressed and seventy-seven percent out of them are depressed because of the ill nature and rude behavior of their wives.

It is said that a lady involved in illicit sexual relations is a prostitute while a man keeping sexual relations with other lady is sexually debauched. In context of prostitutes, it can be said that prostitute is a lady whom with anyone can perform sexual course just by paying her fees for the sexual services she provides. A lady, who provides sexual satisfaction to men by taking some financial or other kind of benefit from them, is a prostitute. As per the technical definition, a lady who earns by providing her sexual services is a prostitute. This definition seems to be very simple but in fact it is not because if a man can get the sexual services of a lady by paying her then she is a prostitute for him but if the other man can not get the sexual services of that lady even by paying her then she can not be said to be a prostitute for him. Hence as per literal definition, all prostitutes are sexually debauched ladies but all sexually corrupt ladies are not prostitute. A sexually corrupt lady is a prostitute only for a man who can get her sexual services by paying her. If a lady makes illicit sexual relations for the sake of pleasure only or does not take any financial advantage from her sex-partner or pays him for sexual courses like middle aged ladies then she can not be considered to be prostitute. A lady, living with a man as her husband and performing sexual courses with him only, after marrying properly either through the customs of any religion or through the legal acceptance of the judiciary, is neither sexually corrupt nor a prostitute. Again a married lady performing adultery is sexually debauched not a prostitute and she is considered to be a prostitute when she takes money or any kind of financial profit for providing her sexual services and she is a prostitute only for the men with whom she takes such financial benefits. Hence a married lady, keeping illicit sexual relations for the sake of pleasure or money, is in fact a prostitute from the point of view of her sexual relations with her husband if she is taking any kind of financial or other assistance from her husband. Again ladies involved in illicit sexual relations just for the sake of sexual pleasure or the ladies providing money or other kind of financial profits to men so that they may keep sexual relations with them are not prostitutes.

The judiciary as well as the society personally consider the illicit illegal deeds or crimes done by someone in the society hence if a man keeps illicit sexually relations with a lady by paying for her sexual services then such a lady itself becomes a prostitute in the opinion of the society and judiciary. As we justify or define an attitude in the similar way as it is defined by the society organized by the judiciary hence we too consider a lady to be a prostitute if she is involved in illicit sexual relations. The basic difference in the performance of a prostitute and a sexually corrupt lady apart from their financial attitude is that a prostitute has nothing to do with the appearance or looking of her client because actually she keeps very little charm for achieving sexual pleasure from the clients while a sexually corrupt lady always seeks men of her own liking for sexual plays because she is desirous to achieve sexual pleasure only. A man plays no role in making a lady to be a prostitute or adulterated because these two terms are defined by the sexual attitude of ladies and their objectives behind keeping the sexual relations.

Some ladies say that men treat their wives as prostitutes or behave them as they are prostitutes. To get the veracity of this, it is essential to know about the definition of prostitutes defined by ladies. As per the ostentatious disposition or moral opinion of ladies, a lady is said to be prostitute when she keeps illicit sexual relations in her unmarried life or is a widow keeping sexual relations without remarrying or performs adultery. Hence as per their opinion, if a lady keeps sexual relations with a man other than her husband in whole of her life span then she is a prostitute. Again no man can make a lady prostitute because by all opinions, this term is defined by the attitude of ladies only. Whoever keeps sexual relations with her husband only is not a prostitute hence if she says that she is treated like a prostitute, it is a mere confession done by her regarding her illicit sexual relations with other men either done in past or in parallel to her married life. We can classify prostitutes on the basis of their financial status and living style in following sections-

The category of the prostitutes who is available to very renowned or wealthy men and itself belongs to rich families is considered to be very high level prostitutes. Society can never imagine about such ladies being prostitutes. Such prostitutes belong to very high class families or possess high financial backgrounds and are involved in high class business or employments hence to call them prostitutes is out of the capacity of society or judiciary. Their presence in high class functions and the dancing or some other performances shown by them are also a part of their business of prostitution. These ladies seldom ask for any fees for providing their sexual services in order to enhance their contacts and high-profiled social circle but they are always paid a very big amount. Like a normal prostitute, they are paid more for the dancing performances shown by them in comparison to sexual plays. They are very efficient and are able to get any kind of political help but again no one can prove that they are very high leveled prostitutes. They are also seen in touch with big Mafias. They always perform prostitution behind the shade of their glorified business and leave prostitution once get married with some renowned person. While choosing their showy profession behind which they perform harlotry, they give preference to the fields of acting, dancing and modeling. Again very high class and renowned men take their sexual services. They have their pre-defined charges as a fixed package. Under this package of lakhs or millions of rupees, they provide indecent dancing programs like a striptease and to offer sexual services at the end of program is often included in the services that are provided for such packages. Some newcomer renowned ladies are unaware of the unwritten regulations of such packages and easily become ready to provide their indecent dancing services for such alluring packages but when at the concluding of the ceremony, they are asked for sexual plays then they pretend to be stunned. One of such a big organizer told that while performing such functions and inviting some renowned dancer or actress for her dancing etc, they have to pay a lot of amount to the concerned lady and the amount is defined by the lady herself as her package. He said that almost of the celebrities affiliated to such programs are very familiar with the fact that the package decided by them is for their dancing or amusement services as well as sexual services.

The second category is of high class prostitutes and their populace is sufficiently more than the very high class prostitutes. Such prostitutes are also not easily available to a middleclass man. Such prostitutes charge around seventy-five thousands to ten thousands rupees for a sexual play trip for a single man. Girls studying in convent schools, who are involved in prostitution, charge near about twenty thousand rupees for providing sexual services. The beautiful and attractive girls studying in the colleges of higher education in well developed cities can often be seen involved in prostitution. Like very high class prostitutes, they too never perform harlotry because of any kind of financial problem. The extreme desire to live a luxurious life, making higher contacts among politicians and local mafias and desire to live a peculiar restrained-free life are the major factors provoking them to adopt prostitution. Lots of girls affiliated in the filed of fashion designing, interior decoration, journalism and management are involved in prostitution and fall in this category of prostitutes. Such ladies seldom perform prostitution after marriage but always seen to be involved in adultery. These are termed to be high priced call-girls.

Middleclass prostitutes can be further differentiated in lower middleclass and higher middleclass. Such prostitutes available to normal men are either students or married ladies. The upper middles class prostitutes charge up to five thousand rupees while the charges taken by lower middleclass prostitutes go up to one thousand rupees. Higher middleclass prostitutes are often utilized in the political lanes as a bribe. It is a very common tradition in India that government officers often provide the sexual services of their wives to their seniors for the sake of achieving promotions or other kind of official benefits and unfortunately wives become willingly agree for this. Such wives are also considered in the category of upper middleclass prostitutes. Some of such prostitutes provide their services to the authorities to make a financial deal in their favor. When someone in debt provides the sexual services of his wife to compensate for the interest and principal amount then such wives are also counted in this category of prostitutes. Ladies working in normal beauty parlors can be achieved for sexual pleasure just by giving amount of one thousand to five thousand and lie in the middleclass category. Girls, who are living in working women hostels or other girls' hostels, are often supplied in mass scale for the purpose of mass sexual entertainment and such girls stay in this category. Often such girls wear veil or *Burka* irrespective of their community so that they may not be identified by others while their visit to perform harlotry. A survey was conducted in *Lucknow* city and the facts revealed were shocking. More than ninety-five percent of the girls, who do not wear helmet while driving but wrap their *dupatta* or other piece of cloth around their face, do this for the sake of hiding their identity and almost of them are having illicit sexual relations and are directly or indirectly involved in prostitution. Lower middleclass prostitutes perform harlotry just for sake of money though this is also true that prostitutes of all the categories achieve financial advantages from prostitution and consider this to be the easiest and shortest way of earning. Lower middleclass prostitutes often provide their sexual services free of cost to advocates and police officers so as to achieve security and protection. Middleclass prostitutes are also made available in renowned hotels or guest houses.

Next category of the prostitutes is lower class and these are available to men belonging to all categories. They claim for eight hundred rupees to thousand rupees for providing their sexual services but are ready to get bargained. They can be managed to come to two hundred rupees. These are also available in the middle standard hotels but there the client or customer has to pay their fixed rates. Almost such prostitutes are locally available and are married ladies. This is the only category of the prostitutes who always keep precautions like condoms to make themselves protected from the sexually transmitted diseases though all kind of prostitutes available in hotels also keep such precautions. They pressurize their customers for using condoms but when they feel that the customer is newcomer in sexual performances, they say him to remove condom to attain full natural excitement.

The last category of the prostitutes is the very low class category which includes of the lady servants working in the houses for cleansing utensils and sweeping floor etc. Such prostitutes provide their sexual services in hundred rupees and somewhere they ask up to the two-hundred and fifty rupees depending on their beauty. Middle-aged prostitutes of this category become ready for sexual plays for fifty to twenty rupees only. Such low priced prostitutes charging twenty rupees can be seen in the small towns and villages where they provide sexual services in their very small dovecot like rooms or they just stood up in narrow lanes taking the support of wall while the customers perform intercourse with them from their backside. These includes of female beggars, garbage collectors and scavengers. Almost prostitutes in the role of lady servants go to the residences of their customers in the absence of ladies of the families and provide their sexual services. They are often seen involved sexually with the gents of the families where they work as a servant. Such lady servants are the tremendous examples of the prostitutes because they provide their sexual services to their financially poor husbands, very low class laborers working on daily wages, the drivers of the manual rickshaws and to men of middleclass or higher class families where they work as servants. Such female servants never wear undergarments while working in residences and seldom get complete naked while performing the mating. They avoid wearing panties so that they may save time while performing copulations. They just pull their *Sari* and petticoat up and men perform copulation with them. They try to sexually draw the attentions of the men of the families where they work. While sweeping the floor, they bend to sit on floor and hence their breasts come out of their upper garment because they never wear bra and similarly they pull *Sari* or the other lower garment up to their thighs so as to sexually excite men of the family and always pretend very innocently that they are unaware about all of this. They perform pilfering whenever they are aloof of the sight of the ladies of the house and when men are alone; they perform sexual courses with them and take money or other domestic items as the price of the sexual services provided by them. Like few concubines, they are the only prostitutes who emotionally blackmail their customers and often take money to hide their relations from their wives. If a lady belonging to lower middleclass or lower class or very lower class possesses extraordinary physical beauty then mostly she becomes concubine of some powerful man when she enters in the field of prostitution. Again beautiful and attractive ladies of lower class families almost become prostitutes or concubines and continue this even after their marriage.

A peculiar term, used in the ancient time regarding ladies involved in prostitution, "*Ganika*" seems to be disappeared in the present society. It is said about *Ganikas* that they perform sexual plays with the men of their own desire but they are not prostitutes because they never take money for their sexual services. *Ganikas* were considered to be expertise in the indecent dancing like striptease and all sexual postures or arts hence they earned money by teaching other young ladies the art of sexual plays etc. Somewhere expertise aged prostitutes become *Ganika* and start teaching sexual skills to young newcomer girls but still it is said that they perform sexual plays not for earning money. In the present society, the term *Ganika* has been replaced by the term "Aunty" and such aunties can be seen as the organizers of small scaled or big brothels running currently in almost all over India. The only difference is that the ancient *Ganikas* were morally high in spite of being involved directly or indirectly in harlotry while the present day aunties in the role of *Ganikas*, have no morals. An extensive survey conducted during end of year 2009 in specific part of almost all of the cities exposed astonishing facts regarding such aunties. In *Lucknow* city, there were approximately four thousand and two hundred such aunties running brothel secretly in their own houses. In *Delhi*, this figure was more than sixty-five thousand. In *Kanpur*, the figure was eleven hundred and twenty only because most of the prostitutes are freelancers. In *Haldwani*, this figure is one hundred and fifty only while in *Deharadoon*, this figure is one thousand and sixty one. These figures of the

Haldwani and *Deharadoon* seems to be doubtful because in fact *Almora* and *Haldwani* are far ahead in prostitution or adultery in comparison to capital of *Uttrakhand Deharadoon* but again almost prostitutes are freelancers not affiliated to some local brothel or aunties. The ratio of keeping illicit sexual relations by ladies is very high in *Almora* and *Haldwani* in comparison to *Deharadoon* but less percentage of ladies are involved in taking money for such relations instead they do it for the sake of pleasure. Similarly seventy-eight percent ladies of *Kanpur* are involved in illicit sexual relations or harlotry. Allahabad is not far behind in this context from *Kanpur*. The worst condition is of *Chennai, Siligudi*, specific areas of West *Bengal*, North Eastern areas, *Bhopal, Agra, Noida*, Interior locations of *Bihar* and *Maharashtra*. The ratio of adultery or harlotry or prostitution is found to be more than thrice in villages or interior rural areas in comparison to urban areas of all the states but *Uttrakhand* state was the only exceptions of this because there the prostitution is number of times more in cities or developed areas in comparison to rural areas. Ladies living like paying guests are found to be involved in harlotry in seventy-eight percent cases and all of the arrangements are done by the aunties or the female owner of such residences. One of such Aunty told that they just have to pay a definite amount weekly or monthly in the concerned police station and they often provide sexual services of their prostitutes to the police officers so as to get security and to run their business smoothly. They are informed by the local police to change residence or the way of dealing to clients when some social hindrances occur. Ladies are set free by police officers at police stations' level either by taking bribes or sexual services or they are released on bail by the police officers even when their offence is deplorable and this happens in almost around forty-thousand criminal matters happening per month in the country.

A prostitute is a lady willingly immerged in the marsh of harlotry having an alluring golden ring of sexual skills to allure men by invoking sexually excitement in them. A sexually excited man approaching them desires for sexual satisfaction. Such man, who has gone through prostitution, keeps the opinion that he did mating with prostitute but in fact he is sexually molested by the prostitute who allows him to go after taking his morality, chastity and money. After finishing of such sexual plays, prostitute remains where she was but a man, newcomer to harlotry, falls in the marsh of prostitution. It is said that brothel is a place where the garbage of unsatisfied perverted sexual feelings of men is thrown but in fact the concept of brothels is kept with the intentions of protecting decent society and progenies from sexual debauchment. It is assumed that perhaps the sexually corrupt prostitutes may not spread adultery in the society if they are provided some specific areas as a shelter for their profession of providing sexual services. The very clear illustration of this can be seen in the organized brothels situated in big cities. Almost of such brothels are situated near the road and normal public uses such routes in performing their daily routines. When decent men or minor guys go through such routes, they face the indecent comments and gestures expressed by the prostitutes. To avoid such embarrassing situations they just bow their heads and start walking rapidly. Again when a father and daughter or a mother and son or a brother and sister go through such routes, they become shocked hearing indecent comments done by the prostitutes. Now if such situations happen in whole of the city then what will happen, can be easily imagined. Hence brothels are not made with the intentions to throw garbage of sexual craving of men over there instead brothels are made so that the garbage of such sexually and morally corrupt ladies may be confined in a specified area.

A lady involved in prostitution said, "Everything is managed and governed by us. Very few ladies are compelled for harlotry because almost of us are willingly involved in this business. If suppose I too am caught red handed by police then I will say that I was compelled to perform harlotry. All of us just to declare the name of some men and speak lie that we were forced by them because rest of our favor is taken by media. I was caught when first I tried to escape from my house with my lover. I blamed him though I did the attempt of escaping as per my desire. We all have to save us by blaming some men and prove ourselves innocent doesn't matter if some men are falsely blamed for this because nobody knows that we are willingly selling our chastity since we were of fourteen to fifteen years. We all directly or indirectly perform harlotry because we are always disloyal and unfaithful. If police men arrest us then they take money or sexual pleasure from us to leave us. If we deny bribing by cash or kind then they arrest us under immoral traffic acts. Now judiciary member either takes money or sexual services of us to relieve us. If some honest person is there then also he becomes helpless as we get the services of advocates, who are regular clients of us. No one can be assured about the chastity or sexual purity of his mother, wife, sisters and daughters hence all of aforementioned authorities release their sexual frustration by sexually abusing us. Police officers can often be seen brutally torturing the guys whom they arrest as an offender of even counterfeit or never happened sexual assaults on the complaint of some cunning lady. Again they all release their family frustration provided to them by morally corrupt female members of their own families.

There was a time when prostitution was adopted by ladies as a career because of their poverty and lack of other options, to earn livings. As the ladies were not so educated so that they may get some job hence almost of them prefer harlotry instead of doing physical labor to earn. Now the conditions and the situations have been entirely changed. A very wide survey is secretly performed regarding the financial conditions of the prostitutes, their past and the reason for which they choose such profession, without making them realized about the intention of survey. As per the figures sorted out, it is found that out of the numerous groups of hundred prostitutes, around eighty-eight adopted prostitution so as to achieve luxurious life, higher ambitions and restrained free life while around seven of them adopted such profession because of the financial crunches. The three out of the remaining five were forcefully or deceitfully engaged in prostitution by their own relatives. Out of which half percent of them were deceitfully sold to brothels by their husbands or lovers. The remaining two adopted this after getting betrayed in sexual love obsessions one by one because they were of the opinion like the other ladies that sexual relations are the only ways by which they can get triumph over men. Hence least of them were having reasons like poor financial position or any kind of compulsions behind their performing harlotry.

Prostitutes call the men approaching them for the sake of sexual pleasure as "customers". The word customer is used in every business for the person who purchases something. The cost of a purchased item varies depending on the quality of the item. Similarly prostitutes charge different amount for providing their sexual services. Sometimes a businessman takes different price of the same thing from different customers depending upon the paying capacity of customers similarly sometimes a prostitute charges different amount from different customers. Sometimes customer need a machine for some hours hence he takes that machine on lease for some duration from the owner instead of purchasing it forever and returns it back by paying him some amount. The concept of prostitution runs on the same principle. This is like an item packed in appealing covering so that customers may get attracted towards it and once they open the packing, they have to pay for it even when the material inside is third class. Mostly the quality of the prostitutes is judged by their age, physical beauty, body figure and the innocent expressions of their faces.

Nimbleness in sexual plays does not enhance the price of a prostitute for a strange customer because this can be known after the sexual course that how much she was expertise. A group of customers give preference to prostitutes who are expertise in sexual plays while the other group gives preference to a novice or newcomer prostitute. As the later one category of customers seldom get any prostitute novice in sexual plays hence they seek less experienced prostitutes by looking their appearances, gestures and physical built. Generally lesser the age of prostitutes and higher the other aforementioned qualities, higher are their charges.

If customers ask to prostitutes about their names, family members and the reasons behind their choosing prostitution as a profession then hundred percent of them speak untruth. All of them tell their pseudonym and says that they were compelled by their relatives to perform harlotry or their parents sold them in a brothel or their parents are handicapped and no one was their in the family to earn money or they are orphan etc. All of such descriptions done by them are false just like their pseudonym. Compelling ladies to perform prostitution or selling underage ladies for the sexual services are only performed in very well organized brothels running under the shelter of police, administration and politicians. A big count of girls escapes from their residences every year and their complaints of being lost are registered in the nearby police stations. This can be seen in almost all part of the country. Fifty-nine percent of them leave their residence and run to *Mumbai* for the sake of being actresses in the film industry out of which more than fifty-eight percent adopt harlotry as their profession. Twenty-eight percent escape for adopting prostitution as a profession willingly because they in their city or town are having restrictions of their parents. Eleven percent escapes with their lovers for love marriage and never come back. One percent commit suicide and their bodies are never found. Around one percent ladies are sold by their relatives or lovers in the hand of others and then they file false complaints in the police stations. The shocking facts are that in more than seventy-eight percent such matters parents are aware about where their daughters have gone but they pretend to be unaware and file fake reports in the police stations. Around eighty-eight percent of such ladies escape because of their high ambitions of earning money by any means and charm of living a free sexual life.

Almost prostitutes become nude in front of their customers mechanically and hence they possess least sexual feelings or excitements. They even perform sexual plays without any emotions as if they are machines. Hence they do not experience seminal discharge even after performing sexual union with number of men one-by-one. They never let themselves to reach the peak of sexual excitement though some of them pretend to be excited by producing artificial indecent hissing sounds. Very high class or high class prostitutes and concubines are exception to this as they experience pleasure while performing intercourses and are willing to perform oral sex while other prostitutes compel client to wash penis from water or cloth before taking it in mouth or sometimes clean it themselves. Before making sexual plays if a prostitute intakes alcohol then the sensitivity of her vagina becomes almost nil though she pretends to be sexually excited by shouting indecent and vulgar phrases.

The men visiting to prostitutes for their sexual services mostly includes of widowers and middle aged men. Men of the age group of thirty years to sixty-five years can often seen visiting harlots. Above this age group mostly rich, intellectual and renowned over-lustful men are seen involved in prostitution. Some old aged men intake ash of gold or some peculiar intoxicants to exhilarate their sexual craving as well as capacity and take the services of prostitutes to attain sexual pleasure. Similarly the count of men, who watch indecent erotic movies or blue-films, mostly includes of the men lying in the age group of middle age to old age. It is said that men take the help of prostitutes when they find themselves unable to fulfill their natural or unnatural sexual desires shown in such erotic movies from their wives. Again the virginity of young guys is mostly molested by sexually corrupt married ladies and less than three percent of such guys take the services of prostitutes either alone or in group with their friends.

When young guys, unaware with the sexual courses, visit some prostitute, they hesitate to express their requirements. Almost prostitutes disrobe themselves in a traditional way without wasting time. Newcomer guys feel anxiety and embarrassment hence either they do not feel any excitation in their penis or their seminal fluid discharges just by looking at the nude prostitute. Only experienced men can perform mating with a prostitute who disrobes herself. Most of such newcomer guys do not experience sufficient tightness in their penis to insert it in the vagina of prostitute and some of them do not face the discharge. They feel uncomfortable while using condom to protect themselves from the probable sexually transmitted diseases. Prostitutes try to erect their penis by rubbing or sucking but again the moment they use condom, penis loses stiffness and becomes loose. Somewhere while performing intercourse, condom falls inside the vagina. Prostitute call such instances in their jargon as "meter down" or "uncharged battery" or "fuse bulb" and the newcomer customer gets mentally depressed. After this, prostitutes are unable to bring sexual excitement or erection in the penis of such clients. Some of such prostitutes emotionally blackmails such guys and take more money from them for not informing about their failure in performing copulation to their friends sitting in other rooms. Prostitutes take some additional money from such novice customers after performing complete or incomplete sexual plays and call this as *"Muh Dekhai"*. Though such *Muh Dekhai* tradition is in fact the ceremony of unveiling a bride's face to her relatives-in-law after marriage and the bride is paid by gifts or money for this. In context of the prostitutes, this is used for revealing the vagina in front of a new customer. It is found in some organized brothels that the prostitutes snatch money, precious wearing, watch and even garments of such novice customers and kick them out after incomplete sexual plays.

The men, expertise in the sexual relations or who had experienced the services of some prostitutes in past, do not get embarrassed in front of prostitutes and instruct them not to disrobe themselves because a peculiar sexual excitation invokes when a lady is gradually disrobed by a man. If a prostitute disrobes herself then sexual feelings vanishes and it appears to be happening mechanically. When a strange customer disrobes a prostitute gradually then she also gets sexually excited and embarrassed. Almost men desire from a prostitute to act like a newly wedded bride. Most of the experienced men make prostitutes sit on their laps and press their breasts and just by this they guess about the quality or standard of them. Then they make them sit on knees to perform oral sex. While performing sexual intercourse, experienced men let them sit like an animal and insert penis into their vagina from their backside. Men seldom perform lip kissing the prostitutes and even prostitutes avoid this though the prostitutes of very high class or high class and concubines are exception to this. All of the prostitutes chew some edible item consisting of tobacco so as to avoid the taste or smell felt while sucking penis. To invoke sexual feelings in a prostitute, it is essential to make her body moving while performing mating hence experienced men let a prostitute lie upon them and say her to make intercourse by pushing herself up and down. Such movements or push-ups performed by a prostitute while sexual intercourse brings natural sexual excitation in her. The prostitutes available in the hotels are expertise in various techniques of oral sex and themselves ask to customers for oral sex calling it "French" etc. They pick the edge of the penis from their lips and produce excitation by rubbing it through the tongue. They smoothly lick and suck testis by taking them inside mouth but remain in mechanical mode without any feelings of sexual excitations in themselves.

Some of the sexually perverted customers compel prostitutes to take semen inside mouth and intake it. Some of them excrete urine over their faces, breasts and vagina. They ask prostitutes to pass urine over their penis and face. Some of them just masturbate on the breasts or face or vagina or undergarments of the prostitutes. Few sexually perverted men ask prostitutes to beat them or do the same act with the prostitutes. They perform anal sex with prostitutes and uses saliva of them instead of using some oily substance. Such prostitutes performing anal sex in blue films go through enema to make the anus route clear for penetration.

There is no limit of hatred disgusting acts in sexual plays. Somewhere a prostitute performs sexual plays with number of clients together while some sick customers ask them just to walk being entirely naked. Perverted or mentally sick customers seldom perform normal sexual course with them instead they compel them to perform ridiculous acts. Some of them just make them nude and sit in front of them conversing for hours while some just put an edible item and wine on their naked body and intake that. Some of such men take an object resembling as the shape as of penis and insert it to their vagina to masturbate meantime they insist them to pick their penis to perform mutual masturbation. Newcomer prostitutes perform oral sex with the help of lips only and avoid touching penis by tongue because of hatred feelings. Gradually some expertise prostitutes make them learn or they themselves become habitual in performing proper oral sex.

In the guesthouses and hotels of the big cities like *Chennai*, the manager or workers including waiters often ask to customers if they need sexual services of prostitutes. Somewhere they ask indirectly whether customer needs someone to massage the body. The men willing to take the services of prostitutes declare openly for this otherwise staff members allow prostitutes to sit on the bench outside the room occupied by the customers so that they may have a proper glance of alluring prostitutes and feel free to choose anyone of them. This all is done just to invoke sexual lustful feelings in the customers. Unfortunately the young students arrived in the city for the purpose of giving some competitive exams like the exams of railway services etc when stay in such hotels, are sort of sexually compelled to take the services of such harlots. Again this is very common in *Chennai, Mumbai, Siligudi, Bhopal, Pune* and some areas of west *Bengal* etc where the centers of such competitive exams are declared. Such kind of prostitution is so organized that the managers or the staff members of the hotels openly ask the demand of customers without the fear of administration or local police. Somewhere albums of the prostitutes are shown from which a customer may select the desired one and a staff member arranges that specific call-girl within half an hour. As this facility of showing albums of prostitutes is provided at very organized scale hence almost customers are happy because the girls chosen through the album are almost more attractive than they appear in the photographs. Such prostitutes keep little bit knowledge of English while some of them are very efficient in speaking English. In some hotels, a beautiful lady collides with the customer on the stairs or in the gallery by-mistake and says sorry for this and another lady brings ordered edible item in the room and prepare it while bending her body to show almost of her breasts and later attendant asks to customer whether he should send the lady confronted on the stairs or the one who visited room with the order. All of this seems to be ridiculous but such arrangements for the meeting of a customer and a prostitute are done in a very organized way. It is noticeable that providing a prostitute to a sexually desirous customer is a very normal process but demonstrating the alluring prostitutes to sexually excite customers and then compelling them to take the services of prostitutes is also very popular.

The places or the locations where one can visit prostitutes are clearer in big cities in comparison to small towns. Mostly prostitutes have their own colonies or society and their locations are in the knowledge of men willing to take their services. Almost cities and towns have specific defamed red-light areas where prostitutes live in groups. Again such red-light areas are in the knowledge of the local public and outsiders. Somewhere such places are very near to bus stations or railway stations. Less than one percent of the total prostitutes live in such areas while more than ninety-nine percent of them live in the society pretending to be decent and virgin.

In the big cities, there are thousands of places where one can visit prostitutes waiting for customers. Typical wearing, peculiar style of standing by little bit titling legs or making cross-legs and the way of swinging lather purse or key ring are the normal postures shown by prostitutes waiting for the clients. One can guess about them by looking them chewing some item and standing by taking the support of pillars or trees or cars. They can be seen in *Mumbai* railway station wearing garland of flowers on wrist and hair and chewing areca nut, vegetable extract, lime and tobacco wrapped by rolled betel-leaf. They themselves ask to customers whether they need their sexual services. In such cities men avoid visiting red-light areas or brothels instead they prefer to go near to prostitutes standing aside of the road, bargain about their charges and let them sit in the car or three wheeler. They go to their residences with the prostitutes or the ladies themselves inform them about some secure place. Otherwise they just seek a lone place aside the road and stop the vehicle to perform sexual plays either in the vehicle or in some nearby garden. Somewhere two friends take the service of a prostitutes and one take the charge of driving the vehicle while other performs sexual plays with her on the back seat and when he has done, they changes their locations so that the other man can perform sexual plays. Now it has been very difficult to assume about a lady being prostitute just by looking her wearing or walking style because only registered or very professional harlots give such indications. At present almost of the prostitutes includes of decent and studious looking college girls, laborious and dedicated ladies working in private sectors and so called faithful housewives.

Ladies often take the shelter of religious priests termed as *Baba* to run their business of harlotry smoothly. A kind of media person affiliated to some TV channel told that one of his colleagues did sting operation to disclose the sexual involvement of a so called Baba. In the country like India, illicit sexual relations or harlotry is said to be strictly forbidden as per the norms of judiciary because they are said to be immoral. Such acts are banned by Hindu religion, society and judiciary. He said that almost ladies started performing adultery but the religion is still unadulterated. Our religion did not get blemished even when temples were demolished, ancient Hindu voyages were forbidden because of the religious sentiments of Muslims, mosques are made just adjacent to almost all of the temples and Hindus were compelled to intake urine and shit of Islamic traitors. Even now the people of other religion deceitfully feed beef to Hindus. When ever a Hindu visits the residence of a person of other religion with the feel of universal sodality, he is offered edible items in which illiterate ladies spit before offering. With all of these stuffs, Hindus are happy because the existence of the religion is maintained but if a Baba provides employment offers or customers to some sexually corrupt ladies then Hindu religion gets adulterated because he is playing with the emotions and trust of Hindus. Some renowned Babas told very personally that the ladies visiting to them sometimes cross all the limits of nudity. They said, "If we do not allow ladies to enter in the premises then we are falsely blamed by them and if we allow them then also we are blamed." One of such Baba said that once he put a board outside of his cottage that ladies are not allowed entering in the premises then few ladies belonging to some organization threatened him by saying that he can not keep such restrictions on women. Some ladies spread the rumor that he was homosexual and was involved in sodomy under the shade of religion with young underage visitors. When the familiar media person was asked about this then he confessed that people of his profession, basically belonging to some channels, often send hired prostitutes to the cottage with the instructions to_sexually seduce Babas. He said that all channel are dying to increase the T.R.P. For this, they are eager to perform anything doesn't matter it is legal or illegal. Few media persons affiliated to different channels told that they are ordered by their authorities to let crime happen and even make the circumstances to let crime happen so that they may get sensational coverage. This can be considered to be the unstated oath of current deformed structure of journalism that a dedicated generalist, involved in making live video coverage of crime, should let the crime happen and should never save the victim even when he can do so because restricting the crime happening or being an obstacle in happening of a crime is not his duty. Unfortunately people have lost their conscience and they do not differentiate in between fame and defame because they are just willing to achieve popularity. It will not be surprising if in future some terrorist group will inform some channel to make live coverage of death of thousands persons in the attack or bomb blasts that he will be going to perform in India. Our journalist friend told that his team got a tip regarding something illegal happening in a mosque. He said that he could not find a single Muslim to help for sting operation, even when he tried to pay a sufficiently big amount to them. Ultimately he realized that Muslims are truly dedicated to their religion and they have strong indivertible faith for their religion. He said that if suppose the same_operation is to be done at some temple or at the cottage of some Hindu Baba then almost all of Hindus would have become ready by taking money. Perhaps our religion is inferior or our feelings are shallow or our devoutness is mere ostentation. Even a single Hindu does not resist to such channels when they tear to shreds Hinduism. Perhaps the blood flowing through the veins of Hindus have become water and we ourselves are ready to blemish our religion. Such tendency of Hindu men is also a big cause behind the moral and physical degradation of their ladies.

In fact almost people engaged in the business of earning money through forecasting or fortunetelling or horoscope analyzing or religious teaching are sexually corrupt, doesn't matter whether they are married or unmarried. It can be seen in all over the world that extraordinary persons are sex maniac but they never perform sexual assaults or rapes. Such men are allowed to live peacefully in other countries because people have nothing to do with their personal lives but in India, people take the advantage of such men and are eager to blemish their character by intruding in their personal lives.

The ladies involved in prostitution should be registered and all of them should be given unique registration numbers so that they may be compelled to go through regular medical checkups to avoid spreading of sexually transmitted diseases. Prostitutes are caught red handed by the policemen and are kept in custody for few hours and then they are set free by them after enjoying their sexual services or after taking bribe or because of some pressure from higher authorities. In all of such instances, normal public is unaware about the ladies living in their proximity and involved in harlotry. Such prostitutes boldly perform harlotry and after some time get married because they know that their respective husbands would never come to know about their pasts. It makes no sense to arrest a registered prostitute because she herself admits that she is a prostitute. The only way to stop young ladies performing prostitution is that the name of all of such ladies should be made public so that no one may dare to perform harlotry in future. When the names of married or unmarried male or female, who are caught red handed performing illicit sexual relations, will be disclosed then the percentage of prostitution will itself go down. All innocent and virgin unmarried guys and girls have right to know whether their would-be spouse had ever been involved in such illicit sexual relations. In all of such instances, the names of the girls or married ladies caught red handed performing illicit sexual relations is made secret so that their future and family life may not get disturb though either their sexual services or a sufficiently good amount of money is taken for this by policemen hence such ladies become daring to perform harlotry because they know that their names will not be highlighted. A police officer told that whenever they catch any girl involved in immoral acts, some of her well-wisher approaches and offers money to leave her immediately. He said that number of school girls involved in prostitution are having so powerful contacts that whenever they are caught, they have to leave them immediately because of the pressure of senior officers or ministers and the most drastic fact is that the parents of such young girls are unaware of the powerful contacts of their so-called innocent and virgin daughters. This is true that the concept of earning by making illicit sexual relations or adultery or harlotry is equally spread in the higher class society as in the lower class but the only difference is that the prostitution is done by the ladies of lower class category for the sake of financial benefit while in higher class this is done just to fulfill illicit sexual craving and unending ambitions. A familiar lady with her boyfriend met on Valentine day in a lone place, less popular among pairs. Her disheveled hair and wearing were sufficient to indicate that she was sexually enjoying the day. While conversation, when the routine of her father, who was a police officer, is asked then she said laughingly that he was on the duty to arrest love couples performing indecent behavior in the parks and hotels while enjoying Valentine day. Such routine inspections done by policemen can often be seen in the cities. The prostitutes escaped from *Uttar Pradesh* and *Bihar* and doing prostitution in *Mumbai, Calcutta* and *Pune* told that they are quite safe in such cities because in their hometowns they have to pay weekly bribe to police officers and the policemen from home-guards to higher officers enjoy their sexual services free of cost.

The basic problem with the policemen of a country like India is that once they are given the rights and responsibilities to maintain codes, they become autocratic and hence overrule the regulations themselves. They even harass love couple or husband and wife conversing while sitting in alone and often take money from them and behave indecently. Such policemen when catch some love pairs sitting in alone then they physically harass men while perform sexual indecency with ladies. They sexually enjoy by indecent touching and abusing to such ladies of the couples. When such a lady takes bold step and starts shouting on them then they escape from there. Some pairs, when trapped in such situations by the policemen, the ladies tear their own cloth on the indecent behavior shown by policemen to frighten them and this technique is found being almost successful. Again all the prostitutes, who are in the knowledge of policemen, are sexually utilized by them without paying them and they regularly give a fixed amount of money to the concerned police station for the sake of preventing themselves from being harassed by policemen. The second category that enjoys the sexual services of prostitutes without paying them is of their pimps. As open harlotry or brothels can not operate without being in the knowledge of policemen hence almost policemen perform the role of a pimp in context of prostitutes.

The disastrous situations of sex market in India can be imagined by this fact that foreigner ladies are coming here for prostitution. There is plenty of money and bright prospect in the field of sex-market in India. Commonwealth games-2010 is going to be conducted in *Delhi*, the capital of country. There are two hundred and nine groups of prostitutes, specially made for this occasion. Every group has two hundred and fifty high-class Indian prostitutes. This all is arranged by the high leveled brokers and pimps whose network of harlotry is spread in all over the country. A lady studying in management college of *Delhi* told on the assurance of privacy that she is engaged from three days before to three days later of the occasion and is being paid eleven lakhs for her sexual services. Her broker will charge three lakhs from her for providing all kind of securities. Such groups are made on the basis of the charges of prostitutes. Total probable business of sex-market of Indian girls during commonwealth games is supposed to be of around ninety-four crore rupees. Isn't it unbelievable! Unfortunately this is true. Young girls from cities and villages have been booked even two to three months earlier, in advance, for their sexual services. The high leveled organizers of sex-market of our country have an agreement with such organizers of eleven countries. The prostitutes are transferred from other countries to that country, where some function is going to be organized. Perhaps nobody will believe this but again this is true that such ladies and gents, involved in organizing sex market, usually import and export prostitutes with these eleven countries. Twelve thousands prostitutes are supposed to be imported from these countries for commonwealth programs. The charges taken by brokers for well maintained foreigner prostitutes vary from five lakhs to fourteen lakhs hence if we suppose that around ten thousand prostitutes are imported then the money that will be charged from them reaches to minimum five hundred crore rupees. Isn't it perfectly unbelievable? People have ordered their demands in advance. Around seven thousand virgin girls are required. Again no one will believe but this is true that filthy rich Muslim foreigners have already kept their demand for Hindu virgin girls and for that they are ready to pay fifty lakhs per girl. A panel of twenty doctors is already paid for verifying the presence of virgin knot or virginity of girls. Such virgin girls are being kept in safe places. Clients, demanding for virgin girls, have been assured that they will be charged when they will get assured about the virginity of the girls. Why the authorities are not taking any step against such chaos created by sex syndicate? Why ladies organizations are not shouting on this? A lady affiliated to all of the management of sex market said," We have fixed the rates of all the concerned officers, local politicians and nearby welfare organizations so that they may not create problems for us. We will pay the amount as bribe to seven hundred sixty two officers, popular persons affiliated with women welfare organizations and local politicians. Three hundred and twenty nine male authorities refused to take cash and have demanded for young girls." One of a high ranked government officer engaged in the preparation for the commonwealth games told that the sex-market or wide scaled prostitution helps out hiding the drawbacks of management from public and media.

Indian Panel Code on Women

The basic and the great concept of the law that an innocent guiltless man should never get punishment even if for this numerous culprits are set free on behalf of the concept of benefit of doubt, is always broken in context of the family crimes related to ladies. The sections of Indian panel code which are mostly utilized by women to pester men are as following:-

According to Indian panel code section 304-B, where the death of a woman is caused by any burns or bodily injury or occurs otherwise than under normal circumstances within seven years of her marriage and it is shown that soon before her death she was subjected to cruelty or harassment by her husband or any relative of her husband for, or in connection with, any demand for dowry, such death shall be called "dowry death", and such husband or relative shall be deemed to have caused her death. This section was included in the panel code by an amendment done in 1986.

According to Indian panel code section 305, if any person under eighteen years of age, any insane person, any delirious person, any idiot or any person in the state of intoxication, commits suicide, whoever abets the commission of such suicide, shall be punished with death or imprisonment for life, or imprisonment for a term not exceeding ten years, and shall also be liable to fine.

According to Indian panel code section 306, if any person commits suicide, whoever abets the commission of such suicide, shall be punished with imprisonment of either description for a term which may extend to ten years, and shall also be liable to fine.

According to Indian panel code section 312, whoever voluntarily causes a woman with child to miscarry shall, if such miscarriage be not caused in good faith for the purpose of saving the life of the woman, be punished with imprisonment of either description for a term which may extend to three years, or with fine, or with both; and, if the woman be quick with the child, shall be punished with imprisonment of either description for a term which may extend to seven years, and shall also be liable to fine. A woman who causes herself to miscarry, is considered in this section.

According to Indian panel code section 313, whoever commits the offence defined in the section 312 without the consent of woman, whether the woman is quick with the child, or no, shall be punished with imprisonment for life, or with imprisonment of either description for a term which may extend to ten years, and shall also be liable to fine.

According to Indian panel code section 354, whoever assaults or uses criminal force to any woman intending to outrage or knowing it to be likely that he will thereby outrage her modesty, shall be punished with imprisonment of either description for a term which may extend to two year, or with fine, or with both.

According to Indian panel code section 361, whoever takes or entices any minor under sixteen years of age if a male, or under eighteen years of age if a female, or any person of unsound mind, out of the keeping of the lawful guardian of such minor or person of unsound mind, without the consent of such guardian, is said to kidnap such minor or person from lawful guardianship.

According to Indian panel code section 363, whoever kidnaps any person from India or from lawful guardianship, shall be punished with imprisonment of either description for a term which may extend to seven years, and shall also be liable to fine.

According to Indian panel code section 366, whoever kidnaps or abducts any woman with intent that she may be compelled or knowing it to be likely that she will be compelled to marry any person against her will, or in order that she may be forced or seduced to illicit intercourse, or knowing it to be likely that she will be forced or seduced to illicit intercourse, shall be punished with imprisonment of either description for a term which may extend to ten years, and shall also be liable to fine; and whoever, by means of criminal intimidations as defined in this code or of abuse of authority or any other method of compulsion, induces any woman to go from any place with intent that she may be, or knowing that it is likely that she will be, forced or seduced to illicit intercourse with another person shall also be punishable as aforesaid.

According to Indian panel code section 366-A, whoever, by any means whatsoever, induces any minor girl under the age of eighteen years to go from any place or to do any act with intent that such girl may be, or knowing that it is likely that she will be, forced or seduced to illicit intercourse with another person shall be punishable with imprisonment which may be extend to ten years, and shall also be liable to fine.

According to Indian panel code section 375, a man is said to commit "rape" who, except in the case hereinafter excepted, has sexual intercourse with a woman under circumstances falling under any of the six following descriptions-

a) Against her will.
b) Without her consent.
c) With her consent, when her consent has been obtained by putting her or any person in whom she is interested in fear of death or of hurt.
d) With her consent, when the man knows that he is not her husband, and that her consent is given because she believes that he is another man to whom she is or believes herself to be lawfully married.
e) With her consent, when, at the time of giving such consent, by reason of unsoundness of mind or intoxication or the administration by him personally or through another of any stupefying or unwholesome substance, she is unable to understand the nature and consequences of that to which she gives consent.
f) With or without her consent, when she is under sixteen years of age.

According to Indian panel code section 376-A, whoever, has sexual intercourse with his own wife, who is living separately from him under a decree of separation or under any custom or usage without her consent shall be punished with imprisonment of either description for a term which may extend to two years and shall, also be liable to fine.

According to Indian panel code section 376-B, whoever, being a public servant, takes advantage of his official position and induces or seduces, any woman, who is in his custody as such public servant or in the custody of a public servant subordinate to him, to have sexual intercourse with him, such sexual intercourse not amounting to the offence of rape, shall be punished with imprisonment of either description for a term which may extend to five years and shall also be liable to fine.

According to Indian panel code section 497, whoever has sexual intercourse with a person who is and whom he knows or has reason to believe to be wife of another man, without the consent or connivance of that man, such sexual intercourse not amounting to the offence of rape, is guilty of the offence of adultery, and shall be punished with imprisonment of either description for a term which may extend to five years, or with fine, or with both. In such case the wife shall not be punishable as an abettor.

According to Indian panel code section 498, whoever takes or entices away any woman who is and whom he knows or has reason to believe to be the wife of any other man, from that man, or from any person having the care of her on behalf of that man, with intent that she may have illicit intercourse with any person, or conceals, or detains with that intent any such woman, shall be punished with imprisonment of either description for a term which may extend to two years, or with fine, or with both.

According to Indian panel code section 498-A, whoever, being the husband or the relative of the husband of a woman, subjects such woman to cruelty shall be punished with imprisonment for a term which may extend to three years and shall also be liable to fine. Here cruelty means:-

a) Any willful conduct which of such a nature as is likely to drive a woman to commit suicide or to cause grave injury or danger to life, limb or health of the woman. Or

b) Harassment of the woman where such harassment is with a view to coercing her or any person related to her to meet any unlawful demand for any property or valuable security or is on account of failure by her or any person related to her to meet such demand.

Crimes Related to Women

Abortion

An induced abortion is a criminal act which is not permitted by the laws of the country. Perhaps this is the only crime for which society gives permission but judiciary is almost against of it. More than eighty percent of the abortions are performed by unmarried ladies, underage girls, divorcees and widows. If such abortions are strictly prohibited by the government then the children taking birth will be illegitimate because the men responsible for that are already married somewhere else or are underage. As explained earlier, most of the young girls perform sexual unions with the married men or with the men very elder to them so that they may achieve sexual pleasure and proper security from them while widows or divorcees keep the illicit sexual relations with men of their proximity. All widows or divorcees, who keep illicit sexual relations, go through abortion because they have no way to justify their pregnancies but as they are very accustomed of such situations hence they do not face any kind of trouble in this. They themselves take contraceptives or directly visit to some gynecologists to take proper advice for abortion. Very less percent of the abortions are done with the intentions to remove the female child though it is assumed that in almost such instances, ladies go through ultrasound to know the gender of the fetus and perform abortion once they come to know that they are carrying a female child.

Young girls involved in illicit sexual relations when someday find their menstruation discharge not started even when the due date is crossed, they become anxious. They inform to their lovers and sometimes take the advice of experienced female colleagues or friends. They bring pregnancy test stripes from medical shops on the advice of some experienced friend and take few drops of their urine to perform test. Performing such test has been very easier nowadays because of the availability of such stripes in almost medical shops. After performing the test, they carefully see the results and meantime read several times the instructions mentioned about judging the result of test. If they find the test result to be negative, they become happy and continue their sexual relations. If the result is positive, they become frightened. If this is happening with them first time then on the advice of some friend, they perform the test again on some different strip. They take medicines to terminate pregnancy and to start menstruation cycle if either of they or their lovers have already faced such situations earlier. If such a girl and her boyfriend, both are novice then they visit to some lady doctor or gynecologist. They pretend to be just married husband and wife and say to doctor that they do not want children so early. Before going to doctor, the lady adorns herself with the peculiar items used by married ladies like necklace and vermillion etc. Experienced lady doctor knows that they are not husband and wife but she remains quiet and somber and gives them the prescription of the medicines to abort. Before this she asks her about the duration of the occurrence of last menses and carefully examines the status of embryo through ultrasound. Again, lady doctor knows that they are not husband and wife and they are telling their pseudonym. She is familiar with the fact that the only relation they have is illicit sexual relation but she becomes neutral and informs them the method to take medicine after taking her normal or above normal fees from them. She does formality to advise them not to go through abortion and tells them about the probable bad consequences of aborting first baby. The lady and her so called husband pretend paying attention to the advices given by doctor. When the lady intakes medicine, she goes through abortion and the pieces of embryo comes out through menstruation discharge. This process is painful for the duration of twenty minutes to half an hour. Sometimes when it has crossed two months then performing abortion through medicines becomes more painful and the broken pieces coming out through menses can be seen and often ladies become embarrassed to look at that. Experienced ladies adopt various techniques for not conceiving pregnancy. Such ladies, who reside in interior villages, after performing sexual courses sit on toes and contract their lower abdominal portion in a peculiar manner to make all of the ejaculated fluid of themselves and their sexual mates out of their body through the vaginal route. They have an opinion that by doing this, they will not conceive and shockingly they are found to be successful. Again the parents of the girls living in the villages prefer to take the help of local remedies instead of consulting doctors when they get about the pregnancies of their unmarried daughters. Married ladies, who conceive pregnancy but are not willing to carry it, also adopt such locally popular methods. In this the pregnant ladies are given edible items producing heat in the body. Such items includes of honey, lump of raw sugar or boiled sugar-cane juice etc. These kinds of remedies are only applicable up to at most three months of the pregnancy. Though the ladies of the families residing in the villages become aware of the pregnancy of the unmarried girls of the family but somewhere they come to know about this when it has been more than five months. In such matters, where it has been late to take the help of local medicines, to get rid of unwanted pregnancies, parents send their unmarried daughters to the relatives residing in the cities and perform their abortion so that no one in the surroundings may come to know about this. Though being pregnant of unmarried ladies is considered to be unpardonable offense in the countries which in actual run on the basis of moral conducts and religious norms but unfortunately in India, there are no specific punishments for such ladies who become pregnant while performing sexual plays with other men. The advantage of such incapability of the judiciary is taken by the almost young sexually corrupt unmarried girls, widows and divorcees. If some law seems to be strict in context of ladies performing abortions or keeping illicit sexual relations then this is mere a delusion because in parallel of such laws, there are numerous laws which provide uncountable ways to such ladies for protecting themselves from the punishments by putting the blames of such all wrongdoings performed by them on the concerned men.

Parents, when find their unmarried daughters suffering from some physical problems; take the advice of some lady doctor. When in such matters, doctors inform them that their daughters are pregnant then they become shocked. Somewhere fathers of such girls die from heart attack and somewhere they commit suicide because they are frightened from the probable defame. If doctors advise them to let their daughters give birth to child for the sake of their safety then such children take birth and almost of them are either thrown in the sewage lines or dustbins or are kept near orphanage. In some matters, parents to such girls talk with the guys responsible for the pregnancy and by mutual understanding of both the sides, the marriage is decided. Somewhere mothers to such guys, who are blamed by the parents of the pregnant unmarried girls, blame such girls proving them to be prostitutes, willing to put the responsibilities of their pregnancies achieved because of the illicit sexual relation with other men on their so called innocent sons. Again when the men responsible for such pregnancies are already married or are in very close relations, the marriage of such ladies with them is not possible. Somewhere childless married couples, who are in close relation to such girls, take the responsibilities of such infants by adopting them but again this happens seldom because no one wants to adopt a child who is proved illegitimate. Almost of the children, thrown by their mothers after birth because of being illegitimate, are adopted by the very low class families or the beggars for the purpose of earning from them in future. Most of them, if remain alive, are adopted by the eunuchs and are compelled to undergo through painful process of making sexually impotent. In such process, the sensitive layer near the vagina including clitoris of the female child is brutally cut to make out from the body with the help of knife and similarly the male child are made sexually impotent. After this, they undergo through a long process by which their voice is changed by compelling them to drink some acidulous substances. Almost of such kids kidnapped or adopted by eunuchs belong to other cities and the kids of eunuchs are never seen because of the fear of them being identified. A big count of such orphans, sheltered by professional beggars, is made handicapped so that they may draw the attention of public and may earn more money by begging. Again such kids go through painful process done over them to make them physically unfit and ugly. Somewhere their tongue is cut by a knife so that they may never speak while somewhere their legs or hands are cut to make them maimed or cripples. Some of them are made permanently blind by putting acid in their eyes. Again the logic behind such inhuman behavior done with them is to get mercy feeling of the public for them so that they may earn more money by begging. They are given insufficient food by the men under whom they work and hence all the money they earn by begging is taken by their so-called owners. Such cruelty in the field of begging is almost faced by the boy children only because orphan female children are either sold in brothels or to eunuchs or beg under the shelter of their beggar mothers.

An incident happened in Assam where a lady kept illicit sexual relations with a man. She got pregnant and the man responsible for her pregnancy helped in her abortion for her safety. This seems to be normal as it usually happens because both of them were willing to keep such relations. Then the lady compelled him for marriage while he denied. The lady filed a case against him that he forcefully did her abortion. She said that she kept sexual relations with him because he promised her for marriage. Now judiciary took that lady to be of very high morals and the man was considered to be guilty. Ultimately that frightened man married with that lady. That lady then took her complaint back as he was now her husband. This is a very nice example of judicial blackmailing. An advocate said that suppose thousands of men would have promised her to marry then she must have kept sexual relations with all of such men. Such instances of blackmailing done by ladies through men on behalf of their illegitimate children or pregnancies can be seen in whole of the country and it is much better to term such incidences as judicial blackmailing instead of emotional blackmailing.

Rape

Sexual molestation or sexual abuse or sexual harassment or the extreme of all of these that is rape, is considered to be a social crime and wherever the norms are followed, this is said to be highly immoral act and is strictly forbidden. Though in some places, forcibly breaking the virginity by demolishing the virgin knot of the young girls through some wooden object is religiously accepted but there also this is done so as to protect them from black magic and harmful incantations done with malicious intentions to exploit their virginity. The literal meaning of rape is sexual assault including sexual union performed forcefully with a lady by making her physically or mentally helpless. A sexual course performed with a lady is only considered to be rape of her when it is done forcefully with her without her consent and she has struggled utmost to resist the concerned man. Her silent acceptance or consent for mating or not resisting properly to the man performing sexual mating is not considered to be her unwillingness. Hence to prove the unwillingness of a lady or to justify that she is raped, there should be proper indications of the resist done by her or her helplessness to oppose. What exactly is the opinion of the society and the judiciary regarding the sexual rape and when it should be considered to be an unpardonable offense, is a subject of contradictions. We can categorize all kind of sexual rapes faced by ladies, which come into the knowledge of society because of getting disclosed or are hidden from being public, into different sections on the basis of the age of the victim ladies, actual situations and the number of men who performed such rapes, as follows:-

In the first category of the rape, the age group of the victim is of less than sixteen years. Most of such rapists are mentally and sexually perverted but it is seldom seen from their personality and behavior. Such men allure minor girls by providing them toys or candies or gifts and make them come to a lone place. They do indecent touching to such underage girls and disrobe them. When the girls come to know that something wrong is going to happen with them, it is already too late. Small girls of the age group of less than eight years are unfamiliar with even the premonitions of such misshapes and hence they never realize what is going to happen with them till the penis is inserted into their vagina. They are not having the capacity to resist and they become unconscious bearing utter pain and sometimes die. Some of such perverted rapists slay the girls after sexual course because of the fear of disclosing their identities or just to satisfy their sadistic behavior. In some of such matters, they cut the victims in to pieces to hide their body. All of such offences of raping underage girls should be considered to be unpardonable whether they are performed by a group or a single man and the concerned rapists should get the death sentence publicly even if they are proved to be mentally retarded so as to make a fear in the unconscious or conscious mind of sexually perverted men.

Somewhere underage girls of the age group of around fourteen to sixteen years give their consent for sexual plays because of curiosity, sexual excitation and lack of conscience as well as lack of discretion. When such girls are allured by the aged sexually corrupt strangers or relatives, they become ready. Almost of such girls are ignored and not properly cared by their parents therefore they seek the affection that they should get from their parents elsewhere and hence sexually molested by men. The parents of such underage girls are equally responsible and should be equally punished as the men who sexually molest them.

The sexually perverted rapists molesting the girls of the age group of less than ten years are almost illiterate, mentally sick and sadist. Again they perform complete or incomplete sexual course with girl children by enticing them for some edible item and bringing them in a lone place. In fact such rapists are of extreme hatred mentality and lack mannish qualities hence they need a piece of loath to make their sexual perversion released. They are utter coward and find themselves impotent to satisfy their sexual desires from a lady of their age group. Though almost of them are sick but they should immediately get severe punishment equal to death sentence or whole life imprisonment without showing any kind of mercy so that they may be kept away from the human society. They often pick underage girls of three to eight years and make them nude by telling them that they are showing them the hole where ants live and then lick their vaginal area. Then they insert their penis and make minor girls either unconscious before it by hitting something on their head or tie their mouth so that they may not shout and attract people.

The second category of the rapes includes of mass rapes in which more than one man perform copulation forcefully with a lady. Normally offended girls are not physically wounded to make unconscious in such rapes because one man sits over their breasts or holds them tightly while the other one performs mating with them. All of the men perform copulation with the victim one by one and after second forcible sexual course, the resistance power of affronted girl becomes weak. Again the mass rapes are performed by the men who are sexually perverted and sadist hence other perverted disgusting sexual acts are also performed in mass rapes. Such rapists do not bound lady to perform oral sex because they are frightened that the helpless lady may cut their genital organs. Such rapists often excrete urine over the face and genital organs of the victim lady after performing sexual rape with her. Mass rapes are again unpardonable offenses and all of the rapist should be equally and severely punished so that men with such sexual perversion may get frightened to perform such acts of satisfying their sexual perversion. Unmarried and virgin girls are worst effected by mass rapes as this often make them frightened in context of normal sexual courses and they take time to even be normal with their husbands after marriage during intercourse. The ill physical consequences of mass sexual rapes are remedied after some period but the victim usually takes years or even more than that to overcome from the psychological side-effects of it. Mostly mass rapes are faced by married ladies or the ladies expertise in sexual relations because in almost instances, mass rapes are done to take revenge when married ladies deny continuing their illicit sexual relations with a previous sex partner while keep such illicit sexual relations with other men in parallel to their marital life. The mass rapes, faced by married ladies or the girls already having sexual relations, mostly invoke sexual perversion in them and the consequences of this is actually faced by their husbands or blood relatives.

In some instances, married or unmarried ladies are sexually raped by their boyfriends along with their friends. In this, a guy performs mating with his lover and the same is done one by one by his friends but such instances seldom happen. Again almost of the instances of mass rape happen just for the sake of taking revenge. Somewhere a lady is raped by some guy along with his friends because of the betrayal she has done with him or the false blame she put on him in past. Almost of such instances are faced by ladies because of their previous love affairs or enmities and in more than ninety percent of such instances, they themselves are directly or indirectly responsible for their sexual rape hence it is more genuine to call it as mass sexual performance rather than mass rape. Still this is true that such mass sexual performances or rapes should be considered as serious offences if it is sure that the victim was not a lady of ill sexual character and she is compelled for such relations.

Whatever is the assessment of the scholars familiar with the sexual relations and women psychology regarding sexual rapes but this is true that without performing violence, two men can not rape a lady. A lady can be raped by two men only when they tie her by rope or perform violence to her by physically wounding her or make her unconscious either by some injury or by some intoxicant or give her drugs to sexually excite or compel her by the threaten to kill some of her close relative. If aforementioned situations are not seen then only three or more than three men can rape a mature lady. If it is found that the lady, mass raped by men, was virgin and lost her virginity because of the rape then the culprits must be punished severely even when aforementioned situations are not seen with her. Here, the only indication of virginity is the presence of virgin knot. If a lady, keeping illicit sexual relations, blames that she is mass raped then definitely she is also responsible for this.

The third category of sexual rapes is one where a lady is raped by a man. In such matters, the age of the victim is more than sixteen years. Again in such instances, if the lady is raped after giving her the medicines providing sexual stimulation or made unconscious by medicines without her knowledge then she should be considered to be raped. Ladies raped by a man after making physically helpless by providing injury or by other means, are also considered in this category. A lady, who willingly intakes wine in the company of a man and afterwards blames him for her sexual rape, is equally culpable. Almost of the blames of sexual rape put by ladies on single man are false when there are no symptoms of the proper resistance shown by them though in all of such matters, the so-called liable men are punished by the judiciary. It is seen practically that a man can not sexually rape a physically fit lady unless he utilizes at least one of the aforementioned ways. A rape performed by a man by fatally injuring a lady or by binding her with a rope after making her unconscious is also considered to be an unpardonable offense. Compelling a lady for sexual course by threatening her for killing some of her relative as younger brother, is also considered to be in this category but there should be proper evidence like the so called relative should be in custody of that rapist. Deceitfully making a lady intake some intoxicant mixed in some edible item and then performing copulation with her while she is unconscious or unable to resist, is also considered to be a serious and unpardonable crime. A lady willingly taking alcohol or some other intoxicant in the proximity of her boyfriend or some other guy, if sexually coursed by him then this can not be considered to be her sexual rape because in context of a country like India, the virginity is supposed to be the most precious wealth of ladies and if a lady, keeping such precious wealth, involves in the activities where the safety of her valuable wealth is not assured then she herself is responsible for that because she is taking risk in spite of knowing that she should not involve herself in such activities where she is skeptical about securing her wealth. If a lady invites or allures a man to perform sexual plays presenting her as an object to attain sexual pleasure then she herself is only responsible for the indecent behavior shown by him towards her. If a lady disrobes herself in front of a man or sexually seduces him or unnecessary reveals her body parts by wearing indecent garments then she is also culpable for any kind of sexual harassment she faces because she is going against Indian culture. If a lady shows some scratch marks on her body as a proof of the struggle done by her to protect herself during the sexual rape of her done by a single man then this should not be considered to be her rape because the history is witnessed that Indian ladies sacrificed their life when they felt that they were going to be sexually molested. The simple scratch marks on the body of a lady should be considered to be the indications of her consent for sexual course rather than any kind of resist done by her. If it is clear that the lady was compelled or injured during sexual course or she injured the man who was trying to perform sexual course with her then this should be considered to be her sexual rape or an attempt of sexual rape respectively and the concerned man should be punished severely. Again if sexual course is done by a man without the consent of a lady and the symptoms as wound or injuries can be seen on the body of victim as an indication of the resistance shown by her then this is a serious offense and the concerned man should get severe punishment. In the matters of rape, there should be clear indications of the force applied by accused as well as the forceful resistance shown by the victim. If it is not proved that the lady resisted so-called accused forcefully then it should be considered to be sexual relations formed with mutual consent and if such a lady blames a man for sexual rape then she should be punished for false blaming, committing harlotry and being false witness of her so called rape. Often ladies themselves tear their cloths and make scratches on their breasts and faces just to falsely blame innocent guys but again this should not be considered as an attempt of rape. All of such matters, where a lady is blaming a guy for attempt of her sexual harassment or molestation, should be deeply scrutinized and if ultimately the guy is found to be guilty then he should get severe punishments while if it is found that lady lied regarding such blames then she should get more severe punishments.

Ladies and school girls are available if one is desirous to trap a man in the false blame of sexual harassment and rape. This is not a joke because in *Lucknow*, girls are available from forty thousand rupees to eighty thousand rupees, depending on the status of man whom one is eager to blame. After taking the required money, such girls arrange the meetings with the men, whom they have to blame on the directions of some other men, in order to make closeness with them and then suddenly someday blame them for sexual assaults or rapes. Charges taken for this job varies from one lakh to five lakhs in *Delhi*. Now, to file forged complaint of sexual assaults in police stations, there are different rates again depending on the status of the men whom one has to blame. Such payments are given by the men who are desirous to blame someone with the help of specific ladies. The amount taken by responsible police officers for filing a fake complaint of sexual assault vary from thirty-five thousands to five lakhs. Number of cases happens in the country where outsider ladies give money to maidservants working in the residences to blame for sexual assault to men of such residences. In a matter, recently happened in the country, a maidservant was caught red handed while pilfering and then she was advised and paid by the lady who helped her appointing in that house to falsely blame for sexual assault to man of the house. Again this is very common and can often be seen in the country. Whenever maidservants are caught in stealing, they often counter-blame men of the families for sexual assaults. Though almost all of the maidservants are sexually available still they blame when aforementioned situations are created.

Now again we are taking the example of *Lucknow* city. Ladies and school girls involved in prostitution, use their own jargon. Code three means the client will be available at *Lucknow* polytechnic gate near the turn of *Gomti Nagar*, code five means in front of *Mayfair* cinema hall, code eleven means in front of IT girl's collage etc. Similarly WD means whole day booking and NH means night halt. Such abbreviations are frequently used by school girls. Recently the District Magistrate of *Lucknow* announced that school girls and boys in the school uniform are prohibited to enter in the shopping malls, cinema halls, restaurants or hotels and parks. Indeed, it was a very wise decision because guys in the school uniform go to watch indecent adult movies instead of going to schools and often can be seen smoking or taking alcohol in the parks. Even school girls go to visit parks or restaurants with their lovers and often can be seen performing harlotry. Poor parents think that their innocent children are in the schools. Such smart students bunk their schools once and twice in a week so that their attendance may not get short. School girls belonging to an area go to visit another area which is at long distance from their residences hence they are never caught red handed. They often keep another dress in their school bags so that they may change their school uniform while roaming with their lovers. Unfortunately when the decision was given by the District Magistrate, the female Chief Minister dismissed and made void that order on the same day by applying her veto power. One of senior government officer told that if school girls are prohibited to visit here and there in the school uniform then availability of such girls during day time for sexual plays will become difficult and this will ultimately increase the financial corruption because in the higher level authorities, the bribes are taken in the form of hard cash or some favor of another kind or sexual services of young girls.

The fourth category includes of the sexual rapes where the offender kills the victim either before or after performing sexual course. Such disgusting acts are done by mentally retarded and sexually perverted men. Somewhere such rapists cut the breasts of the lady and damage her vaginal area or anus with a sharp weapon then perform sexual course while somewhere they just make lady unconscious and perform sex then destroy her body organs. Offended lady dies painfully and the rapist gets overwhelmed while seeing blood coming out from her breasts and vagina. They soak their penis into the blood of the lady and suck her breasts by biting it through teeth. Some of the shrewd men rape some lady and destroy her body so as to pretend that to be an act of some mentally sick men. Though the actual rape is itself an act performed by sexually sick men but lustful men of normal temperament are also found performing rapes. In some of such instances, the men perform rapes in such a peaceful manner by hiding the clues that they can never be considered to be mentally sick. Somewhere such serial rapes are performed by a rapist and he is never caught red handed by the police because of his awareness. Somewhere such serial rapes are performed by perverted men just like a puzzle and they play this with the police and administration. They keep a sort of challenge in front of the police to catch them and consider this as their nimbleness. Though this category of rapes is seen very rare in the Indian society but this is true that such rapist doesn't matter whether he is mentally sick or not, should be condemned to death.

In the fifth category of rapes, the rapist performs sexual course with a lady who is in destitute or is helpless. Though the symptoms of force or compelling are not seen in such rapes but as the victim ladies are already helpless hence it is assumed that they are not in the position of resisting. Ladies admitted in hospitals for some medical cure are sexually abused or raped by the staff member or the ladies arrested by the police and raped in the police stations, are considered to be in this category. Such crimes are extremely serious but in almost of such instances, victim is compelled by the administration to withdraw her blame. This is true that the incidents of actual sexual rapes happening in the society are very less in comparison to the rapes performed in the local police stations under the custody of responsible police officers. Unfortunately less than one percent of such rapes happening under the custody of police are highlighted. Again it is often seen that whenever some policemen find a love couple sitting alone, they abuse the guy and take money from him while bring the lady away. They sexually abuse the lady and compel her to perform oral sex. Both of the guy and girl are threatened that if they speak against of this then their parents will be informed about their love affairs and it will be said to them that they were caught red handed performing sexual course or immoral act. All of such ladies request not to inform their parents and permit them to perform oral sexual plays with them. This is very common in North India and in the evening hours, some policemen can be seen visiting parks to seek for love couples. Though they are appointed to stop performing indecent performances but unfortunately some of them behave indecently and perform sexual plays under the shade of pretending themselves busy in stopping such acts done by the couples. Up to what extent, ladies are ready to perform sexual plays with the unfamiliar policemen so as to hide their love matters from the parents, can be imagined by this that out of around more than hundreds of such instances happening everyday only in the *Lucknow* city, no complaint is filed against such policemen by the so called victim ladies.

In the sixth category of the rape, the girl is incapable to disclose her sexual molestation because the offender is her close relative. Such rapists are found in the families of the victim girls. They often play sexually with the girls of the family while they are sleeping. When relatives perform such indecent act of pressing breasts or massaging at the genital organs, the girls get embarrassed and never inform to their parents. Again they make sexual relations with the young girls of their relations because they know that such underage girls will never tell about this to parents because of shyness. Such rapists are often found making unnatural sexual course with animals though all of the perverted men performing sexual plays with the animals are not incest. Such men desire to perform sexual course with their cousin sisters, sisters-in-law and other indirectly related female relatives and often masturbates on their undergarments. They are eager to perform copulation even with a female cadaver. Somewhere the staff member or a medical student performs sexual plays with the dead body of ladies kept for the dissection purpose in medical colleges. As a dead body or an animal can not express consent or refusal while sexual course hence the level of punishments in such crimes are difficult to judge. Again performing sexual course with an animal or a corpse is a disgusting inhuman act but can not be considered to be sexual rape. The sexual molestation of a girl done by her stepfather or brother is considered to be in this category and is an unpardonable crime. The lustful relatives often perform sexual plays with the young girls instead of sexually raping them. The severity of such sexual plays should be considered to be equivalent to a rape as per the opinion of the judiciary and the offender should be punished if caught. Young girls are deceitfully indecently touched by the relatives at breasts or thighs under the shade of emotional affection. Such relatives often compel girls to perform oral sex with them. Again along with the offenders, the parents or specially mothers of such girls are equally culpable and should be punished because of being careless for their girl children.

Fourteen matters were surveyed where young or minor girls blamed men for the sexual harassment in some vehicle like in bus or car or train. It was said that the girls were raped in all of such instances. Out of such fourteen matters, nine were said to be performed in the personal vehicles as private cars and all of such blames were false. In a recent matter happened in *Delhi*, a school girl of around eighteen, blamed a middle age man for her rape. She said that she was waiting for the bus when the culprit asked some address from her and offered her lift to her destination. She became ready and during the journey, the man stopped the car in a corner and raped her. Sounds very shocking and unfortunate but astonishingly she was lying. The blind media broadcasts such matters without any delay and even police officers stand in favor of such girls without using commonsense. In rest of the five matters, two were actually happened out of which one was performed in a bus and another was in train. The remaining three matters, said to be happened in trains, were bogus. Why young ladies or even underage school girls are falsely blaming men? The reason was told by some girls, of the same schools, who were familiar with the so called offended girls. They said that in almost of such instances, the so called culprits are the mature or over age sex partners of the affronted girls. The girls keep sexual relations with such men for the sake of pocket money and unending expenditures and when they seek new partner, they kick them. After keeping sexual relations till sufficiently long duration with such school girls, men have already spent a lot on money on them and they have been emotionally attached with these girls. Hence the moment the girls declare that they are quitting, the conflict takes place and the girls blame them for never happened sexual harassment or rape. An incident happened in west Bengal, in which the culprit was hanged to death as a punishment of raping and murdering an underage girl, is important to mention here. He was a guard of a residential complex and he raped and killed a girl living there. The offender and the victim both are dead now hence it would be a disgrace for the demised to discuss about that. The day before the execution, victim confessed that he murdered that girl but he did not rape her. When he knew that the very next day he was going to die then it can not be assumed that he was lying because this confession was not going to avoid his death sentence. It was indeed a very crucial confession done by the man blamed for sexual assault and murder of an innocent girl. Anyone responsible for such murder of an innocent girl, should get punishment of death and that he got but suppose for a moment that he was right because he murdered that girl but he did not rape her then it has lots of meanings. Perhaps this was not liable to be considered in the category of cold blooded murders. Sometimes in such situations, offended girls are very intimate to such culprits and unfortunately some situations take place which cause hot argument and one is killed by other. Somewhere culprit men are aware of the illicit sexual relations of such girls and hence they pressurize or blackmail girls to keep sexual relations with them. Almost every year, such incidents happen especially in west Bengal and often main culprits are out of the reach of administration. A shocking incident of West Bengal happened many years before, in which a Muslim guy killed a fourteen years girl to take revenge and he slotted her into pieces so as to hide the body. The culprit was caught by the police and got simple imprisonment. This was the crime that would have been defined in the category of cold blooded offence and the criminal would have been punished by the death sentence. There are numerous such instances where men, killing underage children are simply punished by imprisonment and never got death sentence. That means in the aforementioned criminal matter, the culprit was hanged to death because he raped that girl not because he killed her. If this is true then shockingly he did not rape that girl. Unfortunately judicial decisions also get affected by the social pressure, political pressure and higher influences.

In the society, there are mischievous men, eager to perform sexual assault on innocent ladies and underage girls and ladies have to be expertise and bold enough to face adverse situations. Again sexually hungry wolf in the shade of men's skin can be seen roaming in the society and ladies have to be morally strong and active to avoid and oppose them, though the count of such men is very limited. The rough behavior and attitude adopted by ladies to deal with such wolfs become troublesome for their blood relatives, would-be in-laws and husbands because they can never get rid of such aggressive temperament that is needed to deal with aforementioned men of ill-feelings and hence they start utilizing the concepts of such behavioral nudity on their family members. It can be often seen that innocent girls or ladies living alone in the society, separate from their residences because of achieving higher studies or their jobs, face adverse situations caused by such wolfs. Out of twenty percent morally high ladies, around sixteen percent are very innocent and such ladies can be seen in the society. They are indeed worthy of utter respect and even their parents as well as their husbands get rid of all of their sins just by the proximity of them and this is ritualistic as well as spiritualistic truth. Unfortunately the count of such virtuous ladies is continuously decreasing. Guys, who are fairly busy in their studies or legal earnings, never get the time to tease or humiliate ladies. The ill acts or teasing is done by the guys whose parents have earned lot of money by illegal ways but unfortunately they are proved unworthy to give proper guidance and ethics to their sons. Such parents are responsible for making a battalion of these ill mannered boys because they provide them all the facilities that should not be given to them while they are underage. Again shockingly, it is always seen that mothers to such wolfs stand in favor of them when they are found involved in harassing some innocent lady. More than ninety-eight percent children, who get diverted from the right track of morality, are favored by the blind affection of their mothers. Sixty-eight percent fathers confessed in a survey that they are bearing the sin of giving birth to iniquitous daughters or sons because their wives are in support of their children and are only responsible for the misdeeds done by them. A popular lady psychologist told during very personal conversation that either the milk of the breasts of the mothers has been adulterated or the blood of the children they give birth is impure because of crossbreeding, as mothers are not giving birth to worthy youngsters. Nowadays, decent men are afraid of helping destitute ladies. Often such men avoid giving lift to ladies or assisting them in trouble if they are alone or not accompanied by some gents. People avoid keeping girls in their houses as paying guests or tenants. Wise men never take kids from the arms of ladies because they may be blamed by ladies for indecent touching at their breasts. Nowadays only those men dare to help ladies, who are either very innocent or are very cunning with malicious sexual intentions. Almost men, helping to ladies, are falsely blamed by them for sexual harassment. Again the notorious guys involved in harassing or eve-teasing decent girls should get strict punishments and their parents should be informed about this so that they may keep control over them but if girls are found blaming falsely some guys then they and their parents should get punishment. Sexual involvement of ladies and gents before marriage is illicit hence such pairs, whenever caught red handed, should get equal punishment irrespective of their gender. This is the only way by which the rate of adultery or debauchment can be controlled successfully. There should be fear of judiciary and administration in ladies because then only they will stop making illicit sexual relations and falsely blaming men.

When a virgin girl is actually raped by a man or men she never comes out of the depression and grief. Though society keeps sympathy and mercy feelings for her but the feelings of hate and disgust reside behind such mercy. Such a lady is treated strangely by her relatives and friends. Her friends keep a distance from her and relatives warn their children not to be intermingled with her. She always carries a kind of inferiority complex. She feels neglected in the family functions because relatives or friends converse with her factitiously. As per the lustful experienced men, she is easier to get for sexual course while the guys impractical in sexual relations afraid of her. If she is unmarried then the probabilities of her arrange marriage in future becomes almost nil. If a man of strong morals and idealism, dares to pick her hand for marrying her then this is found seldom because no mother permits her son marrying with a lady, who has faced rape. The renowned ladies associated with women welfare organizations and always pretending to be in the favor of widows, victim of sexual assaults or rapes, prostitutes and the daughters of prostitutes never dare to marry their sons with such ladies. Victim ladies of sexual rapes bear humiliation and harassment done by other ladies in whole of their life. When married ladies undergo sexual rape then husbands of them never become able to behave emotionally normal to them in future.

In some instances, it is found that sexual rapes decrease the sensitivity of the vaginal route of victim ladies. Such ladies are often scared of the nightmares. Some of such ladies are so frightened that during sexual courses with their husbands after marriage, they excrete urine or perform farting. Such ladies are extremely conscious in context of their daughters in future and keep strict control over them. Some of the unmarried girls, who have faced mass rapes, stare at the infinity for hours and the desire for living in them diminishes. They get frightened from the dark but in actual are desirous to live in dark. They are found cured when given proper guidance and assistance from some male well-wisher. If they have faced judiciary in context of their sexual rape then they hate from the system, judiciary and the society.

Dowry

Somewhere the followers of the other religions criticize Hindu religion by blaming that newly married ladies are burned alive and physically harassed for the demand of dowry. The active ladies, affiliated to women organizations, seem to be united in such topics and take steps to protect the victim brides. To protect young married ladies from the probable harassment for the demand of dowry, there are very strict laws termed as "Anti-dowry acts" already mentioned in the previous chapters. During a hearing in *Delhi* High Court, judiciary declared that the laws which are made for protecting ladies from the dowry problems are mostly misused by ladies to harass in-laws and husbands. In this hearing, the husband was falsely blamed by his wife for asking dowry because he was not financially much strong to provide luxuries to her. Though the aforementioned statement given by a renowned judiciary member is itself sufficient to express the veracity of the dowry matters but still it is essential to know about the circumstances under which such true or false blames are put upon the husbands and in-laws.

Most of the young girls marry and come to the residences of their husbands with the feeling of possessiveness and desire of ruling over there.

If husband to such a lady follows the instructions of her then the family runs smoothly. The problems and the complications appear when husband does not follow her instructions by not allowing her disrespecting or humiliating other family members. In such situations, a corrupt wife insists her husband to live in another house by leaving parents alone. If husband strictly denies leaving his parents and young brothers or sisters then such a wife adopts various techniques, almost used by immoral ladies, to mentally and physically harass the husband. When husband requests her to adjust with other family members then she threatens him for committing suicide. Almost of such ladies warn their in-laws that they will falsely blame them for the physical harassment for dowry. Some of them put kerosene over themselves and attempt to suicide so that they may blame to in-laws. Hence almost of the dowry cases filed in police stations are forged or the married ladies are themselves responsible for that. Unfortunately parents to married ladies teach them to misuse the anti-dowry act and other acts, which are actually made for the safety of innocent women. Almost married ladies know that if they put false blame on their husbands or in-laws for physical harassment for dowry within the span of seven years from the date of marriage then persons blamed by them will be arrested immediately by the police. If they physically harm themselves and approach to police station pretending that they are beaten for dowry by in-laws then all of the in-laws or family friends whom they blame will get imprisonment. Ladies are familiar with the facts that the innocent husbands often accept all of the ill attitudes of wives so as to protect their aged parents from probable false blames put by the wives. A man facing such awful situations created by his own wife knows that a lie or false blame put by his wife, who is provoked by her parents, will make the social life and the dignity of him as well as of his parents ruined. Almost men live under pressure of their wives because they know that the life of their virtuous parents and well-wishers will become hell if wives falsely blame them for asking dowry or for other kind of harassments. Wise men wait for the seven years and after that they take any appropriate action against of their wives but unfortunately the span of seven years is a big period and till that duration, they have ruined their ethics and personalities. Again all men involved in illegal ways of earning money are in fact irritated from their wives and live in frustration and depression. As such depression always comes out in the form of something immoral hence such men make themselves busy in earning money by illegal ways. They compensate their lack of family comfort by earning money though they never accept this in public. Hence ladies are only responsible for all the financial or social corruptions spread in the society and this is entirely true in context of a country like India.

In the medium class families, dowry system is represented as a horrible incurable disease. According to the views of the grooms' side, no one asks for unlimited money in the form of dowry from the parents of the brides. Such demands vary from thousands to lakhs depending upon the paying capacity of a bride's parents. A fourth class employee gives money in thousands as dowry in his daughter's marriage but he is asked for more if groom's side is very assured that he is having much black money earned by taking bribes. If a man, who has earned money from the illegal ways or bribes, if asked for little more money as dowry then nothing is wrong in that. It has been a custom in India that all corrupt fourth class or third class government employees, who earn lot of money by taking bribes, hide their financial status by living simply and their actual financial level is seen when they become retired from the service because after the retirement, they expend their money explicitly for themselves. Almost of the government servants engaged in taking bribes, can be seen after their retirement involved in making illicit sexual relations with the girls even less than or equivalent to the age group of their own daughters. Again parents of the bride voluntarily give dowry even more than their capacity when they marry their daughters with the comparatively rich guys or government servants. In this, they always keep the thought of achieving financial assistance from the would-be in-laws through their daughters, after marriage. In a survey, it is found that in ninety-seven percent dowry matters, the demand for the dowry is either directly done by the mothers of the grooms or they compel the fathers of the grooms for asking dowry. In all such situations, the grooms or their fathers just act as a medium to either express the desires of the ladies or give silent consent on the demands mentioned by the ladies of the family. Such hundred ladies, who were having sons as well as daughters, were found to be strictly against of dowry while marrying their daughters but ninety-eight of them took dowry on the marriage of their sons. In the very intense and personal survey done regarding the dowry matters disclosed the fact that eighty-seven percent young unmarried girls were in favor of the dowry while thirty-eight percent of the young guys were in favor of dowry. Such figures are very shocking and incredible to believe but this is bare truth that the give and take of the dowry is done by ladies while fathers related to brides' side give the dowry on behalf of their daughters and fathers related to grooms' side just verbalize the demand of dowry expressed by their wives. Hence dowry has nothing to do with gents and it can be seen that the ladies, who are against of dowry because they are losing money, stand in the favor of dowry when they gain it on the occasion of their son's marriage. One more shocking fact is that all unmarried ladies desire to get dowry from their parents because it is their legal right while they call it illegal when such demands are put by their husbands or in-laws. Again married ladies are always against of dowry and say it illegal when they have to give that at the time of the marriage of their daughters while they say it to be perfectly legal and their primary right, when they marry their sons. Now let us see the opinion of judiciary in such matters. Judiciary is biased to take favor of women hence the custom of dowry has been declared to be illegal but again all ladies desire for dowry hence the amendments are done to provide the parental property's right to married women. This is the extreme of the lack of conscience in the law makers. If a married lady asks for money from her parents then she is perfectly right but if the same demand is kept by her husband or in-laws then they should be punished but Why?

One more fact related to dowry is surprising. At the time of betrothal, the family members of the boy's side keep their demands in front of the family members of the girl's side and the parents of the girl give the acceptance of it. As the Hindu marriage is carried in number of steps hence the parents of girl assure to give dowry in steps before marriage. Sometimes they give a part of dowry at the time of engagement and promise to give the rest part at the time of marriage. Now, at the time of marriage ceremony, girl's parents often give only a part of the rest of the amount and say to give the remaining after marriage. If the parents of the boy's side agree to it then the rest of the process of marriage is performed otherwise conflict occurs. In case the parents of the boy deny performing the remaining process then parents of girl request them and promise to give remaining part after marriage. If still the parents of the boy do not agree then parents of girl blame them for asking dowry though they themselves are culpable because they promised at the time of betrothal. Parents of the girl know very well that after marriage, the emotional inclination of the boy towards his newly wedded wife arises and hence he seldom asks for the remaining amount. If parents of the boy believe on the parents of the girl and perform the remaining ceremony then after marriage, mother of the boy insists him to ask for the remaining amount. Now this situation causes trouble and complications. It is noticeable that in almost of such instances, the lies told by parents of the girls become the main cause of conflicts. The main cause of distress of young guys is not the false commitment done by the in-laws instead they are more shocked when they hear from the other relatives that the in-laws are making rumor that they gave more than decided amount though in fact, they even did not give that much amount which they promised. Again it is found that not even four percent parents of the girls speak truth about the exact amount that they give as dowry to their sons-in-law and more than ninety-six percent parents of the bride tell multiple times more amount given by them as dowry than what they actually gave.

In some matters, where the parents of the girls deny giving the remaining amount about which they promised earlier to give at the time of marriage, parents of the boys refuse performing marriage ceremony and then girl's side take the help of anti-dowry act. As the act of denial done by the parents of girls at the time of marriage regarding the promise made by them earlier, is not considered to be any kind of offense and judiciary never provides justice to grooms' side in dowry matters hence in almost of such circumstances, either the boys marry with the same girls because of the fear of the judiciary or are send to prison with their aged parents in the offense of remembering girls' side regarding their promise. The moment guys are pressurized to marry in such situations because of judicial pressure, the concept of marriage ends. A renowned advocate once said during an exclusive conversation," This is the basic problem of our judicial system. Judiciary thinks that marriage is a one-day relation and guys can be compelled to marry with peculiar girls. In almost of such instances, guys are forced to marry with such girls though in fact they should be allowed to quit in the beginning if the conflicts occur at the time of marriage. Our Hindu religion provides inspiration to live a peaceful married life while our judiciary imposes the restrictions on gents. Religion is unbiased in context of marriage matters while judiciary is entirely biased in this. It is appropriate to say that judicial system is against men in marriage matters instead of saying that judiciary over-supports women." A familiar female media person said on this," At present, it is absolutely rubbish to say that girls are ill-effected if their marriage is not accomplished at the eleventh hour because of dowry-conflicts because all of the parents of brides' speak lies when they themselves deny giving dowry about which they had promised earlier. Again parents of the brides' as well as brides themselves lie regarding dowry, doesn't matter whether marriage is performed or cancelled. Parents of the brides always keep safety measures and stock of false blames to protect themselves hence if the marriage is not performed at the last moment, they and their daughters are nowhere defamed, instead the parents of guys and guys themselves are ill-effected because of getting falsely blamed by the brides' side. Before denying giving rest of the amount of dowry, all of such parents of brides' side have planned earlier what they will do when grooms' side will deny marrying because of betray done by them." In such seventy matters, where bridegrooms' family members asked for money or other goods at the time of marriage and denied to marry unless the demand is fulfilled, it is found that in sixty-eight matters out of them, girls' side did the promise to provide that amount or some item but refused at the last moment. Again the girl's side lied earlier with the intention that the grooms' side would not dare to refuse for marriage at the last moment because of the one-sided laws favoring girls and their parents in context of dowry. Girls' relatives spread the rumor that the parents of the boys kept new demands but in fact it was not true because the promise to fulfill those demands was made by the girls' side at the time of betrothal. It is found that the one sided biased laws and illogical support of judiciary provoke the girls and their parents to tell lies, betray and ditch and motivates them to perform family crimes.

The situations or circumstances under which a lady commits suicide basically depend on two reasons. The very first is that if a lady finds herself depressed and is unable to transfer her depression on others, adopts the ultimate way of suicide by which she is able to depress and distress her well-wishers. For example a girl failed in some exam finds herself unable to inform her parents because of the fear of the probable aggression of the parents or breaking of the high expectations of her parents for her result, commits suicide because she could not distribute her depression to others. Similarly a lady betrayed in love affair or when rejected by some man of her choice, gets depressed. If she does not seek any other boyfriend as a replacement or compensation or option of the previous one, she finds herself unable to distribute her depression hence if she is not in the position of informing her parents about her mental disposition because of the conservative environment of her family, she attempts suicide. She knows that she will get free from all of her troubles by suicide but her well-wishers will be cursed to live in depression and distress.

The second reason behind this is that, the ladies having mannish attitude become mentally sick and aggressive because of the internal contradictions. Normally such symptoms are not seen in the behavior of the ladies but the moment they are depressed they become aggressive and perverted. The tendency of taking revenge suddenly rises in them and hence they adopt sadistic nature and tendency to commit suicide. The basic aim behind their causing pain to self or performing suicide is to make others distressed. Such ladies appear to be very gentle and no one can even guess about the killing-tendency in them. More than ninety-five percent ladies performing suicide or burning themselves in so-called dowry matters are mentally sick and are governed by the second reason. Though their parents and the society never accept them to be mentally sick but the husbands and the lovers, to such ladies, who have sexually coursed with them and have spent sufficient duration in their physical proximity, are familiar with the abnormal attitude of them. Three percent of the ladies perform suicide in their marital life because of their escaping tendency while performing family responsibilities or bearing even small stresses. Around two percent ladies are burned by their in-laws or are bound to commit suicide because of the humiliation and harassment of them done by the in-laws or husbands. Again even in love affairs, the moment a guy comes to know about abnormal tendencies of his lover or about her being mentally sick, he escapes immediately by quitting from the relationship.

Fifty instances of dowry matters were surveyed extensively then the figures disclosed were shocking. In nineteen of such families, the blames of asking for dowry, put by married ladies on husbands and in-laws, were false and the only intention behind such false blaming done by ladies was to mentally harass the in-laws. Out of these nineteen matters, eight brides often found intimidating to in-laws regarding committing suicide. Out of the rest of thirty-one matters, in six matters men came to know about the illicit sexual relations of their wives and when they asked for clarification then wives blamed them for harassment for the sake of dowry. In three matters out of aforementioned six instances, husband caught red handed to their wives performing adultery. In thirteen matters, the parents of the ladies provoked them for false blaming to in-laws because their husbands were not ready to leave their aged and physically incapable parents. In one matter, the lady was getting treatment of mental problem by a psychologist from the unmarried life and committed suicide after marriage. In five matters, the parents of the ladies did not pay the amount as they promised to give before marriage hence mothers-in-law to such ladies usually humiliate them by asking for the remaining amount of the dowry. In three matters married ladies quarrel almost everyday with in-laws and one day they put kerosene on themselves and commit suicide to make frighten the in-laws. One of such lady died at the spot even after the full effort done by her in-laws to save her while rest of the two died in hospital and mentioned in their false dying declaration that they were burned by in-laws. In two matters, husbands were of poor family background and hence often ask for dowry. In one matter out of aforesaid two matters, lady was tied by rope and burned alive by mother-in-law and sisters-in-law. In one matter the husband was alcoholic and often used to torture his wife physically for asking for dowry. Out of such fifty matters, when the behavior, temperament and attitude of ladies were scrutinized thoroughly and the opinions of the expert psychologists were considered then the fact exposed was that the thirty-eight of such ladies were mentally sick because the behavior shown by them was not normal. A renowned psychologist told that only a lady can dare to speak untruth by falsely blaming someone in her dying declaration.

Two instances, where the dowry problem took disastrous form, must be mentioned here. In one of such matter, the innocent lady was physically as well as mentally tortured by her in-laws. She was beaten regularly and asked to bring money from her parents and unfortunately parents did not help her even when they were financially capable. She was cauterized by hot tongs on thighs and buttocks just as a punishment. She was made tied from the bed and cruelly beaten by lather belt and sleepers. Such all inhuman behavior to her was done by her mother-in-law and two sisters-in-law. Ultimately she committed suicide to get rid of her in-laws and morally impotent husband. In another popular instance happened, the lady was beaten brutally by in-laws. She was made nude and raped by her brothers-in-law one by one, in the absence of her husband. She was compelled to drink urine and her mother-in-law performed lesbian relationship with her. She was burned alive by her in-laws. A similar case happened in *Delhi* but the authenticity of that matter is doubtful because lady was quite healthy in comparison to her mother-in-law and brother-in-law, whom she blamed for her immoral harassment and she was having numerous ways to get free from her so called harassment. In fact these two matters should not be intermingled with dowry matters because these were the examples of hike of moral and sexual perversion as it is found that in both of the matters, so called mothers-in-law of the affronted young brides were having illicit sexual relations with their own sons.

To get the precise ratio of such instances and the chaos in the families, a new method of survey based on population of the country is applied which revealed the following interesting facts. On average, out of ninety-eight families, in one family, husband beats his wife for her mistakes. Out of twelve hundred families, in one family husband beats his wife without proper cause. Out of three hundred and twenty families, in one family husband beats his wife because of her conflicts with her in-laws. Out of five thousand families, in one family the mother-in-law physically punishes her daughter-in-law for mistakes. Out of fourteen thousand families, in one family mother-in-law physically harasses daughter-in-law while hot argument. Out of eighteen thousand families, in one family she is taunted regarding dowry by her mother-in-law. Out of one lakh and twenty thousand families, in one family she is scolded by her father-in-law for her mistakes. Out of six lakhs families, in one family she is beaten by her father-in-law on her blunder mistakes. Out of thirteen lakhs families, in one family she is scolded and harassed by all the family members on her faults. Out of seventy lakhs families, in one family she is sexually harassed by the family members. Out of fourteen crore families, in one family she is either burned alive or suicides herself because of actual harassment of her.

The figures regarding the activities of the brides are as follows. Out of hundred families, in eighty-six families the ladies as brides unnecessarily create complications and conflicts. In seventy-four families, they unnecessarily humiliate and scold their in-laws. In seventy-six families they beat their children to take a kind of revenge from their husbands. Out of one hundred and twenty families, in nineteen families wives physically torture their husbands and tear their cloths while conflicts. Out of every thousand families, in twenty-six families wives physically torture their in-laws. Twenty-one percent ladies secretly keep illicit sexual relations with the nearby relatives of the husbands. Seventy-six percent ladies, even after being housewives, never prepare food at appropriate time and ninety-three percent of the husbands to such housewives prepare the bed-tea themselves because their wives are sleeping.

The dowry matters are mostly seen in middleclass families. The occurrence of such matters is quite less in lower class families in comparison to the middleclass families. In higher class families, such matters of dowry are seldom seen. It is said that the middleclass men are satisfied by their life styles because they have a limited charm and desire for earning money while higher class families are never satisfied by the money hence they are always busy in earning money. If this concept is followed then there should be more instances of dowry matters in higher class families but this is not seen to be true. The custom of dowry is in fact accepted by all categories irrespective of their financial status. Again almost men take dowry as per their social and financial level and similarly almost parents of young girls give dowry willingly or unwillingly. While defining dowry, demand has nothing to do with this because if a bride comes to her husband's house by wearing the garments given to her by her parents then this is also dowry. A lady brings one rupee or one million rupees with her, both will be considered to be dowry. Again she comes to husband's residence wearing simple metallic necklace or silver necklace or golden necklace with diamonds embedded to it, all will be considered to be a part of dowry. Hence even when men say that they are against dowry, they are in fact taking dowry. If some lady, married to financially higher class family, blames her in-laws for asking for dowry then such ridiculous blame put by her might be highlighted by the media but in fact the relatives, society and the concerned judicial authority immediately come to know that she is lying. This is the main cause that such instances in very higher class or high class families are seldom highlighted.

The instances of dowry demand are less in lower class or very lower class families because in almost of such families both of the husband and wife are earning. A rickshaw driver drives whole day for earning while his wife earns as a maidservant working in middleclass residences. Hence if the wives are working then both of them are busy in earning their livings. Almost of the ladies of the lower class or very lower class are involved in prostitution in parallel with their jobs. Somewhere idle husbands help their wives in performing harlotry. Husbands are beaten by the wives and wives are beaten by their husbands. Women of this category confessed that if they are not beaten by the husbands then they will start performing harlotry, openly. It was very embarrassing taking interviews of the very lower class men. Such men said that they perform hard core physical labor on daily wages and are scolded by the owners. They come to home in the late evening hours where again they are scolded by the wives. They said that they usually take alcohol to maintain themselves physically fit and give the remaining salary to the wives. Though such earned money is sufficient for running the family still they are humiliated by the wives. Wives join some work of maidservants in the other comparatively rich houses to earn money for their luxury. They said that they all are familiar with the fact that their wives are involved in prostitution but whenever they say to them not to work for earning then they get harsh reply from them. Wives reply to them that they will leave working if they give them more money to fulfill desires. Hence such poor men have limited options as either leaving their wives or earning more money. They are unable to leave their wives because their society is very strict in such matters and for gaining more money, they have to adopt illegal ways of earnings. Hence ultimately they live with their wives ignoring the indecent acts and misbehavior done by them. They let their wives performing prostitution under the shade of their job of maidservants.

In the residences where such maidservants are working on hour basis or permanently, ladies of the houses perform no house jobs and they make maidservants work like hell. In such houses, maidservants are not allowed to sit or to go lavatory. The ladies of the house do inhuman behavior with them. When hundred of such maidservants were interviewed then all of them said that it is very difficult to work under ladies because they keep disgusting behavior for maidservants. All of them said that those maidservants are very fortunate who work under the rule of men of the houses. All of such maidservants were found to be involved in pilfering money, jewelries, utensil and edible items from the houses where they work. When the owner of the houses were interviewed then they said that only a lady can handle properly to a maidservant because all of them are utterly indolent and kleptomaniac.

In the lower or very lower class category, the violence in-between husband and wife and the big count of children are the factors which help ladies to be associated with their husbands. It is found that if such ladies do not give birth to number of children and are not punished by their husbands on misdeeds, they are unable to stay with one man as their husband. Again almost ladies of this category are of loose character but they afraid of their husbands. If such ladies quarrel with their husbands and go to their parent's house leaving husbands alone then they seldom get shelter by the parents for long. Ultimately they have to live with their husbands and hence they can not falsely blame their in-laws for dowry demand. If the parents to such ladies belonging to financially poor class families, start giving shelter to their married daughters and provoke them to unnecessary raise the voice against husbands then dowry matters will start arising in this category also. A peculiar tendency is found in the ladies of these categories that they often can be seen changing their husbands and for this they never go through the process of divorce. As mentioned above, this facility is not available to men of this category as their society is strict on quitting from family obligations only for men. A lady of these categories, when feels uncomfortable with her husband or seeks another suitable man, leaves her husband and children and starts living with the other man. In fact the anti-dowry act and other acts made for protecting ladies are not biased or wrong. Such laws become biased and iniquitous when ladies start false blaming and misusing such rules for the sake of harassing in-laws and husbands. This is because at present, no lady want to marry with a man being his life partner instead all ladies desire to rule their husbands and in-laws.

After marriage, husband and in-laws are legally not authorized to ask for dowry from the bride and her parents and if such act is done by them then this is an offence. This is true that young married ladies are harassed and humiliated by in-laws for the demand of money or some assets in the form of dowry and somewhere such brides are burned alive by in-laws but in fact in very less percent of the total dowry matters such situations appear because in almost of such cases, young married ladies put false blame on the in-laws and husbands. In some instances such ladies blame the in-laws in their false dying declarations. Some of them are saved by doctors but the acute pain of burning is experienced by them. Almost ladies, who commit suicide either to harass in-laws or because of being in extreme depression, blame the in-laws for this. The tendency of taking revenge is so strong in ladies that they desire to blame all of the persons whom they do not like or whom they could not suppress or whom with they could not perform sexual course even after having infatuation for them. Fortunately they can not do this and hence they blame to surrounding in-laws or other relatives whom they dislike, for their so-called harassment. If a lady dies in an accident within the span of seven years from her marriage then the parents of that lady threaten the husband and in-laws of her and often take big amount of money for not filing a false police case on them. Almost of such parents are found taking money from the in-laws of their demised married daughters thereby earning on behalf of the dead-bodies of daughters.

If a wife performs indecently, unnecessarily quarrels with the family members and threatens for blaming for dowry or for committing suicide then the wise lawyers advise her husband to go through medical checkup of her by a psychologist. They advise to keep all such documents safely which can prove that the lady was in depression and was mentally sick so that if she commits suicide in future then it can be proved that she was mentally abnormal. Such precautions are seldom taken by the husbands to immoral wives because they deny visiting a psychologist. Some wise husbands, anxious and depressed by the threatening of their wicked wives, pretend to visit some physicians with their wives while actually take the services of psychologists and keep required data, including medical prescriptions given to wives in written, with them so as to protect themselves in future. Wherever a decent married lady is harassed in actual sense by the in-laws, there she is harassed till her mother-in-law becomes physically incapable because of being aged. The humiliation and harassment of the married ladies done only by their husbands is seldom seen while the harassment of husbands done by the wives is very common and can be seen in almost families. In almost of the instances where the ladies get the free environment in husband's family, they become despotic and hence start ruling over their husbands and in-laws.

In almost of the disputes occurred between husbands and wives, either compromises are done by the husbands and they bear the ill nature of their wives considering it to be a part of destiny or the complications took disastrous form and the parents of the wives intervene. To cross-check the data of the men and women compromising for the integrity of the families in urban areas, another survey is performed in thousand families then it is found that out of such one thousand families, where husband or wives were living together by performing compromises or kind of sacrifices of the own feelings, in seven families wives were compromising with their husbands while in sixteen families both of them were compromising for living together. In the rest of the nine hundred and seventy-seven families men were compromising with their wives of robust and ill nature. It is very shocking to know that in such matters if the parents of the lady intervene then almost of them give improper advice to their daughters. Almost of such ladies with the help of their parents, take the advice of the advocates to make a pressure on the in-laws and all of such lawyers ask them the date of marriage so that they may falsely blame their in-laws by the dowry act.

Ladies possess acute ego problem and hence they never accept their mistakes and keep arguing with the husbands or in-laws. It is entirely useless to expect for repentance and atonement from ladies. Almost men never physically punish their wives and hence ladies took the advantage of this and become shameless and aggressive. An aged lady told that a lady bear whole of the weight of man while performing sexual course hence it is useless to improve her by giving her physical punishment because such punishments make her more brazen and daring. Women are like a puppet of heavy weighted base with light upper part filled with air. When one hits such puppet it falls and immediately gets up to acquire previous position. Hence women are least affected by the proper guidelines, fear of the elders and physical punishments once they are spoiled because they become shameless like the puppet.

In the context of dowry, a lady advocate was interviewed. During the sufficient long conversation, she said," Very few percent married ladies are actually harassed by their male in-laws or husbands because either they are lying or are being harassed by their female in-laws. Often popular ladies belonging to some organizations or commissions say that the rate of sexual assaults, rapes and humiliation of ladies at family level has been increased and government is doing nothing on this. In fact this all is rubbish because nowadays husbands are not having the guts to even stand against their iniquitous wives. Our country is women dominating and this can be seen in all residences. Obviously no lady is going to protest against ladies. You must have never seen even a single case in which such female heads of the organizations oppose some wrongdoer lady. All ladies including me too need freedom. We all say that the rules and laws should be very strict for the men performing eve-teasing or sexual assaults on ladies but we never say that ladies should get severe punishment if their involvement is seen by any means. The reason behind this is almost of us are sexually or morally corrupt. We never care for the social norms or ethics. When a newly married lady accompanied by her mother approaches to me to get the legal advice by which she can trap her in-laws then I say to her to file a police complaint against her husband on male in-laws. Almost of such ladies say that they are not troubled by the husbands or other gents of the family because the cause of their distresses are their mothers-in-law then I advise them that they have to falsely blame their husbands or other men of the family because then only public opinion will become in their favor. I advise them that they will get the support of women organizations only when they blame on their husbands or male in-laws and by blaming the male members, they can further trap the female in-laws in the false blames. I tell them that they can never get justice if they blame only to their female in-laws. This is basically the secret of our profession that we should do anything to make our clients win the legal matter doesn't matter whether they are genuine or not and doesn't matter how many men are falsely blamed for that by producing false witnesses."

Parents, who do not teach codes of conduct and morality to their daughters, get free from their responsibilities after marrying their daughters while they make the life of the young guys and their parents like hell whom with they marry their immoral daughters. Such ladies with lack of discretion, lack of conscience, excessive aggressiveness and false ego, make the life of their husbands and in-laws ruined and somewhere commit suicide to blemish the in-laws forever. The affliction and the anguish of the parents of a married lady, who has committed suicide, stand nowhere in front of the sorrow of her husband. All men marrying with a desire to get a simple and sober wife, when find a morally corrupt lady of aggressive and quarrelsome temperament as their wife, get shocked and consider it to be a part of their misfortune and hence live the life with uncountable compromises.

In many surveys, married ladies accepted that their husbands just desire for love, faithfulness and performing family duties from them. Husbands earning sufficient to run the family seldom desire their wives to get involved in business or jobs for earning. Husbands who let their wives working in field for earning mostly do this either because of their poor financial position or they are compelled by their wives willing to work outside. Some men are familiar with the fact that ladies sitting idle become the reason of complications and conflicts hence they permit their wives working outside so that they may be busy. Almost men keep limited desire from their wives but women keep unlimited desires from their husbands and such desires of them are unpredictable. In fact a lady herself does not know that what exactly she wants from her husband.

The Essence

It is not true that today's women is literate and women in past were illiterate. If literacy means the knowledge of few words of the advanced foreign languages, exposing nudity of the body parts and performing harlotry then it can be said that almost women are literate at present. If ladies define the patronages and facilities provided to the ladies of ancient period as confinement then at present they have only achieved moral degradation by performing adultery as a symbol of freedom. Women can never get rid from the slavery of men because they were never slaves of men. Women are slave of their immoral habits, uncontrolled sexual lust and other women and this situation is from the beginning of the era and will sustain till the end of human race. This is an absolute delusion that women are harassed by men. Normal parents give same facilities to their sons and daughters. A girl child gets the same meal that is given to her brother. Mothers have more affection for their sons instead of daughters still they do not perform partiality while breastfeeding to them. The affection of father is more achieved by a daughter. A son and a daughter both are provided education the only difference is that if the girl child is unwilling to study then she is allowed to quit from this while a boy child is compelled to go for schooling even when he not willing. Parents have to expend more money while marrying their daughters while in case of the marriage of their sons, the expenditures are least. A guy has to have money with him while being in love with a girl while a girl is free from such social or economical obligations.

Teachers often give severe physical punishments to the male students while they do not dare to touch girls. Female teachers even punish male students and seldom punish girls. If a girl is caught red handed performing some local crime like pilfering then she is generally left by giving warning while if the same act is done by a guy then he is brutally beaten by the public. Almost in all the fields including public conveyance, women are given preferences. Again in the culture of "Ladies first", the ladies are always given first chance. In the queues made for some objective, ladies have their separate queues even after that they barefacedly enter the queues of the gents. In married life, ladies are harassed by other ladies either in the role of their mothers-in-law or daughters-in-law. In both of the situations, men as husbands are always harassed. Contrary to aforementioned situations, if ladies are found to be harassed by the gents of their family then it rarely happens. All men desire to gain wealth so that their wives and kids may live a comfortable life. If wives or daughters are physically not well then men devote whole of their efforts to cure them and make them happy. These are the situations that normally occur in the life and if ladies seek their harassment in this then nothing is left to say. Apart from all of these, judiciary keeps merciful views for ladies. Women are provided reservation in almost of the fields. There are so many facilities which are provided only to women in India that if all of them are discussed here then it will make a big treatise.

If we include the sexual assaults under physical harassment then also at family level, in-between the relationship of husband and wife, less than three percent ladies are harassed mentally or physically by their husbands while more than eighty-nine percent men are harassed by their wives. Unfortunately the instances of harassment of men very rarely get highlighted. All ladies know that they are having precious gift or by-birth quality as their *Yoni* or vagina hence almost of them never hesitate to utilize this gift for earning money. A renowned lady told that the ladies, who are able to utilize their sexual skills for earning wealth, need not worry to work somewhere else till the entire span of their life while the ladies, who are failure in earning money even after providing their sexual services, usually say that they are sexually molested by men. Almost ladies are desirous to adopt the shortest route of harlotry for achieving success and this is the reason that at present more than eighty percent ladies are ready to keep illicit sexual relations to achieve social and financial benefits.

Wherever women pretend to lose, in fact they gain there. Generally the justice is given or done to them who lose something and it is considered that in the almost crimes affiliated to women, they are the losers. This is the biggest misconception spread in the society because as explained earlier, almost ladies who pretend losing their virginity, have already lost it numerous times by making illicit sexual relations willingly. If some thing is sold in market then obviously it will attract buyers and the same happens with the so-called never existing chastity or virginity of ladies. Punishing buyers is not going to give any solution unless sellers are punished hence adultery or illicit sexual plays will end up only when women are punished for that. Only judiciary can control over the situations by strictly punishing the ladies and gents, who are the prime cause of ruining the Indian culture and society. Though such decisions taken by judiciary may seem to be brutal and in-human but that is the only solution to improve the current morally degraded status of society. I would like to state here the wordings of my female journalist friend. She once said to me," If anywhere in the country, ladies are harassed then that is because of other ladies. As the offended ladies fear to blame other ladies hence they just blame the men, of the surrounding of wrongdoer ladies, who in fact have nothing to do with the imposed blames. There is a secret of the world of women. All of us know where we are wrong and if we are right then where the other ladies are wrong. You can never find any lady publicly menacing the misdeed of other lady in front of media unless she is anyhow affiliated to that matter and is against of her. Like every profession or organization, we too have our unmentioned oath that we have to shout on the beat of drum that we are always harassed by men. A big crowd of men, who is morally impotent or flirtatious, stands in favor of us. All of us and the men society know that we are wrong but if even after that, the society and judiciary take our favor then where is our fault? Only a woman can successfully oppose other woman hence I usually advise to decent ladies to get gathered to oppose the ill-deeds of other morally corrupt ladies. I incite all of the virtuous ladies, doesn't matter if they are young or aged or physically sick, to come forward to oppose wicked ladies, who are disgracing all ethical women by wearing the veil of brazenness and performing physical or moral harlotry, because this is the only solution to improve the degraded chastity of women. This is absolute false that we are running through the phase of 'survival of the fittest' because nowadays men have to save their chastity from sexually corrupt women and women are almost safe. This is the phase of hyper feminism which is extremely dangerous for the families as well as for the society. If the same rate of degradation of morals of ladies and their involvement in illicit sexual relations is maintained then within twenty years, India will appear as the biggest market of sex workers on the international platform and the entire country will become a brothel"

Glossary

Abla: Women are often said to be *Abla* which literally means one who is helpless and is always harassed.

Bhasmasur: A demon, who was devotee of lord *Shiva*. He was blessed by lord *Shiva* that, whose head he touches by his palm, will immediately burn and turn in to ashes. For testing the authenticity of the boon, he tried to put his palm on the head of lord *Shiva*. Lord *Shiva* fled but he chased him. Ultimately Lord *Vishnu* appeared in the form of a beautiful lady and *Bhasmasur* felt in love with her without recognizing Lord *Vishnu*. Lord *Vishnu* in the form of lady made *Bhasmasur* dance with her and in a dancing step made him put his hand on his head hence *Bhasmasur* burned in to ashes.

Buddha: The founder of Buddhist religion born at *Lumbini*, a part of ancient northern India. He also considered being embodiment of lord *Vishnu*.

Burka: A loose outer garment worn by Islamic women to hide their body parts when go out in public. It is worn over the usual clothing and removed when women are back to their houses. It covers whole of the body and the area covering the eyes is made of semi-transparent cloth.

Daan: It means a kind of donation with no self interest.

Dojekh: It literally means hell while the reverse of this *Jannat* is the paradise. *Dojekh* is specially made for the non Islamic people while *Jannat* is reserved for Muslims.

Dupatta: A long multipurpose scarf worn by South Asian ladies along with suits. It is traditionally worn across both shoulders.

Durga Puja: The literal meaning of *Durga* is the one who is incomprehensible or beyond the imaginations. Goddess *Durga* is worshipped for her gracious and terrifying aspect. She is worshipped by different names among her devotees.

279

Dwapar Yug: The third among four *Yugas* or eras. The duration of this was of 864,000 years and the average life span of human being was of 1000 years. Lord *Vishnu* incarnated in the form of Lord *Krishna* in this era.

Ganesha: The most widely worshipped deity of Hindus with the head of an elephant. He is the lord of beginnings, troubles and remedies. He is worshipped before almost all of the rituals and ceremonies.

Gandhi: *Mohandas Karamchand Gandhi*, the father of the nation of India, was a pre-eminent and spiritual leader of India during Indian Independence movement. He is considered to be a man of superlative virtues. India is in fact known abroad by the country of Gandhi.

Ghunghat: A kind of veil or head scarf worn by Hindu ladies to cover their head and face. It is considered to be a symbol of modesty and bashfulness. A corner of *Sari* is kept overhead in such a way so that the face should be hided when coming in front of the elders. Even *Dupatta* is also used for this purpose and wrapped around the head. Ladies often make a *Gunghat* when they visit some synagogues or pay respect to some elder or perform some religious rituals.

Gotra: This is the lineage assigned to Hindus at the time of their birth. In most of the Hindu families, marriage in the same *Gotra* is prohibited because people with same *Gotra* are considered to be siblings. Gents have the *Gotra* of their father in their life time while ladies have the *Gotra* of their father before marriage but of husband after marriage.

Gilli danda: A popular game usually played by two wooden sticks. The longer one is termed as *Danda* while shorter one as *Gilli*. The *Gilli* is put on the ground and *Danda* is used to strike it.

Janmashtami: This festival is the celebration of lord *Krishna's* birthday.

Kalash: A pitcher as a Vedic symbol made of either metal or soil. It is worshipped during almost sacred rituals. It is placed on the earth, facing the north.

Kanche: These are marbles used as small spherical toys and are specially made of glass. A sphere or curved zone is drawn on the sand and one has to hit the marbles of others lying outside the spherical area from inside.

Kanyadaan: A part of marriage ceremony in which bride is given to the groom by her father or male guardian. *Kanya* means a virgin and *Daan* means virtuous donation.

Karvachauth: A traditional Hindu festival in which married ladies take fast for the enhancement of the age of their husbands.

Lakshmi: The goddess of wealth and prosperity.

Matrika: An acronym for motherhood, knowledge and spiritual power. They are female deities worshipped during lots of religious ceremonies of Hindus.

Moksha: It means liberation from the cycle of the death and rebirth. This is the final release from one's worldly conception of shelf by attaining the true affection of the God.

Panchayata: It literally means the assembly of five wise men selected by a village or community to take care of the welfare of that villagers or community. Traditionally they settle the disputes between the individuals and the villages. *Panchyati Raj* is a system of governance in which gram or village *Panchayatas* are the basic units of administration. It has three levels as village, block and district. At village level this is termed as *Panchayata*.

Ram: The seventh incarnation of lord *Vishnu*. He is the most popular God of Hindus, worshipped all over world. He was the embodiment of truth and morality.

Ravan Dahan: Lord *Ram* killed *Ravan*, a brilliant intellectual king living in the form of ten headed demon. The effigy of *Ravan* is buried every year on the day and termed as *Ravan Dahan*.

Salwar Suit: A versatile type of clothing presently used by ladies. *Salwar* is the lower wearing like pant while suit is upper part like a shirt.

Sari-Blouse: Sari is around six yards long piece of cloth draped in a peculiar fashion by ladies. Blouse and petticoat are the essential garments worn along with a Sari.

Sati Savitri: One of the most chaste and loyal woman of ancient Indian period. She forced lord of death to resuscitate her demised husband.

Satsang: It means the company or proximity of the truth or the virtuous men. This is traditionally used for the assemblies where the religious and ethical knowledge is provided by some spiritual Guru to the audiences.

Seshnag: The serpent God worshipped in India. It is said that the earth is balanced by it's hood.

Swayamber: A custom popular in ancient India, where life partner is chosen by a girl among number of worthy guys.

Talak: It literally means to untie the matrimonial knot by articulating a word denoting divorce. If a Muslim husband utters the word on his wife, they get divorced automatically.

Varun: The God of sky, water and Celestial Ocean. He is also considered to be God of law.

Vivekanand: The chief disciple of the saint *Ramkrishna Paramhans* and the founder of *Ramkrishna* mission. He is best known for his inspiring speech beginning with "sisters and brothers of America" through which he introduced Hinduism at the parliament of the world's religions at Chicago in 1893.

Yoni: It literally means vagina or female genital organ. It also means incarnations or embodiments.

From The Author

अति सर्वत्र वर्जते | The excess of everything is forbidden because it ultimately causes chaos in the social structure. This is a general law applied to almost all of the aspects. Truth can not be adulterated by amalgamation of lies in it because after this, it becomes fabricated and truth exists nowhere. There are lots of aspects about which we need to tell truth to ourselves. Truth needs no support because it itself is the only support to the virtuous deeds. Once a man lies or betrays others, first of all he has to cheat himself. One can only live with the truths when he comes out of the pseudo norms made by himself and leaves the ostentatious way of living life.

India is going to be the second strong-most power of the world and perhaps in future, we will become the most economically powerful but what will be the exact achievement of this, is difficult to predict. The actual prosperity and development of the country take place when the count of men lying below the poverty line becomes nil not by the ostentations done at international platform. In the past recent years, the drastic fall in the economy of almost countries took place which ultimately effected to Indian market but as per the opinions of the economists, we have controlled over the situations and continuous growth can be seen in the different indexes affiliated to market. We are happy that men of our country are making new records. We are breaking the records in the field of games like cricket, movies and nudity etc. There is nothing to be proud on it because the actual victory can be declared only when we will be able to say that every child of India is literate, the selection criteria is only and only the worthiness, no one is bound to sleep with empty stomach, no one sells her daughter for the sake of removing his poverty and financial problem is not a hurdle in marrying innocent girls. Is it difficult to achieve all of this? Perhaps not. After accomplishing all of this only we can get the right to present ourselves on international platform. Freedom is not only for us instead it is more for them who are starving and seeking jobs here and there even after being qualified and worthy because they are not having plenty of money to bribe. Though it is not true that every country presenting itself at international level has achieved such goals but we belong to India and it is still assumed that our foundation is based on ethics and morals.

When a foreigner tourist comes to India and takes the pictures of some destitute ladies and gents in torn cloths then we strictly oppose this through our public opinions. We are not ashamed because the situations of poor and helpless men or beggars might be sketched by foreigners to make an amusement among their people instead we are bothered because this discloses our nudity and brazen attitude. It discloses that the harassment of our poor or starving people is done by us and we are not even desirous to help needy of our own country. We say that rich people of other countries feel pleasure to watch Indian public in torn clothing and starving or the poverty of India is sold outside the country. They are outsiders and should not be blamed because they are not responsible for such situations. We and our Indian system are only responsible for that because we always blame others and quit when we are asked to help our destitute brothers and sisters. We are more brazen and morally nude in comparison to those who are living in poverty or who are drawing their images for the sake of popularity or making money.

We only release our frustration by living glamorous life and showing ourselves advanced by accepting nudity of western countries. We say that such nudity and brazenness are the gifts of western culture. We could never learn the virtuous attributes of western people. We are not as laborious as they are. We are not as patriotic as they are. In fact we all are opportunistic. Lack of dedication and lack of patriotism swallowed the Indian culture. We have entirely adopted the pompous behavior and ostentatious attitude. We are busy in earning and humiliating our own brothers and sisters though we always talk about universal sodality. Our administrative system or government is busy in earning and making the figures of their never attained goals. We are expertise in paper work and hence are busy showing the figures fulfilled by us. We don't have any concern with the worthiness or disability of applicants because we have to fill the backlogs and the ability of one in India is considered to be his bribe-paying capacity. Whoever is talented and is of assiduous nature or laborious and is willing to live a peaceful life without corruption, is eager to quit from Indian subcontinent because he knows that honesty and talent have no values in India. Who are involved in financially sucking the country or are an inseparable part of corrupt system or are financially unable or are penniless talent, are living in the country. We reproach brain-draining and often say that talented lobby quits from India for the sake of earning more money. We are wrong as more than ninety percent cream quit from India because they are not getting facilities for their researches and the environment of the society has been entirely corrupt. The students of top engineering colleges when selected in civil services or railway services either become corrupt or are killed by the big contractors of the concerned departments or are thrown in remote areas where they are bound to live a life of handicapped. Some brilliant scholars, who are not ready to take bribe, give resign from their posts and join private sectors for utilizing their talents and for the safety of their families.

We misuse our laws and are always eager to take the over-advantages of the facilities provided by government. We are busy in hunger strikes or other kind of agitations. We make our agitations effective by burning some of our brothers or sisters alive and proclaim that they did sacrifice for their agitations. We demand for our own state and keep on going for movements and it seems that we are desirous for the freedom from our own country. All of such made new states make new records in corruption. The ways of putting such demands for autonomous states or for other matters has been mere gateway of the entry in politics. We are very conscious for our right doesn't matter if we have to sacrifice others for this. We have nothing to do with our social and moral responsibilities. Heavy rainfall created disastrous situations in the country but none of us came forward to help our badly influenced people of villages though we all know that if all of us would have contributed then the situations would have been normal. We blame to political leaders and they blame to central government for not providing financial help. This is our culture as we all are beggars even after being sufficient rich. We never lose any chance to earn money. Our people have a very big amount of black-money and the exact figure of that is entirely beyond the imagination. There are plenty of scopes for rising or financially gaining in games like cricket, movies and sex-market in our country India. We spend more money in aforementioned fields in comparison to any other country. Then what is the problem and why our own people are facing starvation and natural calamities? The reason is that our mentality, thoughts and opinions are poor and we always ignore our moral responsibilities. Our mentality and approach, about which we proclaim to be high and sophisticated, is in fact high leveled sheer ostentation of our poor and disgusting mentality.

We have to see before taking meal that no one should be starved in our surroundings. We have to help destitute of our surroundings and have to stand with others in their sorrow before celebrating some festival or other moment at our residences because this is the humanity and the basic of our religion. If our people do not recognize or adopt this then whatever we proclaim about our advancement on the beat of drum at international level, the situation of civil war will definitely take place in near future and no terrorism will be accountable for this because we ourselves will be responsible. Almost of us earn illegally just to make others down. We are involved in the race of unfair competition with our own people but till when? When will our hunger of sensual lust and money come to end? When we will feel ashamed of ourselves? Till when we will be engaged in plundering in our own country? Perhaps we don't know the answer of these. Scholars assume that situations are bad but not worst. If this is true then I advise them just to adopt the policy of wait and watch for ten to twenty years.

With all this stuff, one peculiar change occurred during the past decade in the disposition of Hindus, is important to mention here. We all have been religiously impotent because of our over involvement in making money. If Hinduism is little bit maintained then this is because of backward class, who is ever ready to oppose the ill-demands and massacred done by the fanatic religious men of Muslim community. At the time of freedom of India, Muslim political and religious leaders demanded for their own country and they were allowed to bifurcate India. They formed *Pakistan* and most of them shifted there. Their demand was accepted and it was confessed and assured by their leaders including *Jinna*, that such division or peculiar demand will not be raised in future, even by their those people who were not ready to shift to Pakistan. In spite of that since then till now such efforts of further division of India is continuously made by them either through terrorism or through making chaos in Kashmir border or through asking for *Babri* Mosque. Again at the time of division of India, it was made sure by Islamic leaders that after the division, they and their men will not raise any right on the remaining land of India. It is a big misconception that Islamic men are against of idol worshipping because engraving men and making tomb is itself biggest example of their belief in worshipping dead men. They were not supposed to put any claim in India after the division. Unfortunately they took the advantage of generous Hinduism, misused democracy, morally loose political leaders and absurd judiciary and tried to create social chaos. Again they assured at the time of freedom that they and their demised people residing in tombs, will not make any claim but they lied. To keep enmity or obstinacy in religious matters is not fair but Hindus have to do this because the religion Islam standing as a prime enemy to them, is entirely based on the foundation of ill-concepts and wrong-headedness. Those were not Hindus who demanded for partition. The demand for the partition was made by Muslims and hence after fulfilling their demand of separation, they have no right to keep new demands. All of the mosques are deliberately made near or at the place of temples by demolishing our ancient most religious places and Muslims are very determinant to impose their religion on other religions. As Islamic autocrats forcefully converted Hindus in past by torturing them or presently Christians are converting Hindus by taking the advantage of their poverty, similarly nowadays, Muslims are trying to convert pious religious places of Hindus in to Mosques. This is the biggest conspiracy of Islam against Hinduism and unfortunately it is supported by morally-ill political leaders seeking shelter in Islam to calm down their perversion and to get the strong fanatic vote banking. The existence of *Babri* Mosque at *Ayodhya* had always been the point of conflict among Hindus and Muslims. The history of Mosque is supposed to be of Year 1527 but the birth of Lord *Ram* at *Ayodhya* took place very earlier to that. Islamic past is considered to be a history and considered to be a certified proof but the existence of *Ram* is skeptical in the opinion of people otherwise such long legal dispute would have not carried. Even now, the temples, as a symbol of Hindu deities, are termed by Muslims in their jargon as "*Bavari* Mosques" and it can be often heard in Uttar Pradesh, where the so called *Babri* Mosque exists. Islamic people called Hindus temples as *Bavari* Mosque which literally means "The religious place of insane people". The controversial *Babri* Mosque is in fact *Bavari* Mosque. Again *Bavari* means the insane or mad. Hence at the time of *Babar*, people worshipping at *Ramkot Hill* were said to be mad and were often abused by Islamic men, whose confidence was on peak because of the victory of *Babar*. Hence *Bavari* Mosque doesn't mean the Mosque made by *Babar* but unfortunately in-future, it was misinterpreted by the historians and was mentioned as *Babri* Mosque.(From my probable next book "The

Truth of *Babri* Mosque", chapter "The foundation of Treachery"). Then why didn't they call it *Bavari* Temple instead of calling Mosque. The answer is that mere speaking the word temple was considered to believe in the existence of Hindus and hence Muslims at that period never spoke the word temple. The place was termed by some religiously soft Muslims as *Masjid-i-Janamsthan* or the mosque of the birthplace. This is the clear indication done by the Muslims that they demolished the birthplace of lord *Ram* and the structure was made their just to humiliate Hindus. The historical evidences of *Baburnama*, the book written by *Babar*, nowhere describes the existence of *Babri* Mosque. Few pages of the authentic book *Baburnama* are missing because they were torn by the autocratic men of *Mughal dynasty*. It is said that *Babar* did three confessions in those pages. The very first confession he did was the repent shown by him for partiality done by him with one of his spouse. The second repent he expressed was regarding the adulteration of pious land of *Ram-Janmbhoomi* or the birth place of lord *Ram*, done by his general *Mir Baqi*, The third and last confession done by him was regarding the brutality done by his men on the people of other religions. Somewhere the articles of historians can not be considered as truth specially when they were either fanatic Muslims or were under pressure of Islam or were bribed by rich Muslims. This is the truth that after division of the country, the foundation of *Pakistan* was laid while we could not make remaining India as *Hindustan*. After partition, no other religion was having any right on the land of *Hindustan*. Muslims had already got their rights on the land and now if they desire more then they should be sent to Pakistan. Whatever be the decision of the judiciary in the conflict of Mosque and temple, should be accepted by both the parties because allowing such conflicts to occur or letting Muslims to take the help of judiciary for converting Hindus or Hindus' religious places in to Islamic culture, is itself a big misfortune for Hindus. If perverted Muslims are allowed to consider the pious land of *Ram-Janmbhoomi* as mosque then the remaining faith and trust of Hindus on Hinduism will get broken and perhaps they will prefer to get converted into other religions instead of being a part of handicapped Hinduism. Whatever democracy says but this is true that it has been very essential to make a rule to stop men of other religions spreading their religious garbage in India. The victory achieved by Hindus in the legal conflict of Mosque and temple at *Ayodhya* will be the triumph of humanity while if the victory is achieved by Muslims then that will be the triumph of brutality and will enhance the confidence of Muslims to spread terrorism. (From "The Truth of *Babri* Mosque")

Well, we are not here to discuss about fanatic Muslims instead we are concentrated on the problems of our own people residing in India, irrespective of their religion. We were not socially and morally harassed up to that extent during the period of our slavery as we are in the present scenario of our independent India. It has been more than sixty years after freedom but we could not produce sixty brilliant scientists to serve the country. We can not count the name of sixty doctors from the freedom who sacrificed their lives for the sake of humanity though every year, more than thousands of doctors get their degree. We produced millions of criminals, prostitutes and more than billions of people involved in corruption. There was a time when deities lived in India then human came into the existence. Now wolves are residing in India, eager to intake blood of each others. The bright future is of devils and the beginning of this can be seen in the country. If we would have been in the control of British rule at present time then no one would have taken part in the freedom movement because all of us would have been busy in earning from our slavery. Perhaps the only lobby, which would have come in front for the struggle of movement, would have been of Naxalites, whom we abuse at present. After getting freedom by the martyrdom of them, we would have been enjoying the freedom and would have been proclaiming that we got the freedom with great efforts. Is it so that Indians again need slavery or the regime of some other country? India was definitely worthy of freedom but were the Indian people worthy for getting freedom? Do we deserve for freedom? What were the actual circumstances that happen at the time of our Independence Day and how people misused and misinterpreted their freedom till now, an attempt to express that is done by me in my one of the forthcoming books "The Freedom and Democracy". I would have published my literature in my country India but again as I mentioned earlier, the country has almost lost it's morals and ethics hence it is not possible to change people's mentality and psychology just by literature. For the real improvement, Indian public needs a rule of some absolute ruler or autocrat because republicanism is not the treatment of us. We have entirely misused the concept of democracy. If mere literature or the power of the words would have been capable to ameliorate the social chaos of the country then it would have been done earlier because we have male and female poets and authors, very capable to express the truth. Unfortunately, almost of us could not maintain our country's dignity and have been ruined in the wave of current social trend.

About The Author

Ashok Kumar Pant born in *Mumbai*, a metro city of Indian subcontinent, in 1972. Professionally being ha software engineer he started his journey of literature from "It Is Continued" and "Woman, The Myth". He devoted himself in writing on the subjects like women psychology and moral degradation of the society.